People with learning disability and severe challenging behaviour

New developments in services and therapy

Ian Fleming and Biza Stenfert Kroese   editors

This book draws on the most recent research to examine the ways in which high quality services can be developed for those people with severe learning difficulties and challenging behaviour.

With contributions from eminent researchers and practitioners, the book is divided into three sections dealing with: the definitions and prevalence of challenging behaviour; different forms of service development; and effective therapy of such individuals. Crucial issues affecting work in this area are discussed including: service evaluation; 'aversive' versus 'non-aversive' procedures; and pharmacology.

The book will be of interest to social workers; nurses; psychologists; occupational therapists and educationalists.

Ian Fleming is a Clinical Psychologist with Chorley and South Ribble Health Authority; Biza Stenfert Kroese is Lecturer in Clinical Psychology at Birmingham University and Clinical Psychologist with Dudley Health Authority.

People with learning disability and severe challenging behaviour

New developments in services and therapy

edited by Ian Fleming and Biza Stenfert Kroese

Manchester University Press
Manchester and New York

Distributed exclusively in the USA and Canada by St. Martin's Press

Published by Manchester University Press
Oxford Road, Manchester M13 9PL, UK
and Room 400, 175 Fifth Avenue,
New York, NY 10010, USA

Distributed exclusively in the USA and Canada
by St. Martin's Press, Inc.,
175 Fifth Avenue, New York, NY 10010, USA

British Library Cataloguing-in-Publication Data
A catalogue record for this book is available from the British Library

Library of Congress Cataloging-in-Publication Data
People with learning disability and severe challenging behaviour: new
    developments in services and therapy / edited by Ian Fleming and Biza
    Stenfert Kroese.
        p.   cm.
    ISBN 0-7190-3690-9
    1. Mentally handicapped--Mental health.   2. Mentally handicapped--
Behavior modification.   3. Mentally handicapped--Mental health
services.   I. Fleming, Ian, 1954-.   II. Kroese, Biza Stenfert, 1954-
RC451.4.M47P46 1993
362.2'7--dc20   93-2706

ISBN 0 7190 3690 9 *hardback*

Printed in Great Britain
by Biddles Ltd, Guildford and Kings's Lynn

Contents

Figures

Tables

Contributors

SANDY BERING B.Sc., M.Sc. Clinical Psychologist, Liverpool Health Authority.

RAYMOND CHADWICK B.Sc., M.A., M.Sc., C.Psychol.Clinical Psychologist, Swindon Health Authority

DAVID CLARKE M.B.,Ch.B., MRC.Psych. Senior Lecturer in Developmental Psychiatry, University of Birmingham, and Honorary Consultant Psychiatrist, South Birmingham Health Authority.

ERIC EMERSON B.Sc., M.Sc., C.Psychol., FB.Ps.S. Senior Research Fellow, Hester Adrian Research Centre, University of Manchester.

DAVID FELCE Ph.D. Director of the Mental Handicap in Wales – Applied Research Unit, University of Wales, College of Medicine.

IAN FLEMING B.A., Dip.Psych. Clinical Psychologist, Chorley and South Ribble Health Authority.

DONNA HEAD B.Sc., M.Phil. Clinical Psychologist, Leicestershire Health Authority Child Speciality.

RAY JACQUES M.B. Ch.B., MRC. Psych. Senior Registrar – Learning Disabilities, Mersey Regional Health Authority.

ROBERT JONES B.A., M.A., Ph.D., Dip.Psych. Senior Lecturer in Clinical Psychology, University College of North Wales at Bangor.

JEAN LALLY B.Sc., M.Sc. Consultant Clinical Psychologist and Co-ordinator of Additional Support Team, South Manchester Joint Service for Learning Disability.

FERGUS LOWE B.A., Ph.D., FB.Ps.S (EPC). Professor and Head of Psychology Department, University College of North Wales, Bangor.

KATHY LOWE B.A., PGCE. Research Fellow, Mental Handicap in Wales – Applied Research Unit, University of Wales College of Medicine.

PETER McGILL B.Sc., M.Phil., C.Psychol., AFB.Ps.S. Senior Lecturer, Centre for Applied Psychology of Social Care, University of Kent.

DANUTA ORLOWSKA B.A. Research Officer, Mental Handicap in Wales – Applied Research Unit, University of Wales College of Medicine.

HAZEL QURESHI B.A., Dip.Soc., M.A. Research Fellow, Hester Adrian Research Centre, University of Manchester.

JULIE REED B.Sc., M.Phil. Clinical Psychologist, South Warwickshire Health Care NHS Trust, and Lecturer in Clinical Psychology, University of Birmingham.

BIZA STENFERT KROESE B.Sc., Ph.D., M.Sc. Clinical Psychologist, Dudley Health Authority, and Lecturer in Clinical Psychology, University of Birmingham.

CHRIS TUPMAN B.Sc. Clinical Scientist with Liverpool Health Authority.

HUW WILLIAMS B.A. Trainee Clinical Psychologist, North Wales In-Service Course.

What are days for?
Days are where we live.
They come, they wake us
Time and time over.
They are to be happy in:
Where can we live but days?

Ah, solving that question
Brings the priest and the doctor
In their long coats
Running over the fields.

'Days' from 'The Whitsun Weddings' by Philip Larkin
(reprinted with permission of Faber and Faber Ltd, London)

Introduction   *Ian Fleming and Biza Stenfert Kroese*

The term 'challenging behaviour' was first used in Britain by the Special Development Team of the University of Kent to describe a group of people with a disparate range of behaviours. Its usage became widespread when the King's Fund Centre adopted it in their influential 1987 document 'Facing the Challenge'.

The strength of the term lies in its focus on the relationship between behaviour and environment, and the implication that the analysis of this interaction is a vital component of any successful intervention. Despite its strength, it is nevertheless open to misinterpretation. It is important to clarify that the behaviours are *not* referred to as challenging because of harmful/ challenging consequences for other people, but rather because many current services are *challenged* to give the individuals concerned the quality of life that is their due. A less widespread, yet even more distorted interpretation of the term challenging behaviour is that it refers to actions which are meant to issue a challenge, i.e. 'throwing down the gauntlet'. Obviously, this contradicts the intentions of the authors of 'Facing the Challenge', who hoped that the term would place the focus of discussion on the quality of service provision rather than on the individuals showing the 'problem behaviours'.

While the term challenging behaviour has gained prominence in the past five years, there has been little agreement about what constitutes such behaviour, which services are best suited to reducing challenging behaviour, and which interventions are most effective and most ethically or philo-sophically coherent. The definition formulated by the Special Development Team:

.... behaviour of such an intensity, frequency or duration that the physical safety of the person or others is likely to be placed in serious jeopardy, or behaviour that is likely to limit or delay access to and use of ordinary community facilities.

is not a precise definition.*

* See Emerson and McGill's comment in Ch. 4, p.102.

Although we have witnessed a recent, sudden increase in the UK in services designed for people with challenging behaviour, British research and evaluation in this area is still a faint echo of the research carried out in North America since the late 1960s. It is the intention of this book to address some of the questions still unanswered regarding definition, prevalence, service delivery, assessment and therapeutic interventions, and ethics. Our contributors are all actively involved in research and clinical work and are respected as practitioners as well as academics in their particular area of work. All our authors are currently working in the UK, but this should not detract from the scope of this book as all the contributions are presented in the context of an international knowledge base.

The book is divided into three sections. In the first section Qureshi addresses the issue of definition and emphasises the value of using a definition which focuses on the consequences of a behaviour rather than on a description of the behaviour itself. She discusses the social process of defining challenging behaviour and presents data from a large epidemiological study in the north-west of England. Her discussion of the various service responses sets the scene for later chapters. Of particular interest are the findings that clear interventions which are consistently applied across different settings are rarely available, and that there is an overrepresentation of the 15–35 age group.

The second chapter in this section considers prevalence and persistency of challenging behaviour in children. This five-year follow-up study suggests that the behaviours of some children are very persistent and that this population requires a service response over and above that available in a typical British health district.

Section two describes three different service models which have recently emerged and which are specifically designed for people with severe learning disabilities and challenging behaviour. They all favour a service based on expert teamwork rather than the more traditional model of special units, i.e. they advocate that a service needs to invest in skilled people who are flexible and mobile enough to work in a variety of settings rather than limit itself to beds, bricks and mortar.

Bering, Tupman and Jacques describe the inception and initial period of such a service, augmented with emergency beds. They describe how an operational policy was formulated and the service was founded. Their case studies clearly describe how challenging behaviour cannot be ameliorated by the provision of valued opportunities alone. Well planned, consistent interventions based on psychological theory must be applied to produce lasting change. Also, access to short-term residential care and close collab-oration between psychology, psychiatry and nursing appear to contribute to an effective service.

Bering *et al.* also describe the interface between the specialist team and other professionals from the already existing services, such as community support teams. The creation of specialist teams may produce adverse reactions from existing staff, who could be made to feel that their work is being undermined or removed from them by an 'elite' service.

Emerson and McGill in Chapter 4 provide an account of the five years in which the Special Development Team of the University of Canterbury have provided a service for people with challenging behaviour in the south-east of England. Most of their clients posed extreme challenges for the services. Nevertheless, most of the service plans have been maintained and individuals have remained in a community setting. This chapter provides an excellent insight into the political context in which the service was created, and frankly discusses failures as well as successes.

Lowe, Felce and Orlowska point out that research on etiology and treatment of challenging behaviour often appears to take second place to vague philosophies when services are being planned and developed. There is a discernable lack of understanding of, and aquaintance with, research findings from all disciplines amongst service planners.

The chapter describes a research project which was designed to investigate the workings and effectiveness of two challenging behaviour teams. Difficulties encountered in definition and measurement of challenging behaviours are reported, which underline the points made in earlier chapters regarding the subjective nature of such attempts. The authors make observations about the diversity of the individuals referred to challenging behaviour teams and investigate the relationship between challenging behaviour and intellectual and social functioning. Specialist teams are often faced with difficulties when defining their client group. That is, should they provide a service for people with mild learning disabilities and/or mental illness who often pose the greatest challenge to the services? Individuals with moderate or mild learning disabilities who have at some time have been served by forensic or mental health services are frequently excluded from challenging behaviour services. This exclusion is not without problems, since it is difficult to define the different levels of learning disability. On occasions, learning disability services will work with people whose special needs are not predominantly associated with their intellectual impairment. However, this is often due to the absence of other services rather than the result of a clear policy statement.

Lowe and her colleagues discuss the skills and proficiencies demanded of specialist team members, an interest they have in common with the authors of the previous two chapters. They also discuss the interface between specialist services and mainstream services.

The three chapters describing specialist teams have emphasised the importance of investing in staffing (both in terms of expert and 'hands on' resources) rather than the 'bricks and mortar' specialist unit model. Any service which depends so heavily on competent staff implicitly demands that a great deal of thought goes into the training, management and support of the team members. Lally's chapter expands on some of these staffing issues. She emphasises that staff need to acquire skills in preventing and interpreting challenging behaviour as much, if not more, than skills in containing such behaviour. This necessitates an understanding not only of the relationship between environmental events and behavioural responses, but also expertise in interpersonal interactions and how conflict arises. Lally stresses that staff who work with this client group will need a great deal of managerial and peer support in order to remain motivated. Job stress and ultimately job 'burn out' are particularly associated with this line of work.

Recent years have seen a burgeoning publication of international research related to interventions and therapies for challenging behaviour. However, there often exists a disparity between the depth and variety of the approaches described in the literature and the likely treatment on offer in local services. Procedures derived from applied behavioural psychology are probably the most well known and closely researched, yet paradoxically they are often half-heartedly applied or at worst ill-used. Misuse is often due to misunderstanding, and for this reason alone it is essential that the theoretical rationale and clinical application of such procedures are coherent and clear. Reed and Head address some of these issues in the first chapter of section three. They present a theoretical background to the method of Functional Analysis and describe the procedures derived from it. Some clear case studies are used to illustrate the uses of Functional Analysis and the treatment approaches that can be adopted. Their examples show the usefulness of quantitative data analysis in the context of a single case design. They also go to the heart of one of the most topical debates in challenging behaviour – that of 'aversive' versus 'non-aversive' interventions, setting the scene for the final chapter, which discusses these ethical issues in more detail.

In Chapter 8, Jones, Williams and Lowe present a detailed review and discussion of a treatment strategy which has become known as 'self-regulation'. They observe that therapy purely based on operant principles (often derived from research with non-verbal species) may not only be insufficient and/or inappropriate, but also goes against the widely accepted principles that people, whatever their disabilities, should be encouraged towards self-determination. Their review of the literature concludes that language skills are extremely important in teaching people to respond in adaptive ways. When verbal mediation is beyond the capabilities of an individual, visual stimuli may well be of use when self-regulation is the aim of treatment. The authors conclude that the theoretical framework which now exists has not as yet produced a wealth of clinical applications. They urge that this must be rectified if concepts such as advocacy, real choice, self-determination and equality of status are to become more than just slogans bandied about in policy documents.

Although this book has mainly concentrated on services and interventions derived from a psychological knowledge base, pharmacotherapy is probably the commonest and most consistently applied of therapies for people with severe learning disabilities and challenging behaviour. Clarke reminds us that challenging behaviour is often related to biomedical factors and he reviews the uses of psychopharmacological agents in treating people with challenging needs. He discusses in greater detail the assessment procedures and the pharmacological management of three specific types of challenging behaviour. Clarke points out that it is essential that appropriate assessment procedures are implemented in order to ensure that the drug treatment is beneficial. It is particularly important that the effects of the drug treatments are closely monitored, as people with learning disabilities are less likely to report undesirable side-effects. Furthermore, they are often incapable of discussing or comprehending the risk/benefit ratio of the treatment. Clarke recommends multi-disciplinary treatment reviews in which pharmacists can play a particularly useful role. Such collaboration between different professionals will be essential if a variety of interventions (e.g. psychological, social and educational) are applied simultaneously with the drug regime.

The final chapter deals with ethical issues. It describes the heated debate around the application of 'aversive treatments'. The difficulties in defining aversiveness are outlined and the dilemmas encountered by practitioners when dealing with life threatening self-injurious behaviours are illustrated by examples from the literature. The authors conclude that decisions should not be made solely on the basis of treatment efficacy and that in any case, the conclusions that can be drawn from applied research findings are clouded by the tendency for the publication of mainly positive results. Several themes that have cropped up again and again in previous chapters are repeated here. They include the importance of choice and self-determination, the need for truly accurate assessments, and the vital role of communication training (be it verbal or non-verbal) in the treatment of challenging behaviours.

We have tried in this introduction to summarise the contributions and to identify some of the issues which we felt to be important for future developments in the area of challenging behaviour. We have aimed to provide the reader of this book with a selection of current and topical issues in the context of theoretical discussion and empirical research. We hope that this will stimulate further developments in research and service delivery for people with challenging needs. In particular, there is a great need to demonstrate that community settings can effectively meet such needs. The simple notion that an 'ordinary environment' alone can 'cure' challenging behaviour has now been abandoned by most service providers. However, there is still a great need to identify the most effective ways in which to provide a service which combines structured and consistent intervention procedures with a strong commitment to equal opportunities, dignity, choice, and promotion of self-determination for people with learning disabilities.

Defining the population

1 *Hazel Qureshi*

Prevalence of challenging behaviour in adults

INTRODUCTION

The term 'challenging behaviour' is of relatively recent use. It was brought into prominence in the UK by Blunden and Allen (1987) in a King's Fund publication entitled *Facing the Challenge*. This document presented strong arguments for making the attempt to provide ordinary living environments for people with learning difficulties whose behaviour was a challenge to services. Ideologically it represented an effort to move away from a perceived orientation among service providers towards viewing difficult behaviour, or behaviour problems, as a characteristic inherent in individuals, and towards a focus on services and the ways in which they might respond to the challenges posed by particular forms of behaviour, in the context of a commitment towards de-institutionalisation and normalisation. Such a shift of focus was also strongly promulgated by the Association for Persons with Severe Handicap (TASH) in the USA. Behaviour problems, difficult behaviour, or sometimes 'behaviour disturbance' were terms in widespread use, although it had proved difficult to capture their meanings in ways which could reliably be measured. The change of nomenclature, whilst it may have signalled changing attitudes, did not immediately provide any firmer basis for measurement, although there was a clear implication that attention was to be concentrated on a rather smaller group of people than those identified in conventional studies of behaviour problems. The usefulness of many such existing studies to service planners and providers interested in challenging behaviour was limited, not least, as will be discussed, because of the definitions used.

It may be helpful to distinguish between three different types of definition. First there is an abstract or conceptual definition of challenging behaviour, which reflects the fact that it is ultimately socially defined; second, there are a range of everyday or 'rule of thumb' definitions which are used by people on a day-to-day basis for a range of purposes; finally, there are operational definitions, which are specific attempts to construct methods of identifying and measuring challenging behaviour which can be used to provide quantitative information for use in research, evaluation or service planning. At its most abstract, behaviour which is defined as a 'problem' or a 'challenge' is behaviour which violates the norms of 'proper' behaviour in a given situation, in ways which are negatively viewed. This assumes that there are prevailing norms in a given situation, i.e. shared beliefs about acceptable ways to behave. If not, then different actors will have different views about what constitutes a 'problem', and questions of relative power will be important in determining what comes to be seen as the prevailing everyday definition of challenge or problem. The conceptual definition does have practical use in the sense that it helps us to see that a strategy to reduce the perceived 'challenge' implicit in a particular behaviour does not necessarily have to concentrate on changing or modifying the behaviour. It may in some instances be preferable to redefine the acceptable norms, for example by increasing staff tolerance, or otherwise to change the attitudes of the actors in the situation so that the behaviour is then perceived as acceptable.

The idea that on an everyday basis the concept of challenging behaviour is socially defined is reinforced by the fact that apparently identical behaviour may be seen as challenging by staff in one setting but not in another. Of course there may be differences in the social or physical environment which render a particular behaviour more dangerous in one setting than another, but even in similar environments, whether behaviour is seen as challenging may depend on, for example, the goals which carers may have for a person. Passive, withdrawn behaviour may not be seen as challenging by over-worked staff in an environment where it is a struggle to achieve containment and the meeting of physical needs. However, where staff are attempting to increase the level of a person's community participation, such behaviour may pose considerable challenges. Thus if, in an attempt to assess the prevalence of challenging behaviour, staff across different settings were asked to identify people whose behaviour was challenging, it is likely that this would give rise to a group of people selected by a number of quite different sets of criteria related to existing norms and expectations, the characteristics of the setting and the variety of goals pursued.

Given this difficulty, the impetus in academic studies of the prevalence of problem or challenging behaviour has been to try and impose some consistency of definition across settings, and to eliminate elements of subjective staff judgement as far as possible. This has most often been attempted by the use of checklists of problem behaviours, together with ratings of frequency or severity. Unfortunately, this strategy generates a number of difficulties, centred round the problem of finding meaningful ways to aggregate the data generated by such checklists. Techniques such as factor analysis and cluster analysis have been used to seek consistent patterns of association between different listed behaviours, but little has emerged beyond Nihira's early identification of two factors which he called 'social' and 'personal' maladaptation, reflecting a difference between inwardly and outwardly directed behaviour (Nihira, 1969; Kiernan and Qureshi, 1986). However, checklist methods do not subsequently give rise to any straight-forward definition of challenging behaviour which can be used to isolate the group of interest, because there are a large number of ways in which one might define a 'more severe' group. For example, should there be a concentration on the total number of problem areas indicated, or only the particular areas which the researchers consider intrinsically more serious. Will it be enough to focus on anyone with at least one problem area rated 'frequent' or 'severe' or both? As will be demonstrated, different answers to these questions give rise to quite different estimates of prevalence, as do varying lists of problem areas. In addition, there has been considerable difficulty in achieving satisfactory levels of inter-rater reliability, where this has been tested, even with the most carefully constructed and exhaustively tested lists of problem areas.

Some authors (e.g. Leudar and Fraser, 1986) have questioned whether understanding prevalence in relation to a diffuse umbrella term such as 'behaviour problems' is particularly useful. After all, it may be argued, very little epidemiological effort is devoted to investigating the prevalence of 'cancer'. Instead there is a focus on particular forms of the disease, and their incidence and prevalence, among different relevant groups, say lung cancer among smokers and non-smokers. The forms of challenging behaviour which seem to have aroused most concern among practitioners and most attention in the literature are broadly: aggressive behaviour towards others; self-injury; destructive behaviour; other socially or sexually unacceptable behaviour (NWRHA, 1985; Hill and Bruininks, 1984). Leudar *et al.* (1984) observe that different forms of behaviour exhibit different relationships with other important factors such as age and degree of intellectual impairment, and also, from their own study, that 'different forms of behaviour exhibit different kinds of longitudinal stability'. Additionally, a focus on a specific form of behaviour holds out the hope that a greater degree of reliability in identification can be achieved. There are a range of studies concentrating on specific forms of behaviour, most notably self-injury (for example, Schroeder *et al.*, 1978; Griffin *et al.*, 1986; Oliver, Murphy and Corbett, 1987), although aggressive behaviour has also been singled out (Harris and Russell, 1989a). Operational definitions which specify criteria involving tissue damage to self or others and a precise time window, seem to achieve better levels of reliability (Oliver *et al.*, 1987; Reed, 1990). Concentration on self-injury seems to have produced somewhat more consistent results across studies, with most estimates being between 4 per cent and 10 per cent of people with learning difficulties, and with higher rates of between 10 and 15 per cent in institutions. Self-injury has been shown to be associated with more severe levels of learning disability, and to be more prevalent in younger age groups. A difficulty with these estimates from the service planners' point of view is that unfortunately, unlike cancer, people do not seem to generally show just one form of challenging behaviour at a time. At least half of the people showing self-injury exhibit other forms of challenging behaviour (Emerson, 1991) and these other behaviours may be of greater concern to staff in some cases. Harris and Russell (1989b) reported that 45 per cent of people identified as showing aggressive behaviour also showed self-injury.

These broad descriptive categories may break down when studied in depth, perhaps because what appears to be a description of form easily shades into an ascription of motivation. For example, in a study of the parents of young adults with challenging behaviour (Qureshi, 1990), the destruction of clothing was seen by one parent as aggression, because only the mother's clothing was destroyed. Similarly another parent saw the breaking of light bulbs not as destructive behaviour but as an attempt at self-injury. Finally, a third parent saw self-injury as aggressive because it was a way of punishing parents when the young person was angry with them.

These various difficulties may lead us to question whether the concentration on forms of behaviour, either as checklists, or singly, is the most fruitful way forward for research on challenging behaviour. Blunden and Allen (1987) gave a practical 'rule of thumb' definition which was formulated by the South East Thames Regional Health Authority Special Development Team 'Severely challenging behaviour refers to behaviour of such an intensity, frequency or duration that the physical safety of the person, or others is likely to be placed in serious jeopardy, or behaviour which is likely to seriously limit or delay access to and use of ordinary community facilities' (Emerson *et al.*, 1987, p.8).

This definition makes no reference to the form of the behaviour but instead concentrates on actual or potential consequences for the individual and for others. Extreme consequences such as 'life threatening' behaviour, have been considered in the literature (Hollis and Meyers, 1982), and, perhaps of more relevance in relation to questions of measurement, Nihira and Nihira (1975) demonstrated that only a small proportion (16%) of reported maladaptive behaviours resulted in jeopardy to health, safety, general welfare and/or legal jeopardy. Obviously there is no intention to argue that the form of behaviour is not important for service planners or providers. Clearly it is necessary to know that staff or people with learning disabilities may be in danger of attack, or that a person may be likely to run heedlessly across busy roads if not closely supervised. However, in terms of whether a person is seen as challenging or not, the form of the behaviour may not be the most relevant dimension.

In this chapter it will be argued that a focus on consequences, and on the resources required for control of behaviour, have greater salience in relation to definition and identification of challenging behaviour. Resources for control are mentioned because if negative consequences are prevented by the use of, for example, additional staff, security precautions or strengthened fittings and fitments, then people for whom these resources are needed should presumably be included in any group of people identified for epidemiological study.

Having said this, a degree of caution must be exercised in assuming that people in any kind of special provision do actually need all the features present in that setting. Other information, such as the level of response required to control behaviour, will also be useful as a measure of 'intensity'. Hill and Bruininks (1984) constructed a scale for rating the level of responses to behaviour, beginning with behaviour which elicited no response from staff, continuing through verbal response to physical intervention by one, or more than one, member of staff. They found that only one-third of incidents of problem behaviour required more than a verbal response. Again this suggests the relevance of considering resources required for control, rather than the specific form of the behaviour, in assessing the degree of challenge presented. Frequency of behaviour has often been considered to be a key factor (Nihira *et al.*, 1974), but clearly there is an interaction between frequency and consequences. It is this which makes it difficult to specify appropriate time windows within which particular behaviours should have occurred, in order to be considered relevant at the time of any survey of prevalence. For a behaviour such as 'pinching others' a time-span of 'in the past year' may be too long, for 'life threatening injury to self or others' it may not be. Equally, staff judgement about likely repetition must come into play in relation to serious incidents in the past and their current relevance. Later sections of this chapter will outline the ways in which a team from the Hester Adrian Research Centre (HARC) chose to tackle these issues in a study of challenging behaviour in the North Western Region. First perhaps we should briefly consider the reasons for undertaking research on prevalence at all.

Richardson and Koller (1985) identify the purpose of epidemiological study as being 'to investigate the distribution and determinants of a disease, disorder or condition'. More specifically, there are two broad kinds of reason for undertaking epidemiological studies: first, to seek for patterns of association between the phenomenon of interest and other factors, perhaps in order to improve our understanding of cause, and/or assist in prevention; second, to provide useful descriptive information for service planners and providers, perhaps about present and future service needs, or to gain a broad overview of current service responses. Perhaps unsurprisingly, in the published academic literature on behaviour problems somewhat more effort seems to have been devoted to the first aim than to the second, and the forms of definition which have been used in studies pursuing this first aim have not necessarily lent themselves in any straightforward way to use for the second purpose. In general, epidemiological studies are concerned not only with prevalence (the number of cases existing at a particular point in time), but also with incidence (the number of new cases arising within a specified time period). The latter has not figured largely in studies of problem behaviour, and this is perhaps unsurprising considering the difficulties which are encountered when deciding on criteria which identify the 'onset' of problem behaviour, especially as this may occur at a very early age and only gradually become distinguishable from other features of developmental delay. In addition, unchanged behaviour may become challenging to services because of changes in the person, such as increasing physical strength, or because of changes in services, such as reduction in staff ratios, or the loss of staff with special competence. This chapter will concentrate on prevalence only.

Two basic elements are required to construct an epidemiology of a particular phenomenon. The first is an operational definition of the entity to be studied, and the second is a definition of the base population. In relation to challenging behaviour, as has been discussed, the first of these is problematic, and much of the detail of the rest of this chapter will consider a variety of approaches to this issue. However, the second element also poses some difficulties which have been less widely recognised. As will become evident in discussion of the HARC survey, the use of different base populations can be important in interpreting and making use of epidemiological data. First, however, we turn to the problem of constructing an operational definition, and in the next section a number of commonly used measures will be discussed, and it will be illustrated that there are probably as many estimates of the prevalence of 'behaviour problems' as there are definitions.

OPERATIONAL MEASUREMENT – COMMONLY USED MEASURES

As mentioned, many measurements of behaviour problems, or 'maladaptive' behaviour, rely on a checklist of types of behaviour, and a rating for each of these, perhaps according to frequency or some other judgement of severity. Early work by Kushlick and colleagues in Wessex (Kushlick and Cox, 1968, Kushlick, Blunden and Cox, 1973) used a checklist of six types of behaviour, in a questionnaire designed for self-completion by staff:

1. Hits out or attacks others.
2. Tears up papers, magazines, clothing or damages furniture.
3. Extremely overactive. Paces up and down restlessly.
4. Constantly seeking attention – will not leave adults.
5. Continuously injuring himself physically e.g. head banging, picking at sores, beating eyes.
6. Anti-social, irresponsible and given to petty offences.

Each of these was rated according to a three point scale of which the most serious end, labelled 'marked', was defined as 'this behaviour has occurred during the last month and continues to present serious problems of management'. In combining scores additional weight was given to some behaviours, which the researchers felt were intrinsically more serious (e.g. physical attacks). This research group produced an estimate, which is still often quoted, that there are twenty adults and ten children, per 100,000 district population, who show severe behaviour problems.

The Disability Assessment Schedule (Holmes, Shah and Wing, 1982) is also an instrument for screening large populations, but administered by trained interviewers. The DAS list of behaviour problems includes the Wessex categories but adds a number of additional categories including: screams or makes other disturbing noises, temper tantrums, disturbs others at night, difficult or objectionable personal habits, scatters or throws objects around and sexual delinquency. The ratings for each behaviour are 'Severe', 'Lesser', 'No' or 'Potential'. Severe is defined as 'severe management problem (staff have to intervene, or upsets other residents, or marked effect on social atmosphere. Would be unacceptable in public)'. The instructions to interviewers make it clear that behaviours can be rated as severe by virtue of either frequency of occurrence or severity when they occur. No more detailed information on a behaviour is sought in the DAS, which is a well-respected instrument intended to gather information about levels of disability and ability in large populations of people with a learning disability.

In their study of reliability, Holmes *et al*. discuss the number of difficulties in assessing the degree of agreement between observers with regard to the presence or absence of behaviour problems. They note that the individual's behaviour may be genuinely different across settings, perhaps because of different levels of demand or stimulation. Even within the same setting behaviour towards different members of staff may differ, but also there may be differences over time, with a person showing intense phases of a particular kind of behaviour at apparently unpredictable intervals. They argue that there is no universally applicable way to decide between the relative importance of severity and frequency, and that ideally the criteria adopted should be determined at the stage of planning any particular study, depending on the purpose for which the information is required. They also argue for the importance of considering not only percentage agreement, but also agreements on presence and on absence. If a characteristic is rare, say present in 5 per cent of the population, then a study in which 5 of 100 people were identified incorrectly by a second observer as possessing this characteristic, would still give 90 per cent agreement because of the large number of agreements on absence of the characteristic. Therefore, for rare characteristics agreement on presence is important, whereas for common characteristics agreement on absence is important. Cohen's Kappa (Cohen, 1960) is a measure of the degree to which observed agreement is an improvement over that which would be expected by chance, and may therefore be a more appropriate measure than percentage agreement. Holmes *et al*. do not use this but give percentage agreement figures for the presence/absence of any behaviour problems *at all*. They do not report the reliability of assessment of the presence/absence of particular problems, or the ratings of severity. It seems that if a person were rated as showing severe self-injury by one member of staff and 'lesser' attacks on others by a second staff member, this would count as agreement on the presence of behaviour problems. Bearing this caveat in mind, overall agreement on the existence of behaviour problems seemed to reach levels of over 75 per cent, and the use of the DAS might therefore be one way to conduct an initial screening of the population, with a view to collecting much more detailed information subsequently about those people identified as showing, say, at least one severe problem.

One of the most widely used checklist scales has been the AAMD Adaptive Behaviour Scale (Nihira *et al.* 1974). Part I of the scale is concerned with the skills necessary for independent living. The second half of the scale presents a checklist of what are called 'Maladaptive Behaviours' divided into fourteen groups or domains. Each behaviour, if it occurs, is rated as occurring 'occasionally' or 'frequently'. For example, domain 10 – Self-abusive behaviour, sub-domain 31 – Does physical violence to self, lists the following: Bites or cuts self; slaps or strikes self; bangs head or other parts of the body against objects; pulls own hair, ears, etc.; scratches self causing injury; soils and smears self; purposely provokes abuse from others; picks at any sores he might have; pokes objects in own ears, eyes, nose or mouth; other (specify). Each behaviour occurring frequently is scored 2 and each occurring occasionally is scored 1. A total score for each domain is constructed to give a 'profile' of the individual's maladaptive behaviour. In all there are 452 specified behaviours to rate.

Part II of this scale has been subject to considerable critical comment centred round low inter-observer reliability, the incoherence of some domains, the inadequacy of the scoring system, which does not weight behaviours by perceived severity, and the difficulty of interpreting the resulting 'profiles'. (Bean and Roszkowski, 1982; Clements *et al.*, 1980; Holmes and Batt, 1980; Leudar *et al*, 1984). With a socially constructed concept, inter-observer agreement will be of considerable importance. Conventionally, correlations of the order of 0.8 are required for satisfactory reliability. The majority of items on Part I achieve this, with the lowest agreement recorded in the ABS Manual 1974 revision being 0.71. However, none of the domains on Part II achieve scores above 0.7 and five domains score below 0.5. As might be expected scores for test-retest reliability are much higher (Isett and Spreat, 1979) since these rely on the same observer being consistent over a short period of time. Attempts have been made to adapt the scale to a UK context (Thomas and Webster, 1974) but the difficulties of achieving reasonable levels of reliability remain. The scale does have the virtue that there is a great deal of normative data for comparison, and the reliabilities are at least known, and not conspicuously worse than for other checklist methods. Identification of people showing challenging behaviour from the use of the ABS Part II would have to rely on the overall number of problem areas shown, the researcher's own weightings of the relative seriousness of particular kinds of behaviour, and the frequency ratings.

Much subsequent work, particularly in the USA, has drawn on adaptations of the ABS, perhaps involving use of only the more reliable domains, and/or severity weightings devised by other researchers. As a result of this work it is generally accepted that certain kinds of behaviour problem are associated with greater likelihood of residence in an institution, rather than in the community. Physical attacks on others, self-injury and destructive behaviour have been found to discriminate between institutional and community populations (Eyman and Call, 1977). In an important study in relation to debates about deinstitutionalisation, Eyman, Borthwick and Miller (1981) compared over 400 young people allocated to community and institutional placements and found considerable stability through time in the presence of behaviour problems, which seemed to be unaffected by the type of placement. They considered that this suggested that relocation in itself might not be effective in reducing the prevalence of problem behaviour in the absence of appropriate treatment or programmes for individuals relocated.

EXAMPLES OF ONE-OFF STUDIES, DEFINITIONS AND RATES OF PREVALENCE

Four examples are given below to illustrate the range of definitions and corresponding rates of prevalence which may be found in the literature.

1. *Baker and Urquhart* (1987)
    Operational definition: One question in interview: 'Does this person have any particular behavioural difficulties about which a new member of staff (for example) should be informed?' Open-ended – coded subsequently.
    Source of information: Census of all services for adults with learning difficulties in Scotland.

    Prevalence
Hospital	29%
Community residential	14%
Day centre	9%

2. *Clarke et al.* (1990)
    Operational definition: A checklist of specified behaviours including temper tantrums, self-injury, excessive noisiness, withdrawal, wandering off, physical aggression, destruction of property and attention-seeking (this last one of course is not really a form of behaviour but an ascribed motivation). Staff had to indicate whether behaviours caused the individual or their carer a severe or a mild problem, either occasionally or frequently. Prevalence was calculated in relation to people who were said to show at least one severe problem at least occasionally.
    Source of information: Birmingham Special Needs Register.

Prevalence
Hospital	42.4%
Community residential	36.3%
Family home	41.4%

3. *Jacobson* (1982)
   Operational definition: Staff were given a list of twenty-nine behaviours which were defined as obstacles to placement or provision of services. They recorded up to three behaviours present for the person with an indication of frequency for each.
   Source of information: A database on the developmentally disabled population receiving services in New York.

   Prevalence (defined as those not symptom-free)
Developmental centres (larger institutions)	73%
Community residential facilities	61%
Family home	52%

4. *Koller et al.* (1982, 1983)
   Operational definition: Researcher ratings of in-depth interviews with parents and people with a learning disability, and of information from agency records. Overall behaviour disturbance was rated on a five-point scale, for childhood and young adulthood.
   Source of information: Cohort Study in a British city.

   Prevalence (those *not* symptom-free)
Age under 16	61%
Age 16–22	59%
('severe' behaviour disturbance)	
Age under 16	11%
Age 16–22	18%

With the exception of the paper by Koller *et al.* (1983), no information is given about the reliability of the measures used. It would be unreasonable to suggest that any of these studies saw it as their primary purpose to produce the kind of global overall rates of prevalence which have been quoted. Baker and Urquhart were interested in assessing the balance of care in Scotland in relation to concerns about deinstitutionalisation. Clarke *et al.* were focussed on variations in the prescription of psychotropic drugs. Jacobson was concerned to compare populations of people with learning disabilities who did, or did not, also suffer psychiatric disturbance. Koller *et al.* were interested in comparing people with learning disabilities with a matched sample from the rest of the population. These examples are included in this way to illustrate the degree to which rates of prevalence can vary with the operational definition adopted. In addition they draw attention to the more general finding that using checklists, and reporting the percentage of the population 'symptom-free', will tend to show very high rates of prevalence so that further information is needed in order to enable us to identify the much smaller subset of people whose behaviour is challenging to services.

AN EPIDEMIOLOGICAL STUDY IN THE NORTH WESTERN REGION

In 1986 the Department of Health commissioned the HARC to undertake an epidemiological survey in relation to 'behaviour problems'. It seemed important that this study should use a definition which was relevant to service providers, and should provide an assessment of the reliability of identification. In addition it was intended that the collection of relevant information about individuals would make it possible to focus on a smaller group of people whose behaviour presented challenges to services. The operational definition constructed was based on the use of specific resources within the setting and the individuals for whom these were needed, or the particular consequences of behaviour in terms of injury to self or others, destruction of or damage to property, or severe social disruption which affected the quality of life of others. Thus people were identified through the consequences of behaviour, or because their behaviour was controlled through some feature of the service setting which might avoid or reduce such consequences, for example, strengthened fittings, extra staffing, additional security or segregation (Kiernan and Qureshi, 1986).

An interview was carried out with senior staff in all facilities for adults with learning disabilities, and all residential facilities and schools for children with severe learning disabilities. The survey was conducted across seven Health districts within the North Western Regional Health Authority, which were selected as representative of the types of districts to be found in the North West according to a cluster analysis of districts based on 1981 Census data (Craig, 1985). People originating from the districts but placed in hospital or out-district placement were also screened, although the latter placements were screened by post since they proved more numerous than anticipated. In all, there were 350 screening interviews and 59 facilities were screened by post. Fieldwork teams were also asked to identify any relevant individuals who were not using regular services. Staff were asked to complete a more detailed questionnaire about each person identified. This individual schedule collected background information about the person's level of functioning, and detailed information about behaviour seen as problematic. This included the form of the behaviour, frequency, levels of control needed, perceived causes and consequences, and service responses. At this initial stage of screening, interviewers were instructed to include marginal cases about whose eligibility they felt doubtful, on the grounds that the collection of more detailed information could be a second stage of the screening process. After receiving individual schedules, 8 per cent of those originally identified were dropped from the survey.

RELIABILITY OF THE IDENTIFICATION PROCESS

Two exercises were undertaken to check the reliability of the identification process: one in Social Service settings, and one in a long-stay hospital. In both exercises the setting interview was repeated by a different interviewer with a different member of staff in the same setting. In Social Service department facilities there were eight pairs of interviews, covering approximately 230 people receiving services, and the full two-stage identification process was undertaken, including the completion of detailed individual schedules. In the hospital there were parallel interviews on ten wards housing 167 residents, but, since individual schedules were not sought, the likely number who would have been eliminated at the second stage was estimated from the actual figures observed in the survey (see Qureshi, Alborz and Kiernan, 1989, for full details). This two-stage screening process achieved satisfactory levels of reliability. Cohen's Kappa was estimated as 0.71 in Social Services settings, 0.62 in hospital settings (Cohen, 1960), both of which are satisfactory levels of agreement. Although these levels are satisfactory, differences between observers clearly do remain. In developing the Setting Interview the author held some discussion with staff in Social Services settings about specific differences in identification. It was found that these partly reflected differing knowledge of the clients' histories, and partly differing judgements over the potential consequences of some incidents, such as whether a person who wandered away was or was not in danger if unescorted. The numbers involved were insufficiently large to quantitatively test the reliability of the particular questions in the Setting Interview, therefore the exercise can only attest to the degree of reliability of the identification process overall.

RESULTS

In all, approximately 4,200 people were screened across the health districts surveyed, of whom 896 were in long-stay hospital and 164 were being supported in other residential placements outside their districts of origin. 701 people were identified as showing behaviour which required provision over and above that which would be required as a consequence of their level of learning disability, including 9 who were not using services. Table 1.1 gives the residential locations of the total population using services, compared with the location of people identified as part of the target group, showing that children (defined as those using children's services, therefore likely to be aged up to 19 years) were slightly less likely to be identified than adults, and that adults identified were more likely to be in long-stay hospital than other adults. Of the adult population showing behaviour problems about half were in long-stay hospital.

Table 1.1 *Residential locations of total population with learning disabilities screened in this study, compared with people identified as showing behaviour problems*

	All people (over 5) with learning difficulties (%)	People identified as showing behaviour problems (%)
Hospital	21	37
Community (adults)	51	38
Community (children)	28	25
	(N = 4200)	(N = 701)

RATES OF PREVALENCE OF INDIVIDUALS IDENTIFIED AS SHOWING BEHAVIOUR PROBLEMS

The initial definition identified 16.7 per cent of people, or one in six. This varied across settings as shown in Table 1.2. Note that since people sometimes attended more than one of the facilities listed, the categories overlap and cannot be added to give overall totals of people screened or identified.

Table 1.2 *Rate of identification across different settings*

Location of screening interview	No. identified	Estimated No. screened	% identified
Hospital	279[a]	896	30 [b]
Hostel	79	484	16
Children's home	56	205	27
Day centre	159	1746	9
School	109	1047	10
Other residential	52	578	9

[a] Includes 11 people living in the community
[b] Excluding the 11 people living in the community

RATE OF IDENTIFICATION ACROSS DIFFERENT SETTINGS

Table 1.2 shows the percentage of people identified in different types of setting. Thirty per cent of all those living in hospital were identified, compared with, on average, 13 per cent of those in community facilities. In either type of location, a higher proportion of people were identified in residential settings than in day settings. In hospital the screening of day services added only a very few additional people who had not already been identified on the wards, but did uncover a few individuals living in the community who received hospital-based day care. Almost half (49%) of all people living in wards designated for disturbed residents were identified, whilst the rate of identification in 'other' wards at 19 per cent was slightly higher than that prevailing in community residential facilities. Informal discussion with hospital staff and managers suggested a number of possible reasons why only about half of residents living in wards designated for people who were disturbed were identified. It seemed that some residents chose to live on these wards so as to be with friends who were placed there. Others had lived there before the ward was so designated and were unwilling to move. There were also a number of people who were said to have shown disturbed behaviour in the past but who could not be relocated despite considerable improvement in their behaviour. In a few cases this reflected a wish by the person to remain on the ward, but in others their past reputation stood in the way of relocation to other settings.

Turning our attention to people identified in community facilities, it is evident that in general a higher proportion of people were identified in residential services than day services, although the picture was not consistent across all types of residential service. In general residential services provided in, for example, staffed group homes, contained a smaller proportion of people who were identified as showing behaviour problems than residential services based on larger units such as hostels or children's homes. Given that there were no children (under 18) identified in hospital, it is of interest to note that rates of identification in children's homes approached those prevailing in hospital, whilst rates in adult hostels or other community-based residential facilities were well below this level.

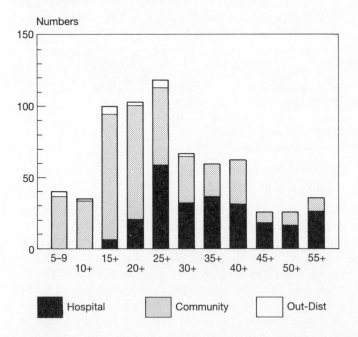

1.1   Residential location of people showing behaviour problems by age (N = 695)

In summary, just under one in three hospital residents were identified in comparison with just over one in four residents in children's homes, one in six residents in hostels and around one in ten people attending schools or adult day care, or other residential services. In addition, nine people who did not attend day or residential services were identified through interviews with fieldwork staff.

Figure 1.1 shows the age and residential locations of people identified. From this one may infer that an increasing proportion of people are placed in hospital with increasing age, but also that the age structure of the population showing behaviour problems will appear quite different to staff in hospitals, as opposed to those in community facilities. In the community the peak occurs in the 15–19 age group and decreases fairly steadily after that. In hospital the peak occurs in the 25–29 age group. Differences in hospital and community adult populations will also be evident with respect to gender. As Figure 1.2 illustrates, hospital staff will see a group of people showing behaviour problems who are predominantly male, whilst in community residential facilities 40 per cent of those showing behaviour problems are women, and staff dealing mainly with families will be almost equally likely to be dealing with women as men.

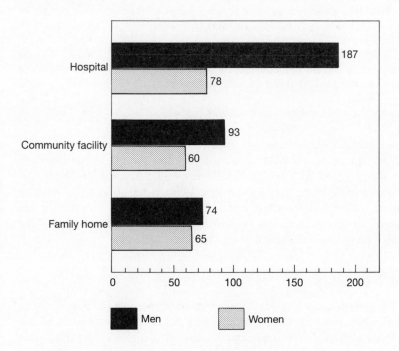

1.2 Numbers of men and women identified as showing behaviour problems in different residential locations (N = 557, all aged 18 or more)

CHALLENGING BEHAVIOUR

Given the range of information available it was possible to construct a number of definitions of challenging behaviour, related to the consequences, frequency or level of control required in each individual instance. For example, of those identified, one in three people in hospital were said to at least sometimes require physical intervention by more than one member of staff, whilst one in four people identified in the community were so rated. This represents 10 per cent of all people screened in hospital and 4 per cent of all people screened in the community. In contrast, 1 per cent of all people in community settings and 2.8 per cent of those in hospital were said to have caused serious injury to themselves or others at some time. Thus, as would be expected from previous discussion, the rates of prevalence of challenging behaviour vary according to the chosen definition. A composite definition of challenging behaviour was adopted here which attempted to combine the various dimensions outlined in a way which would take account of the importance of consequences, frequency and level of control required. This definition was used to select out a smaller group from within the whole group identified, for more detailed study.

People were defined as showing challenging behaviour if they:
Had *at some time* caused more than minor injuries to themselves or others, or destroyed their immediate living or working environment;
OR
Showed behaviour *at least weekly* which required intervention by more than one member of staff for control, or placed them in physical danger, or caused damage which could not be rectified by immediate care staff, or caused at least an hour's disruption;
OR
Caused more than a few minutes disruption *at least daily*.

Of those identified 42 per cent met these rather broad criteria, representing about 7 per cent of people with learning disabilities overall. In summary, 14 per cent of all people with learning disabilities living in hospital, and 5 per cent of adults and of children (considered separately) in the community showed challenging behaviour according to this definition. Figure 1.3 shows the age structure of the group identified as showing behaviour problems, and of the subgroup who met our definition of challenging behaviour.

WHO ARE THE PEOPLE?

Figure 1.4 gives the age and sex breakdown of people identified as showing challenging behaviour by the definition outlined. In total two-thirds, 67 per cent of those identified were male, and 50 per cent of all those identified were between the ages of 15 and 29. Among both adults and children females were more likely than males to be living in the family home, and among adults men were more likely to be living in hospital.

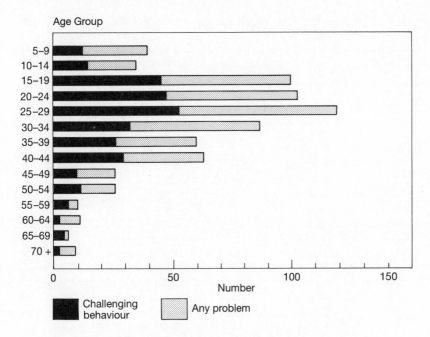

1.3 Age structure of people identified in the survey, showing the proportion of each age group whose behaviour met the definition of challenging (N = 695)

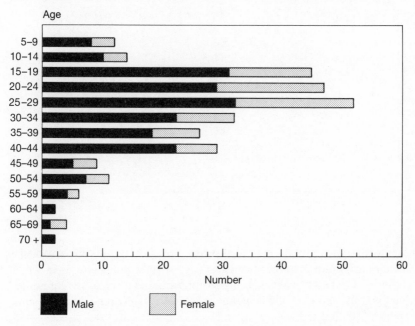

1.4 People identified as showing challenging behaviour: age and sex (N = 291)

Table 1.3   *Residential location of people showing challenging behaviour by gender and age group*

		Men %	Women %
Under 18			
	Community facility	44	21
	Family home	56	79
	N	36	14
18 or more			
	Hospital	57	42
	Community or out of district	26	30
	Family home	17	29
	N	157	84

Table 1.4   *Comparison of age structure of an overall population (Harris and Russell, 1989), and of people identified as showing challenging behaviour in the North West*

Age	Harris and Russell (%)	Challenging behaviour group (%)	Difference (%)
5–9	5	4	−1
10–14	7	5	−2
15–19	9	16	+7
20–24	12	16	+4
25–29	15	18	+3
30–34	9	11	+2
35–39	10	9	−1
40–44	8	10	+2
45–49	6	3	−3
50–54	6	4	−2
55–59	4	2	−2
60–64	4	1	−3
65–69	3	1	−2
70+	6	1	−5
	(N = 901)	(N = 291)	

Since information about the overall age structure of the population screened is not available it is not possible to construct age-specific prevalence rates which might indicate whether particular age groups are under- or over-represented among people showing challenging behaviour. However, there is some comparative data which may be used. Harris and Russell (1989) in their study of aggressive behaviour were able to use information from a Case Register in one health district (not in the North West), and Table 1.4 gives a comparison between people identified as showing challenging behaviour in the current study and the total population of people with learning disabilities using services in Harris and Russell's study. This comparison suggests that the age group 15–34 is consistently over-represented in the group showing challenging behaviour, with the subgroup 15–19 being most prominent in this respect. People aged 45 or more are consistently under-represented. This comparison is not as satisfactory as that which could be made using age-specific rates of prevalence, but it is probably the best which can be achieved with available data. It must lend weight to the importance of careful assessment and service planning for school leavers, especially since the probability that a person showing behaviour problems will be placed in long-stay hospital rises steadily as age increases after the age of 18. The post-school period is a time of significant change in the life of the young person and in the services they receive. For a variety of reasons it is also a key period in relation to family care (Qureshi, 1990).

Figure 1.5 gives the overall figures for the residential location of adults showing challenging behaviour, separating those living in the community into those who live in residential facilities and those who live in the family home. Table 1.5 gives the residential location of people between 15 and 34 divided into five-year age bands, making clear the changing pattern, towards hospital residence, as age increases.

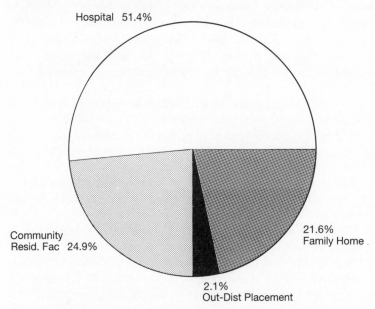

1.5 Adults (aged 18 or more) identified as showing challenging behaviour: where they lived (N = 241)

Table 1.5   *Percentage of each age group living in particular locations*

Age group	Hospital (%)	Location Community residential (%)	Family home (%)	Total N
15–19	2	44	53	45 (100%)
20–24	19	28	53	47 (100%)
25–29	54	31	15	52 (100%)
30–34	81	19	–	32 (100%)

Staff were asked to indicate the degree of learning disability for each person. This was categorised as borderline, moderate or severe/profound, with an instruction that the last category meant an IQ of less than 50. In one in eight instances the level of handicap was recorded as 'not assessed/cannot say'. Of the remainder, 71 per cent were classified as severe/profound, 21 per cent moderate and 8 per cent borderline. A number of studies have suggested that people with mild or moderate handicap are disproportionately represented among adults with behaviour problems. However, as Richardson *et al.* (1984) observe this may be a consequence of the fact that behaviour problems may be the factor which brings people with lower levels of disability into services at all. Those who are mildly disabled and show no behaviour problems may function in society without the assistance of services, especially in adulthood when the specific intellectual demands of the school system are no longer relevant. Thus, because they no longer use services, they will not form part of the base population against which the group with challenging behaviour are compared.

The importance of the presence of additional disabilities in relation to service use by people with less severe learning disabilities is highlighted by the fact that a majority of the small number of people in the 'borderline' category were said to have a mental illness, whereas only 15 per cent of adults with challenging behaviour overall had a definite diagnosis of mental illness. This last figure represented 16 per cent of people in hospital and 12.6 per cent of people in the community. Such rates of prevalence of mental illness are not very different from existing estimates of prevalence among the whole population of people with learning difficulty. For example, Jacobson (1982) reported a figure of 12.4 per cent for a general population of people with developmental disability, and Eaton and Menolascino (1982) found 14.3 per cent of a community-based population were also mentally ill. Thus the findings of the current study do not suggest that people with psychiatric illness are very substantially over-represented among people with challenging behaviour. There are, of course, widely acknowledged difficulties of diagnosis (Reid, 1983), but it does seem that, in contrast to the views of a Department of

Health Study team (DoH, 1989, para. 7.10), the vast majority of people with challenging behaviour do not suffer from psychiatric illness, although people with borderline mental disabilities who show behaviour problems may be relatively more likely than others showing challenging behaviour to be suffering from a mental illness. Fraser *et al.* (1986) also testify to the lack of any strong association between behaviour problems and psychiatric illness in people with learning disabilities, although this is not to deny that people with a dual diagnosis may be a group needing particular attention. Interestingly, in the HARC study, staff did suspect mental illness as a possible factor underlying behaviour problems in 6 per cent of cases where it had not been formally diagnosed by a psychiatrist.

A HYPOTHETICAL DISTRICT

Another way to interpret this epidemiological information is to construct a hypothetical 'average' district and consider the numbers of people with challenging behaviour who would be expected. The average population size of districts involved in the survey was approximately 220,000, the average number of people identified as showing challenging behaviour was 41·6. Using whole numbers, the profile of age and residential location of the 'average' group of people with challenging behaviour is given in Table 1.6.

Table 1.6 *Age and location profile showing challenging behaviour in hypothetical average district*

Age and Location			Number
In Community			
	Age	5–9	2
		10–14	2
		15–19	6
	Adults	(20+)	13
In Hospital			
	Adults	(18+)	17
Placed outside District			2
	Total		42

VARIATION ACROSS DISTRICTS

Within the seven districts studied there was considerable variation around this average picture. The standardised number of people showing challenging behaviour ranged from a low of thirty-one in a district classified by Craig (1985) as a 'High Status Growth Area', to a high of fifty-six in each of two districts containing inner-city areas classified by Craig as 'service areas and cities'. However, much, though not all, of this variation could be explained by variations in the administratively-defined population of people with learning disabilities across different districts. Richardson and Koller (1985) observed that such variations exist and are related to socioeconomic factors, and Fryers (1984) argued that districts with declining populations overall might have proportionately higher numbers of people with learning disabilities, perhaps because of differential migration. In the current study, the two districts which included inner-city areas with declining populations did indeed have higher than average numbers of people using learning disabilities services, and therefore, although the *proportions* who showed challenging behaviour were not markedly different from most other districts, relatively higher numbers were identified as showing challenging behaviour. The use of different base populations therefore gives us quite different information which is useful for different purposes. If our purpose were to allocate resources among districts, then the rate in relation to the districts' overall population would be important, as this reflects the absolute size of the problem. However, to make other meaningful comparisons across districts, for example, to investigate the relative likelihood that people in services were seen as showing challenging behaviours, then the population using services for people with learning disabilties should be used as a base.

One key factor which influences the prevalence of challenging behaviour in community-based services in any given district will be the level of use made of hospital placement in that district. The proportions of adults showing challenging behaviour who were placed in hospital showed a wide range across the Districts studied, varying from 80 per cent of those identified in one District to 39 per cent in another. At the time of the survey the former district contained two large mental handicap hospitals. It was clear that people in community-based services in this district were not dealing with any very substantial level of challenging behaviour because of the very high level of use of hospital placement, at least in the past. Thus if resources were to be distributed amongst districts to develop services for people with challenging behaviours, some districts might appropriately emphasise the building up of community-based services suitable for people discharged from hospital, whereas others might concentrate more resources on the prevention of admissions. Although both aspects would be necessary to some extent in every case, the most suitable emphasis would depend on historical practice.

WHAT KINDS OF BEHAVIOUR DID PEOPLE SHOW?

The four categories of problem behaviour which seemed to have aroused most concern, as has been mentioned, are: physical attacks on others; self-injury; destructive behaviour; other socially or sexually unacceptable behaviour. Staff were asked to indicate which of the four main areas represented the individual's most serious management problem at that time, and which represented a lesser, or potentially serious but controlled problem. All types of behaviour could be rated 'most serious' if appropriate. The following table gives an indication of the extent to which particular categories of problem were rated absent or present, and the proportion of those adults identified as showing challenging behaviour for whom the particular problem area listed was rated as one of their most serious management problems.

Table 1.7 *Adults with challenging behaviour: the proportion that showed any challenging behaviours at all compared with the proportion for whom this was rated their most serious problem*

	Show problem at all (%)	*Rated 'most serious'* (%)
Physical attacks	72	33
Self-injury	54	23
Destruction	61	24
Other	91	58

N = 241

As is to some extent evident from the table above, there is considerable overlap between groups. For example, of people who showed self injury at all, 70 per cent also made physical attacks on others, and of people who made physical attacks at all 52 per cent also self-injured. One in eight people had no problems rated 'most serious' but all of these had at least one area rated potentially serious but controlled. Of those who had at least one area rated serious, in 43 per cent of instances staff had given this rating to more than one type of behaviour. This emphasises the previously mentioned drawbacks to the collection of information about people showing one kind of behaviour only. The particular behaviour chosen may not be the aspect which is currently causing staff concern in relation to the person. Also, a person showing self-injury might have been prescribed psychotropic drugs in an attempt to deal with aggressive behaviour towards others, rather than for self-injury, thus making specific service response to self-injury difficult to assess. Although it is acknowledged that these descriptive categories may break down when analysed in depth, it clearly does help to orient discussion about the group of people identified if it is understood that, for example, for one-third of those showing challenging behaviour, 'physical attacks on others' was rated as their most serious management problem. Those who showed physical attacks but not self-injury were less likely to be rated as having severe learning disabilities, and those who showed 'other unacceptable behaviour' only, without self-injury or attacks, were more likely to live in community residential facilities. However these relationships were not particularly strong, and there were many exceptions to such generalisations.

One important function of epidemiological research is that it can give an understanding of the situation of the majority of individuals in the group of interest. A wealth of literature exists describing behavioural, and to a lesser extent psychopharmacological, intervention used with people who have learning disabilities and challenging behaviour (Singh and Repp, 1988; Gadow and Poling, 1988; Lennox *et al.*, 1988). However, results from epidemiological studies suggest that behavioural techniques are in much less widespread use than might be supposed from reading the practice literature, and that the use of psychotropic drugs is the treatment of choice. Oliver, Murphy and Corbett (1987), for example, found that only 2 per cent of 596 people showing self-injurious behaviour were enrolled on formal psychological treatment programmes, whereas almost half were receiving psychotropic drugs.

Staff in the HARC survey were asked about the use of drugs and behaviour modification programmes with the people identified as showing challenging behaviour. The particular question specified that the treatment should be designed to reduce or prevent the behaviour under consideration, and in the case of programmes stipulated an 'agreed written behaviour modification programme'. Around two-thirds of adults and children showing challenging behaviour were subject to at least one of these, meaning that 37 per cent of adults and 34 per cent of children (under 18) were receiving neither. For adults, there was considerable variation across residential locations in the proportion receiving neither of these interventions. The majority (55%) of adults living with their families received neither drugs nor behaviour modification programmes, and this was also true of 39 per cent of people living in community facilities but of only 24 per cent of people in hospital.

Table 1.8 gives the percentages of adults and of children (under 18), in different residential locations, who were said to be subject to either of these forms of intervention.

These figures may be slightly more encouraging in relation to the use of behavioural techniques than those of Oliver, Murphy and Corbett (1987), but they still indicate a predominance of treatment by drugs among adults, particularly in hospital settings, where a substantial majority of those identified are said to be subject to this form of treatment. Behaviour modification is clearly the treatment of choice for children with challenging behaviour but this position is substantially reversed in adulthood. The question arises as to the degree of overlap between these treatments; Figure 1.6 illustrates this for adults only. It is clear that the majority of people receiving behaviour modification in hospital are also receiving drugs, although there is a greater degree of separation for people living in the community.

Table 1.8   *Adults and children identified as showing challenging behaviour: where they lived and the percentage said to be subject to particular treatments/interventions*

	% of each group said to be taking drugs to control behaviour			% of each group said to be subject to a behaviour modification programme (in any setting)		
Age 18 years or more	Hospital	Community	Family	Hospital	Community	Family
	N = 124	N = 66	N = 51			
N = 241	69	41	31	32	29	24
		Overall 54%			Overall 27%	
Age under 18		N = 19	N = 31			
		5	26	63	61	
N = 50		Overall 18%		Overall 60%		

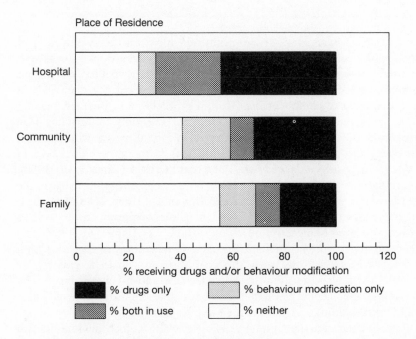

Place of Residence

% receiving drugs and/or behaviour modification

■ % drugs only   ▦ % behaviour modification only

▨ % both in use   □ % neither

1.6   Adults (aged 18 or more) showing challenging behaviour: forms of intervention by residential location (N = 241)

A range of psychotropic drugs are normally prescribed to try and influence behaviour, most prominently the anti-psychotic drugs (*British National Formulary*, 1988). The final section of the questionnaire asked for the names of specific drugs currently being taken, although without making any explicit link to the function of controlling behaviour. Results are given in Table 1.9, and it will be evident that the numbers reportedly taking anti-psychotic drugs conform quite closely with the proportion said to be taking drugs to prevent or reduce behaviour problems. Antiepileptic drugs are not included in Table 1.9.

Table 1.9   *Adults with challenging behaviour: types of drugs currently being taken, by place of residence*

Residence	Taking anti-psychotic drugs (%)	Taking any psychotropic drug (%)	Number in that location
Hospital	69	79	124
Community Facility	39	50	66
Family Home	28	43	51
All	52	64	241

Of course, as Bates *et al.* (1986) point out, high rates of prescription of psychotropic drugs do not in themselves prove that drugs are being misused or over-used. However, Singh and Repp (1988) question whether, given their potentially severe side-effects and limited demonstrable efficacy, drugs should be the treatment of choice for behavioural problems, and whether they are used appropriately with specific clients (p. 273). Certainly concern has been expressed about the high levels of prescription of psychotropic drugs, particularly anti-psychotic drugs, to people with learning disabilities both in the UK (Lynch, 1989; Clarke *et al.*, 1990) and the USA (Rinck *et al.*, 1989). Programmes designed to reduce the levels of use of psychotropic drugs in the States have met with considerable success (Singh and Repp, 1988). Equally a more stringent set of legal safeguards and guidelines on prescribing do seem to have reduced levels of prescription, again in the USA (Rinck *et al.*, 1989). The latter paper reports the case in the USA of an individual with a severe learning disability who successfully sued the institution in which he resided for damages in compensation for the side-effects of anti-psychotic drugs. The court found that negligence had occurred in the administration of major tranquillisers without evidence for the need for such drugs.

Table 1.10 illustrates that among people with challenging behaviour, the use of drugs is most frequently reported in relation to self-injurious behaviour, and behaviour modification is least often used in relation to physical attacks. Emerson (1991) specifically argues in relation to self-injurious behaviour that there is little evidence that psychotropic medication is effective, and that there are indications that some anti-psychotic drugs can lead to serious irreversible

Table 1.10   *Relative use of different treatments/interventions among adults for identified main area of challenging behaviour*

Type of behaviour	Drugs to control this behaviour (%)	Behaviour modification (%)
Physical attacks (N = 80)	53	20
Self-injury (N = 56)	73	27
Destruction (N = 58)	51	28
Other unacceptable behaviour (N = 140)	47	25

side-effects (see also Chapter 9). Insufficient information was collected in the current study to assess the appropriacy of prescriptions but, as has been mentioned, only 15 per cent of adults with challenging behaviour were diagnosed as having a mental illness. Perhaps there is a case for the introduction in this country of American guidelines, which require target behaviours to be explicitly stated, provision for evaluation of effectivenesss to be included in the treatment plan, behavioural changes to be monitored and recorded, and ineffective treatments to be discontinued in a specified time period, wherever psychotropic drugs are prescribed (Rinck *et al.*, 1989).

In Table 1.11 people were counted as subject to a behaviour modification programme if one was applied in any setting in which they were identified. Since 116 people were identified in two different settings it was possible to consider the question of consistency of application of programmes across settings, although in order to generate sufficient numbers, all people who showed behaviour problems are included, not just those identified as 'challenging'. The results are indicated for different identified problem areas.

Table 1.11   *People identified in two different settings: whether or not behaviour modification programmes are being applied in each setting by problem area*

Most serious or potentially serious problem area	N	Number with no programme at all	Number with programme in one setting only	Number with programme in both settings
Physical attacks	32	14	13	5
Self-injury	29	13	11	5
Destruction	24	15	7	2
Other	60	30	28	2

Of course it may be that behaviour differs across settings in some instances, and so there may be some cases where a behavioural intervention may be necessary in one setting but not in another. These numbers are admittedly small, but they do seem to indicate that it is the exception rather than the rule to find an agreed behaviour modification programme which is consistently applied across a number of settings.

CONCLUSIONS

This Chapter argues that there is no one overarching operational definition which will provide the basis for the epidemiology of challenging behaviour. It should not be expected that the 'fuzzy edges' of the concept, which reflect inevitable elements of social judgement in its construction, can be entirely eliminated. Specific operational definitions will have to be chosen which are suitable for the purposes of the particular study. This is not to deny that there will undoubtedly be individuals about whom there is a wide measure of social agreement that their behaviour is a challenge to services. However, there will also be others about whom knowledge and opinions differ among interested parties, among whom may be included both staff and family members, as well as the person in question. On an everyday basis the negotiation of the label 'challenging' is a social process. Although the labelling of individuals may be decried as a possible negative outcome of this process, if this label brings the possibility of additional resources, people are likely to feel that the advantages of its use outweigh the disadvantages.

In practice it is usually the case that people acquire the label because they are referred to senior managers in services as posing particular difficulties. In a policy study associated with the HARC survey (Routledge, 1990) senior managers in Social and Community Health Services were interviewed about their perceptions of challenging behaviour. They felt that the identification of individuals as challenging to services reflected both characteristics and circumstances. They also made a 'rule of thumb' distinction between people whose behaviour would probably be resistant to changes of environment, and people whose problem behaviour they viewed as probably service defined or maintained. The existence of this latter group, it was argued, reflected low levels of staff tolerance and skill, low access to professional support and the general inadequacies of some mainstream day and residential services. The former group was believed to be far smaller in terms of numbers. Given this view, service managers had some reservations about an exclusive focus on a the development of special services. It seemed to them that action at the system level, such as improved staff training, or greater access to professional support, might be more effective in reducing perceived challenging behaviour. Certainly there was a widespread view that if more resources were available for improvements in basic services, this would bring about substantial reductions in the prevalence of challenging behaviour, even though some special services might still be necessary for a few people.

Of course, without implementing and observing such changes, it is not possible to say whether this is an accurate view. However, epidemiological knowledge might assist in focussing attention on particular facilities, or individuals, although results would have to be interpreted in the light of local knowledge. For example, an over-identification of challenging behaviour in one or two particular day or residential facilities might reflect referral policies, or it might reflect poor practice in those facilities. In terms of service planning, a detailed knowledge of the residential location of people identified as showing challenging behaviour might help to ensure that an appropriate balance is struck between devoting resources to the facilitation of hospital discharge as opposed to the prevention of admission. At present, academic commentators and the Audit Commission (1989) have both indicated that preventative work with people in the community is relatively neglected, leading to a perception in some areas that there is a two-tier service, with people who have never been admitted to hospital relatively disadvantaged compared with those who have been relocated (Hardy *et al.*,1990).

If the HARC method of identification is viewed as a reasonable one to use, then it is suggested (although not proved for services outside the North Western Region) that the numbers of people showing challenging behaviour in a given district will be likely to vary according to the socio-economic and demographic characteristics of the district, and their residential location will vary according to past and present practice in relation to long-term hospital placement, although these factors alone will not determine the distribution. The total number of adults and children identified may be expected to vary between 31 and 56 (in a District of 220,000 population). The majority of those identified will be men, but men will be more likely to be placed in hospital, so the relative numbers of men and women identified in the community will be more equal than in hospital. People between the ages of 15 and 35 will be over-represented. Finally the results on the use of drugs and behaviour modification with people showing challenging behaviour, illustrate one important function of epidemiological study: the monitoring of overall service responses to challenging behaviour in order to assess whether new thinking and new methods of intervention do actually filter through in any substantial degree to those people with learning disabilities who might benefit from them.

References

Audit Commission (1989), *Developing community care for adults with a mental handicap*. Occasional Paper No. 9, October.

Baker, N. and Urquhart, J. (1987), *The Balance of Care for Adults with a Mental Handicap in Scotland*, Information Services Division, Scottish Health Service, Edinburgh.

Bates, W. J., Smeltzer, D. J. and Arnoczky, S. M. (1986), 'Appropriate and inappropriate use of psychotherapeutic medications for institutionalized mentally retarded persons', *American Journal of Mental Deficiency*, 90 (4), 363–70.

Bean, A. and Roszkowski, M. (1982), 'Item-domain relationships in the adaptive behavior scale (ABS)', *Applied Research in Mental Retardation*, 3, 359–67.

Blunden, R. and Allen, D. (1987), *Facing the Challenge: An Ordinary Life for People with Learning Difficulties and Challenging Behaviour*, King's Fund, London.

British Medical Association and the Pharmaceutical Society of Great Britain, *Royal British National Formulary*, (1988), London.

Clarke, D. J., Kelley, S., Thinn, K. and Corbett, J. A. (1990), 'Psychotropic drugs and mental retardation: 1. Disabilities and the prescription of drugs for behaviour and epilepsy in three residential settings', *Journal of Mental Deficiency Research*, 34, 385–95.

Clements, P., Bost, L. W., DuBois, Y. G. and Turpin, W. (1980), 'Adaptive Behavior Scale Part Two: relative severity of maladaptive behavior', *American Journal of Mental Deficiency*, 84 (5), 465–69.

Cohen, J. (1960), 'A coefficient of agreement for nominal scales', *Educational and Psychological Measurement*, 20, 37–46.

Craig, J. (1985), *A 1981 Socio-economic Classification of Local and Health Authorities of Great Britain*, OPCS studies on medical and population subjects No. 48, HMSO, London.

Department of Health (1989), *Needs and Responses: Adults with a Mental Handicap and Behaviour Disturbance*, report of a Department of Health Study Team, HMSO, London.

Eaton, L. and Menolascino, F. (1982), 'Psychiatric disorders in the mentally retarded: types, problems and challenges', *American Journal of Psychiatry*, 139, 1297–1303.

Emerson, E., Barrett, S., Bell, C., Cummings, R., McCool, C., Toogood, A. and Mansell, J. (1987), *Developing Services for People with Severe Learning Difficulties and Challenging Behaviours*, Institute of Social and Applied Psychology, University of Kent, Canterbury.

Emerson, E. (in press), 'Self-injurious behaviour: an overview of recent trends in epidemiological and behavioural research', forthcoming in *Current Opinion in Psychiatry*.

Eyman, R., Borthwick, S., and Miller, C. (1981), 'Trends in maladaptive behavior of mentally retarded persons placed in community settings and institutional settings', *American Journal of Mental Deficiency*, 85 (5), 473–77.

Eyman, R., and Call, T. (1977), 'Maladaptive behavior and community placement of mentally retarded persons', *American Journal of Mental Deficiency*, 82 (2), 137–44.

Fraser, W., Leudar, I., Gray, J. and Campbell, I. (1986), 'Psychiatric and behaviour disturbances in mental handicap', *Journal of Mental Deficiency Research*, 30, 49–57.

Fryers, T. (1984), *The Epidemiology of Severe Intellectual Impairment: The Dynamics of Prevalence*, Academic Press, London.

Gadow, K. D. and Poling, A.G. (1988), *Pharmacotherapy and Mental Retardation*, Little, Brown & Co., Boston, M.A.

Griffin, J. C., Williams, D. E., Stark, M. T., Altmeyer, B. K., and Mason, M. (1986), 'Self-injurious behavior: a state-wide prevalence survey of the extent and circumstances', *Applied Research in Mental Retardation*, 7, 105–116.

Hardy, B., Wistow, G. and Rhodes, R. (1990), 'Policy networks and the implementation of community care policy for people with mental handicaps', *Journal of Social Policy*, 19 (2), 141–68.

Harris, P. and Russell, O. (1989a), *The Prevalence of Aggressive Behaviour among People with Learning Difficulties in a Single Health District*, interim report, Norah Fry Research Centre, University of Bristol.

Harris, P. and Russell, O. (1989b), *The Nature of Aggressive Behaviour*, second report, Norah Fry Research Centre, University of Bristol.

Hill, B. and Bruininks, R. (1984), 'Maladaptive behavior of mentally retarded individuals in residential facilities', *American Journal of Mental Deficiency*, 88, 380–87.

Hollis, J. H. and Meyers C. E. (1982), '*Life-Threatening Behavior: Analysis and Intervention*, AAMD, Washington DC.

Holmes, C. B. and Batt, R. (1980), 'Is choking others really equivalent to stamping one's feet? An analysis of Adaptive Behavior Scale items', *Psychological Reports*, 46, 1277–78.

Holmes, N., Shah, A., and Wing, L. (1982), 'The Disability Assessment Schedule: a brief screening device for use with the mentally retarded', *Psychological Medicine*, 12, 879–90.

Isett, R. and Spreat, S. (1979), 'Test-Retest and Interrater Reliability of the AAMD Adaptive Behavior Scale', *American Journal of Mental Deficiency*, 84 (1), 93–5.

Jacobson, J. W. (1982), 'Problem behavior and psychiatric impairment within a developmentally disabled population 1: Behavior frequency', *Applied Research in Mental Retardation*, 3, 121–39.

Jay Committee (1979), *Report of the Committee of Enquiry into Mental Handicap Nursing and Care*, V II, OPCS survey (Table 26) Cmnd. 7468 -II, HMSO, London.

Kiernan, C. and Qureshi, H. (1986). *Feasibility Study for a Survey of the Prevalence and Characteristics of Individuals with Mental Handicap and Severe Behavior Problems* Hester Adrian Research Centre, University of Manchester.

Koller, H., Richardson, S., Katz, M. and McLaren, J. (1982), 'Behavior disturbance in childhood and the early adult years in populations who were and were not mentally retarded', *Journal of Preventive Psychiatry*, 1 (4), 453–68.

Koller, H., Richardson, S., Katz, M. and McLaren, J. (1983), 'Behavior disturbance since childhood among a 5-year birth cohort of all mentally retarded young adults in a city', *American Journal of Mental Deficiency*, 87 (4), 386–95.

Kushlick, A., Blunden, R. and Cox, G. (1973), 'The Wessex Social and Physical Incapacity (SPI) Scale and the Speech, Self Help and Literacy Scale (SSL)', *Psychological Medicine*, 3, 336–78.

Kushlick, A. and Cox, G. (1968), 'Planning services for the subnormal in Wessex', in Wing, J. K. and Bransby, B. R. (eds.), *Psychiatric Case Registers*, HMSO, London.

Lennox, D. B., Miltenberger, R. G., Spengler, P. and Erfanian, N. (1988), 'Decelerative treatment practices with persons who have mental retardation: A review of five years of the literature', *American Journal on Mental Retardation*, 92, 492–501.

Leudar, I. and Fraser, W. (1986), 'Behaviour disturbance and its assessment' in Hogg, J. and Raynes, N. (eds.), *Assessment in Mental Handicap: A Guide to Assessment Practices, Tests and Checklists*, Chapman and Hall, London.

Leudar, I., Fraser, W. and Jeeves, M. A., (1984), 'Behaviour disturbance and mental handicap: typology and longitudinal trends', *Psychological Medicine*, 14, 923–35.

Lynch, S. P. J. (1989), 'Prescribing practice in a mental handicap hospital: 2. Psychotropic medication from 1978–87', *Mental Handicap*, 17, 123–28.

Nihira, K. (1969), 'Factorial dimensions of adaptive behavior in adult retardates', *American Journal of Mental Deficiency*, 73, 868–78.

Nihira, K., Foster, R., Shellhaas, M. and Leland, H. (1974), *AAMD Adaptive Behavior Scale*, American Association on Mental Deficiency, Washington DC.

Nihira, L. and Nihira, K. (1975), 'Jeopardy in community placement', *American Journal of Mental Deficiency*, 79, 538–44.

North Western Regional Health Authority (1985). *Services for People who are Mentally Handicapped: Services for People with Additional Special Needs*. A consultative document issued by NWRHA, Manchester.

Oliver, C., Murphy, G. and Corbett, J., (1987), 'Self-injurious behaviour in people with mental handicap: a total population study', *Journal of Mental Deficiency Research*, 31, 147–62.

Qureshi, H. (1990), *Parents Caring for Young Adults with Mental Handicap and Behaviour Problems*, Hester Adrian Research Centre, University of Manchester.

Qureshi, H., Alborz A. and Kiernan, C. (1989), *Prevalence of Individuals with Mental Handicap who Show Severe Problem Behaviour: Preliminary Results*, report to the Department of Health, Hester Adrian Research Centre, University of Manchester.

Reed, J. (1990), 'Identification and description of adults with mental handicaps showing physically aggressive behaviours', *Mental Handicap Research*, 3 (2), 126–36

Reid, A. H. (1983), 'Psychiatry of mental handicap: a review', *Journal of the Royal Society of Medicine*, 76, 587–92.

Richardson, S. and Koller, H. (1985), 'Epidemiology' in Clarke, A., Clarke, A. and Berg, J. (eds.), *Mental Deficiency: The Changing Outlook* (4th edn.), Methuen, London.

Richardson, S., Koller, H. and Katz, M. (1984), 'Career paths through mental retardation services: an epidemiological perspective', *Applied Research in Mental Retardation*, 5, 53–67.

Rinck, C., Guidry, J. and Calkins, C. F. (1989), 'Review of states' practices on the use of psychotropic medication', *American Journal on Mental Retardation*, 93 (6), 657–68.

Routledge, M. (1990), *Services for People with a Mental Handicap whose Behaviour is a Challenge to Services: A Review of the Policy and Service context in the Seven Districts Covered by the HARC Behaviour Problems Project*, report to Department of Health, Hester Adrian Research Centre, University of Manchester .

Schroeder, S., Schroeder, C., Smith, B. and Dalldorf, J. (1978), 'Prevalence of self-injurious behaviors in a large state facility for the retarded: a three-year follow-up study', *Journal of Autism and Childhood Schizophrenia*, 8 (3), 261–69.

Singh, N. N. and Repp, A. C. (1988), 'The behavioural and pharmacological management of problem behaviours in people with mental retardation', *The Irish Journal of Psychology*, 9 (2), 264–85.

Thomas, D. and Webster, R. (1974), 'The Application of the Adaptive-Behavior Scales in the United Kingdom', paper for the Workshop and Symposium on the AAMD Adaptive-Behavior Scales at the 98th Annual Meeting of the American Association on Mental Deficiency, Toronto.

Prevalence and persistency of challenging behaviour in children

INTRODUCTION

The previous chapter has described a large-scale prevalence study which has brought many important issues to light. We present a more modest attempt at identifying prevalence of challenging behaviour in children with learning disabilities. Our study was carried out simultaneously, but independently from Qureshi and her colleagues. Our target area (Salford) is in fact one of the seven districts included in Qureshi's study. We were particularly interested in the persistence of challenging behaviour and therefore employed a long-term follow-up methodology for our sample of children.

The recent developments in service provision and therapeutic interventions for people with severe challenging behaviour and learning disabilities have been largely confined to adults (see for example, Chapters 3 and 4). Reasons for this may be that (1) challenging behaviour presents more difficulties when exhibited in adulthood; (2) any explanations of it being a developmental problem ('she'll grow out of it') will have been exhausted by adulthood. Despite this, people working in services for children with learning disabilities are concerned about the numbers who display challenging behaviours of one type or another. There is a recognition that parents and carers are coping with difficulties only because of the size and lack of physical power of their child and that the behaviours, if not ameliorated, will develop into a much more serious challenge when the child matures.

It is important that careful research is carried out which examines the contributing factors to maintenance or amelioration of challenging behaviour in this young population. Only then can efficient services be designed. Prevalence and persistency studies are a necessary (but merely first) step in this process. They need to be followed by intervention studies specific to the various types of behavioural disorders identified by the prevalence studies.

There are few studies which report on the prevalence of challenging behaviour among children with severe learning disabilities and even fewer on the persistency of challenging behaviour in childhood and later life. Some researchers (e.g. Birch *et al.*, 1970) have examined the 'psychiatric status' of children with learning disabilities. The prevalence reported in these studies must not be equated with challenging behaviour prevalence, as some psychiatric symptoms may pose no challenge to the services.

In the younger age group (5–14 years) with learning disabilities, Stein and Susser (1975) found that 20 per cent displayed a behaviour disorder. Kushlick and Blunden (1974) reported that in an adolescent population (15–19 years) prevalence is somewhat higher (29%). Koller *et al.* (1983) interviewed young adults with learning disabilities and their parents retrospectively about behaviour disturbances in their childhood and post-school period. They also drew on any records available from support and other public services such as files of health visitors, social workers, schools and courts. They used four categories of behaviour disturbance: 1) emotional disturbance including psychiatric symptoms; 2) hyperactive behaviour; 3) aggressive conduct disorder; 4) anti-social behaviour including delinquent acts. Sixty-one per cent of this sample showed some behavioural disturbance in childhood and 59 per cent in the post-school period ($N = 192$). In the post-school period, the less disabled males (IQ more than 60) often displayed anti-social behaviour whereas the women in this ability group frequently reported emotional disturbance. Prevalence of behaviour disorder in children with severe learning disabilities (IQ less then 50) was slightly higher (at 27%) in this study than in the Stein and Susser (1975) report. Prevalence in adolescence/young adults was slightly lower (at 20%) than the Kushlick and Blunden (1974) findings. All of the categories of behaviour disorder had similar prevalence in the two life periods, except hyperactive behaviour which showed a dramatic decrease (from 12% to 3%). However, no conclusions can be drawn from these data about *persistency* as presence or absence of behaviour disorder was only reported for groups. Also, the findings of this study must be interpreted with caution as most of the information was gathered by *post hoc* interviews and record searching.

A more recent study which has attempted to differentiate between behaviour that is merely disturbing and behaviour that is severely challenging was carried out by Kiernan and Kiernan (1989). They contacted a sample of Severe Learning Disabilities (SLD) schools in Great Britain. Staff were asked to identify children whose behaviour 'presented a significant challenge to their management and education' and subsequently to classify these children as 'extremely difficult, very difficult, moderately difficult, or the least difficult of those identified'. Returns from 79 schools (51% return rate) showed a wide variation but on average 23 per cent of pupils were identified as challenging (giving an average of 14 per school). This rate of prevalence is in concordance with the studies described above. However, of these fourteen children only five (8%) were 'extremely or very difficult' and nine 'moderately or least difficult'. Kiernan and Kiernan estimate on the basis of these data that there are around 2000 children with severe challenging behaviour in SLD schools nationally.

As a result of their recent epidemiological research across seven health districts, Qureshi (see Chapter 1) proposes a typical age and location profile for a group of people with severe challenging behaviour. They suggest that in an average-size health district, ten young individuals (between 5 and 19 years of age) will live in the community and will exhibit serious challenging behaviour.

Jones *et al.* (1988) identified by questionnaire twenty-five children with severe challenging behaviour in the area of Gwent. Their definition for this sample was based on that of the King's Fund Centre (see Introduction in this volume, p.1). The same King's Fund Centre publication refers to a crude estimate that was produced by the 'Wessex Survey' of twenty years ago (Kushlick and Cox, 1967). This suggests that in any population of 100,000 there are approximately ten children with learning disabilities and severe behaviour problems. This estimate agrees with the Jones *et al.* finding that in an average NHS health district (250,000 population) twenty-five such children exist.

A study of children with Downs Syndrome in the Greater Manchester area by Cunningham reported that between 20 per cent and 40 per cent of these children aged between five and ten years had displayed 'severe behaviour problems' at one time (reported in Griffin, 1989). These relatively high prevalence rates may be explained by the inclusion of children who had been severely challenging 'at one time'. They may not have presented behavioural problems at the time of the study, a criteria employed by most recent prevalence studies.

Matson and Gorman-Smith (1986) found that 49 per cent of children identified as aggressive were between the ages of one and ten years. This suggests that the behaviour may be most prevalent among pre-adolescent children. This contradicts the findings by Qureshi (*op. cit.*) who found that severe challenging behaviour was most prevalent among late adolescents. Definitions of challenging behaviour differ across studies and may well account for these contrasting findings.

Large-scale studies on persistence of challenging behaviour are not numerous. Leudar *et al.* (1984), who investigated a sample of 118 adults with learning disabilities over a two-year period, identified six dimensions of behaviour disturbance. They were: 1) aggressive conduct; 2) mood disturbance; 3) anti-social conduct; 4) communicativeness; 5) idiosyncratic mannerisms; 6) self-injury. They found very high levels of persistency and concluded that each disturbance was its own best (and statistically significant) predictor. In particular, aggressive conduct was most resistance to change: 'it seems easier to become aggressive than to stop' (p. 929).

Windahl (1988) found that self-injurious behaviour was very persistent over a ten-year period for people with learning disabilities living in a Swedish long-stay hospital.

This chapter describes an attempt to identify children with learning disabilities and challenging behaviour in one locality and the services available to them. The children identified as having challenging behaviours and a matched control group were followed up for three to four years to establish whether challenging behaviours were persistent. The research developed from a collaboration between the authors and members of a specialist service (the Salford Barnardo's Families Project, which offers a social work service to children with learning disabilities and their families). The collaboration originated from discussions about how to provide a needs-led service to children with challenging behaviour for whom advice from a clinical psychologist was sought.

METHOD

Background

The data source was the case-load of the team members of the Salford Barnardo's Families Project during a two-year period. The team consisted of qualified social workers.

This case-load did not represent all children with learning disabilities in Salford but rather those children and families that were 'open' to members of the project at that time. They were families with identified needs for social work input.

The computerised mental handicap register in Salford indicated that at the time of the research there were 253 children and young adults with severe learning disabilities under the age of 20 living in Salford with families or foster-parents. The number of children receiving a service from the Barnardo's Project was 126 and thus constituted about half of the total.

The project's social workers used a well-defined method of keeping case notes which emphasised the identification of goals. This required them to define their involvement with children and families in terms of the duration and nature of their interventions. This greatly facilitated the systematic searching of files for data regarding presence, nature and persistence of challenging behaviour, as well as information about the involvement of other agencies and types of interventions offered to the children.

Identification of challenging behaviour

For the purpose of the survey, a list of criteria by which to assess the presence of challenging behaviour was developed from a review of the available literature (e.g. Patterson, 1974) and discussion amongst the researchers. They are listed in Table 2.1. The criteria vary in severity, and much of their 'challenge' can be said to be of a subjective nature. For instance, although there is general agreement that violence to another person is challenging, persistent swearing may be severely challenging behaviour to some people but not to others (see also Chapter 1, page 12).

Table 2.1 *Categories of violent or problematic behaviour used to identify challenging behaviour in children with learning diffiuclties*

1. Negative physical act to others.	Attacking or attempting to attack others, potentially inflicting pain.
2. Ritualised threat of negative physical act to others.	Displaying a behaviour recognised to be an antecedent to physical aggression e.g. raising a fist.
3. Negative physical act to self.	Activity which causes or may cause self-injury.
4. Ritualised threat of negative act to self.	Displaying a physical act recognised to be an antecedent to self-injury.
5. Destructive act.	Destroying, damaging or stealing any object.
6. Ritualised threat of destructive act.	Displaying a behaviour recognised to be an antecedent to destructive acts.
7. High rate activity.	Activity which involves gross or inappropriate physical movements and is aversive to others (e.g. running around the house).
8. Obsessive activity.	Repetitive activity which is non-functional (e.g. touching shoes frequently).
9. Non-compliance.	Not doing what is requested and within competence including eating, going to bed or toilet.
10. Yelling/whining.	Frequent yelling, shouting or talking in a high-pitched voice.
11. Crying.	Frequent and/or long bouts of crying with no obvious cause (e.g. pain, grief, teasing).
12. 'Mithering'	Repetitive questioning after an answer has been given.
13. Inappropriate sexual behaviour.	Frequent and/or inappropriate exposure, masturbation or sexual advances.

The goal-oriented records of all the children whose files were open to the Barnardo's team for the period 1985–86 were scrutinised using the criteria presented in Table 2.1. Children were rated as presenting challenging behaviour if any of these criteria were identified from the section of the case notes which deals with problem behaviour.

One or more types of challenging behaviour were recorded in a large proportion (42.1%) of the files. A number of alternative methods were considered to identify from this group of children those who constituted a *serious* challenge to carers and/or services. For example, one can choose to only include children who displayed violent behaviour (i.e. categories 1–6).

Alternatively, one can include children who displayed violent behaviour *or* more than one of the remaining criteria (7–13). The results of these different methods of categorisation are presented in Table 2.2. Other researchers have employed similar methods to define challenging behaviour (e.g. Clarke *et al.*, 1990). Such criteria will always be arbitrary and the most appropriate selection process will depend on the nature and the purpose of the research or survey.

Qureshi (see previous chapter) specified that severity of behaviour problems depended on the consequences of the behaviour and/or the frequency and/or the need for physical interventions by staff or others.

Table 2.2   *Different methods of identifying children as 'challenging' from case notes (N = 126)*

	No. of children	% of total
Presence of any criterion (cat. 1–13)	53	42.1
Presence of physical aggression (cat. 1–6)	28	22.2
Presence of physical aggression (cat. 1–6) *or* more than one of remaining criteria (cat. 7–13)	34	27

Reliability and validity

The reliability of the identification of the criteria from the case notes was assessed by calculating the agreement between two observers on the presence or absence of the specific criteria of challenging behaviour in the files. Agreement was obtained in 92 per cent of cases, which was considered to be sufficient.

The validity of the criteria for challenging behaviour was then assessed by looking at the overlap between the children identified by the search of case notes (i.e. having one or more types of reported challenging behaviour) and the children identified by their own social workers. The latter had been briefed to identify a 'challenging' group in their case-load on the basis of their social work skills and knowledge of the children and their families. The social workers identified forty-two children (39.2% of the case-load) and the agreement between the two methods of selection was 76.6 per cent. We considered this overlap to be an indication that our criteria are reasonably validated. However, for the purpose of this study a cohort of thirty-one children (29% of the sample) was selected comprising those children who displayed any criterion of challenging behaviour *and* who were also identified as challenging by the Barnardo's social workers without reference to the criteria. This particular selection was preferred since it was able to accommodate any type of challenging behaviour, and achieved the best agreement in identification of the children by both methods of selection

Challenging versus control group

From this challenging group, twenty children were randomly selected in order to compare them with a matched control group which was drawn from the population of children without challenging behaviour. The groups were matched for age and sex as far as possible. The families/carers of both groups were then interviewed by means of a set questionnaire. This questionnaire sought details about characteristics of the family and the child, the nature of the child's learning disabilities and the services that the families received.

In an attempt to study the long-term developments of challenging behaviour, a follow-up study was carried out on the two groups three–four years after the original identification period. For this purpose, the files of the relevant children were scrutinised for 1987, 1988, and 1989.

By 1989, of the forty children, fifteen 'challenging' children and thirteen non-challenging children were still receiving the services of the Barnardo's team. Two children of each group had moved to the adult services, and were receiving input from community mental handicap teams (CMHT's) and could still be included in the follow-up phase of the research. Others had moved out of the area.

The files of the children who were still receiving the services of the Barnardo's team were analysed for the years 1987 up to 1989. The procedure described above was again used to identify the presence/absence of challenging behaviour. For the children receiving adult services, a modified procedure was used. This was because the CMHT case files were differently structured from the Barnardo's files. The CMHT key workers were interviewed to determine whether or not in their opinion the young adults were engaging in challenging behaviour. If challenging behaviour was identified, reference was then made to the criteria described in Table 2.1. The key worker was asked to identify what types of challenging behaviour were or had been present.

Information was also collected on significant changes in the children's lives and the services received by them in the intervening years.

RESULTS

Table 2.3 shows the types of challenging behaviour in rank order of the thirty-one children who were identified as challenging by the double selection method in 1985. Non-compliance was displayed by more than two-thirds of the challenging sample, high-rate activity by over a quarter and physical aggression to others by 23 per cent. Average number of challenging behaviours identified per child was 2.1 (range 1–5; median = 2).

Table 2.3   *Types of challenging behaviour displayed by the original challenging group (N=31) in 1985–86*

Type of challenging behaviour	Number of children (%)
Non-compliance	21 (68)
High-rate activity	8 (26)
Negative physical act to others	7 (23)
Yelling/whining	5 (16)
Destructive act	5 (16)
Negative physical act to self	4 (13)
Obsessive activity	3 (10)
'Mithering'	3 (10)
Ritualised threat of negative physical act to others	3 (10)
Ritualised threat of negative physcial act to self	3 (10)
Crying	2 (6)
Ritualised threat of destructive act	1 (3)
Inappropriate sexual behaviour	0 (0)

Females were more likely to be identified as presenting challenging behaviour than males. Of the original 'challenging' group of thirty-one, fifteen were female and sixteen were male. Yet the total case-load consisted of forty-nine females and seventy-seven males. Thus, 30.6 per cent of the female population and 20.8 per cent of the male population were identified as having challenging behaviour. This difference is not statistically significant but agrees with previous prevalence studies (e.g. Matson and Gorman-Smith, 1986).

There were very few differences between the two groups and even fewer reached statistical significance (see Table 2.4).

However, more children in the challenging group lived in one-parent families and more were an only child. There were no significant differences in terms of individual history and disability, except that the children in the control group had more mobility problems (p < 0.05).

Also, it can be seen from Table 2.5 that the children in the challenging group received significantly more respite and psychology services whereas the non-challenging group received significantly more input from the physiotherapy department. There were no significant differences between the two groups in

Table 2.4 *Familial and individual characteristics of the challenging and the control groups*

	Challenging group (N = 20)	Control group (N = 20)
Living with one parent	9	4
Only child	5	3
1 or 2 siblings	9	10
3 or 4 siblings	6	7
Sibling with special needs	2	1
Sedation/Anti-convulsants	7	7
Special Needs:		
Speech	11	10
Visual	2	4
Learning	2	2
Epilepsy	4	6
Mobility*	1	6

* significant at 0.05 level

Table 2.5 *Services recieved by the challenging and control groups*

Services	Challenging group (N = 20)	Control group (N = 20)
Psychologist **	10	2
Psychiatrist	1	0
Physiotherapist*	5	11
Speech therapist	1	0
Respite care**	12	4
Home sitter	13	11
Portage worker	0	1
Special Leisure Service	9	7
Toy Library	0	1
Volunteer	7	3
Neighbours/friends	11	11

*   significant at 0.05 level
** significant at 0.01 level

terms of receiving help from neighbours/friends or professional input such as psychiatry, speech therapy, Portage or special leisure services.

Follow-up

By contacting the adult services as well as the Barnardo's team, it was possible to obtain data for all but three of the children in the challenging group, and for all but five of the children in the control group in 1990.

From Table 2.6 it is immediately noticeable that significantly more children in the challenging group displayed challenging behaviour during 1989 than their counterparts in the control group. These differences were equally significant during the 1987 and 1988 years.

Table 2.6   *Prevalence of challenging behaviour during the follow-up period*

Year	Challenging group	Control group
1987	13 (N = 17)	0 (N = 20)
1988	15 (N = 17)	1 (N = 15)
1989	15 (N = 17)	1 (N = 15)

Note

N = the number of cases for whom data was available. It can be seen that the number of individuals who remained in 'open casework' varied in different years.

The majority of children (12 out of 17) in the challenging group displayed some type of challenging behaviour in each of the years between the original data collection and the follow-up. A further three showed challenging behaviour in two of the years, one child showed challenging behaviour in only one of the follow-up years and a further one in none of the follow-up years. Persistent challenging behaviour was not present in the control group. Only two children from this group showed any type of challenging behaviour and this was, in both cases, one recording of only one type of challenging behaviour. In contrast, most of the children in the challenging group displayed more than one type of challenging behaviour in each of the follow-up years. Average number of types of challenging behaviour per year was 2.4 (range 0–9) for this group.

The most persistent behaviours observed in the challenging children who were followed up until 1989 were: negative physical act towards self, non-compliance, negative physical act towards others and high-rate activity. Particularly, self-injury was most persistent (all four children who displayed this type of behaviour at the onset of the study still self-injured in the last year of the follow-up period).

Children in the challenging group experienced significantly more major changes in their lives during the three follow-up years. These life changes included divorce, the family moving, change of school and death in the family. Numbers of life changes for the two groups are presented in Table 2.7.

Table 2.7   *Significant life changes*

Year	Challenging group	Control group
1987	4 (N = 17)	0 (N = 20)
1988	6 (N = 17)	4 (N = 15)
1989	9 (N = 17)	3 (N = 15)

DISCUSSION

Forty-two per cent of the children on the case-load in 1985–86 exhibited one or more forms of challenging behaviour. When the definitions for inclusion were made more rigorous by including the social workers' opinions, this figure was reduced to 29 per cent. This prevalence rate is in accordance with previous findings (e.g. Kushlick and Blunden, 1974).

However, because of differences in the definitions of challenging behaviour and the size and type of population studied here, it is not possible to make a direct comparison beween our figures and those referred to in the introduction of this chapter directly. Whereas other studies have included total populations of children with learning disabilities (e.g. by contacting SLD schools), this study used only children who were on a social worker's case-load. It can therefore be expected that our study produced a higher percentage of challenging children as the reason for referral to the Barnardo's team may well have been the child's challenging behaviour.

We found no familial characteristics that were significantly associated with challenging behaviour, although more challenging children lived in one-parent families. Unfortunately, we were not able to include parents'/carers' management techniques and their attitudes to their child's learning disabilities, which may well have shown differences between the groups. Challenging children were not receiving significantly more medication than their non-challenging counterparts, although 10 per cent were taking sedatives (most commonly applied as anti-convulsant).

The only additional special need in which the groups differed significantly was mobility, whereby the control group had more mobility problems than the challenging group. This may simply indicate that children who are not able to move around much are less of a challenge when they are unco-operative or aggressive.

The challenging children received significantly more respite and psychology services, whereas the non-challenging group were seen more by the physio-therapy services. These findings are not surprising, especially since the non-challenging group had a higher incidence of mobility problems. It is interesting to note that a large number of children in both groups received help/ support from neighbours, friends and volunteers.

In contrast to the lack of significant differences between the groups in terms of associated characteristics, the two groups differ greatly in terms of the consistent occurrence of challenging behaviours in the follow-up years. Whereas the non-challenging group only shows two reported behaviour problems, the challenging group continues to display problem behaviour throughout the follow-up years. These results suggest that a strong predictor of challenging behaviour in later life is its occurrence in earlier years, a finding already reported by Leudar *et al.* (1984) for an adult population with behaviour disturbances and by Windahl (1988) for self-injurious behaviour in adults. However, our challenging group also underwent more life changes during the follow-up period. The data presented here cannot throw light on causality. It is quite possible that life events may be antecedents to challenging behaviour. But on the other hand, having a child with challenging behaviour in the family may cause more 'turbulence' resulting in divorce, changing house, changing school, etc.

Quine and Pahl (1985) investigated the relative importance of different sources of stress in families with children who had severe learning disabilities. They found that high levels of maternal stress were most strongly associated with severe behaviour problems (especially night-time disturbance). Families with high 'adversity scores' (which incorporate single parenthood, inadequate housing, low income, debt, social isolation and marital problems) *and* a child with severe behaviour problems produced the hightest maternal malaise scores in the study. However, the authors make no observations about the possible causal relationships between behaviour problems and familial adversity scores.

We consider our findings on the persistence of challenging behaviours to be important. As yet there is very little published research on this, so we are unable to compare our data with that of other studies. But despite our small sample size, we have found clear indications that children with challenging behaviour often grow into adolescents and eventually adults with challenging behaviour, despite a wide range of services available to them. It is difficult to comment upon the actual effectiveness of these services here but we feel that this should become an important focus for future research within the growing literature on achieving positive change for people with challenging behaviour.

The King's Fund definition (see Blunden and Allen, *op. cit.*) firmly places the 'challenge' in the court of the service providers. This study indicates that children and young adults with challenging behaviour require more sophisticated and consistent responses from services if these are to provide support and solutions for this group of young people. We are confident that the recent emergence of multidisciplinary specialist Challenging Behaviour Teams for children and adolescents (see Chapter 5) will contribute to the development of more effective services.

References

Birch, H. G., Richardson, S. A. Baird, D., Horobin, G. & Illsley, R. (1970), *Mental Subnormality in the Community: A Clinical and Epidemiologic Study*, Williams and Wilkins, Baltimore, MD.

Clarke, D. J., Kelley, S., Thinn, K. and Corbett, J. A. (1990), 'Psychotropic drugs and mental retardation: 1. Disabilities and the prescription of drugs for behaviour and epilepsy in three residential settings', *Journal of Mental Deficiency Research*, 34, 385–95.

Griffin, J. (1989), 'Overview of a research programme designed to address key issues in the planning and delivering of services for people with mental handicap', *Journal of Mental Deficiency Research*, 33, 477–85.

Jones, C., Murphy, L., Whiteman, J., Gibbs, G. and Robinson, P. (1988), 'People with a mental handicap and challenging behaviour', proposals for a service in Gwent, unpublished paper.

Kiernan, D. and Kiernan, C. (1989), *Survey of Severe Behaviour Problems in Special Schools: Feedback to Participating Schools*, Hester Adrian Research Centre, University of Manchester.

Kings Fund Centre (1987), *Facing the Challenge: An Ordinary Life for People with Challenging Behaviours*, Kings Fund Centre, London.

Koller, H., Richardson, S. A., Katz, M. and McClaren, J. (1983), 'Behavior disturbance since childhood among a 5–year birth cohort of all mentally retarded young adults in a city *American Journal of Mental Deficiency*, 87(4), 386–95.

Kushlick, A. and Blunden, R. (1974), 'The epidemiology of mental subnormality' in A. M. Clarke and A. D. B. Clarke (eds.), *Mental Deficiency. The Changing Outlook*, Methuen, London.

Kushlick, A. and Cox G. (1967), 'Ascertained prevalence of mental subnormality in the Wessex Region', Proceedings of the International Congress for the Scientific Study of Mental Deficiency, Montpelier.

Leudar, I., Fraser, W. and Jeeves, M. A. (1984) 'Behaviour disturbance and mental handicap: typology and longitudinal trends', *Psychological Medicine*, 14, 923–35.

Matson, J. L. and Gorman-Smith D. (1986), 'A review of treatment research for aggressive and disruptive behavior in the mentally retarded', *Applied Research in Mental Retardation*, 7, 95–103.

Patterson G. R. (1974), 'Intervention for boys with conduct problems. Multiple settings, treatment and criteria', *Journal of Counselling and Clinical Psychology*, 42, 471–81.

Quine, L, and Pahl, J. (1985), 'Examining the causes of stress in families with mentally handicapped children', *British Journal of Social Work*, 15, 501–517.

Stein, Z. and Susser, M. (1975), 'Public health and mental retardation: New power and new problems' in M. J. Begab and S. A. Richardson (eds.), *The Mentally Retarded and Society*, University Park Press, Baltimore MD.

Windahl, S. I. (1988), 'Self-injurious behaviour in a time perspective', paper presented at the 8th Congress of the International Association for the Scientific Study of Mental Deficiency, Dublin, August 1988.

Service developments

The specialist support service: meeting challenging needs in practice

INTRODUCTION

This chapter outlines the development and consequent first six months of implementation of community based 'special services' to support adults with learning disabilities and accompanying challenging behaviour/mental health difficulties, following the relocation of hospital services in Liverpool.

We present a detailed description of the model and key service components. An analysis of the initial outcomes is then provided, which includes a detailed examination of process data (i.e. referral information, staff deployment information, and the major activities and services provided for clients and their carers). Case descriptions of four different service recipients are then used to illustrate the reality of how the service functioned for individuals, and the short-term results of such involvement.

This work is then briefly discussed, with a view to identifying the key lessons learned so far in attempting to provide such a local specialist service. The chapter concludes with suggestions for overcoming some of the obstacles and problems encountered locally in Liverpool, and those issues emerging from other similar initiatives in the UK. The intention is to outline the main practical issues to consider when designing a service, training and managing a team of specialist support staff, and delivering effective clinical interventions. It is hoped that readers will be able to make use of this information when considering locally 'specialist support systems', now that hospital options are no longer seen as appropriate.

THE SERVICE CONTEXT

The Need for Specialist Services

There has been a gradual move away from relying on institutional support services and the active implementation of the 'ordinary life' model for supporting people with learning difficulties. This move towards community provision has thrown up a range of practical issues for service providers. In particular, careful consideration is needed in deciding how to provide 'special' assistance at a local level. It is highly unlikely that by themselves, proclamations of intent to achieve valued community options for clients will successfully translate these objectives into reality. However, practical information and guide-lines have been severely lacking (Kiernan, 1991).

Despite this, many service plans appear to give the impression that all that is required is access to ordinary opportunities. Some organisations and individuals appear to advocate an almost exclusive reliance on natural and non-specialised support strategies, and deny the need for any specialist support (Brandon, 1987; VIA, 1990). Such perspectives fail to acknowledge the additional special, and occasionally 'different', needs of certain clients. This is not to deny the importance of the utilisation of ordinary approaches.

The danger of failing to take 'special measures', is that some individuals may be denied real opportunities to live meaningful and valued lives (LaVigna and Donnellan, 1986). So by default, institutional models and punitive interventions may again be proposed as the only realistic options for meeting such complex needs. These unneccesary conclusions have already surfaced in some recent Regional and District plans and have been used to justify the retention and building of congregated and segregated hospital units.

Historical evolution of services in Liverpool

The development of the Specialist Support Service (SSS)
In 1988, in line with planned hospital closure, discussions began to take place about future services for individuals with challenging behaviour. These were seen to include a mix of clients with learning disabilities. That is:

- People with challenging behaviours and/or mental health difficulties who required community-based support.
- People with challenging behaviours who needed to be removed from their natural situations to safe environments.
- People with accompanying mental illness/health problems who needed 'hospital' treatments, during acute episodes.
- People who commited serious offences and required various responses (e.g. Special Hospitals, regional secure units, bail hostels, etc.).

Over the next two years, various proposals were put forward and considered to meet the range of needs of these clients. The main suggestions included:

1. A 20-bedded Acute Unit sited on a District General Hospital site close to an acute psychiatric unit. No proposed upper limits on the lengths of stay were suggested.
2. An 8-bedded Interim Acute Unit on the local hospital site, and a small Behavioural Team to work with adult clients in the community. The proposed upper limit of stay in this Unit was seen to be two years.

3. Four admission beds in one building, registered with the Mental Health Commission, located in an ordinary house in the community. The stay was to be limited to a short-term stay (i.e. no more than a few months), to distinguish this service from long-term social support.
4. Three acute Admission beds in the existing community-based Respite/ Short-term care facility, with staff being based in separate office accommodation when not working with admitted clients. The stay was limited as in (3).

Although option (3) was originally preferred, a number of external factors eventually led to the adoption of (4). These factors included considerations of cost, problems with securing 'mental hospital' status in an ordinary house for any sectioned admissions, and a likely drag on staff time to continually provide cover for the beds. Also, following an analysis of the admissions over the course of the preceding four years, it was suggested that only one–two beds would be used most of the time. As a result, the capital expenditure on such a potentially under-used resource could not be justified to local managers.

A draft Operational Policy for the running of this service was developed in March 1990 (Learning Difficulties Speciality, 1990). This was based on discussions involving clinical psychologists, psychiatrists, senior service managers and nursing personnel, reviews of the relevant literature and an assessment of other service initiatives (King's Fund, 1988).

The development and initial implementation of the service took place between August 1990 and February 1991. During this time, the service design was refined and agreed, potential initial clients identified, the location of the beds agreed and organised, staff interviewed and trained, and the initial evaluation and monitoring procedures developed.

The staff were gradually introduced into posts over a three-month period. This phased build-up of personnel occurred primarily as a response to:

• The external demands of the hospital retraction programme, requiring that in the first instance the SSS offer all the nursing posts to displaced staff.
• Staff only being released to the SSS after the vast majority of hospital residents had been resettled to their new homes in the community.
• The needs of the Induction Training and Support strategy, which required both time and structured opportunities to build the requisite staff competencies, confidence and team commitment.

The clinical psychologist, researcher, psychiatrists and senior nurse who joined the SSS Clinical Team were already in post in the Learning Difficulties service, before these other staff joined.

By 1990, the general community support services for people with learning disabilities developed by Liverpool Health Authority included the key components listed in Table 3.1. The SSS became operational in this service context in February 1991.

Table 3.1   *Key components of the community support services*

4 Locality-based Community Support Teams (CSTs)	Child Support Team (Challenging behaviour)	Respite/Short-term care facility (16 places)
1.5 Consultant psychiatrists	370 'Care in the Community' home places (health-funded), managed by 7 voluntary agencies	

THE SPECIALIST SUPPORT SERVICE MODEL
Principles influencing the service

An important belief that underpinned the service model was a commitment to improving the quality of clients' lives. This was regarded as of equal, if not more, importance with reducing the frequency, duration or severity of the presenting challenges (Meyer and Evans, 1989).

This contrasts with more traditional service responses where the person's activities, relationships and environments may have been severely restricted in order to reduce problems (Guess, Helmstetter, Turnbull and Knowlton, 1987). Such approaches clearly fail to demonstrate a commitment to the notion that all people with learning disabilities have a right and need to be offered the opportunities of a valued ordinary lifestyle (Blunden and Allen, 1987; O'Brien and Lyle, 1987).

The service is also based on the belief that an individual's natural environment is usually the best setting for effective and long-lasting clinical interventions. Special attention was therefore paid to the issues of social validity and cultural acceptability (Horner, Dunlap and Koegel, 1988). The service therefore adopted a 'support model', that is, adding resources to community settings wherever possible.

The people served

It was agreed that a relatively open-door referral policy would initially exist, which could then be made more specific on the basis of actual demand. The only exception made was that a restricted service would be offered to clients with mild learning disabilities.

The service therefore adopted the broad definition of challenging behaviour provided by the Special Development Team of the University of Kent/South-East Thames Regional Health Authority (Emerson *et al.*, 1987, see also Chapter 4), that is, 'severely challenging behaviour refers to behaviour of such an intensity, frequency or duration that the physical safety of the person or others is likely to be placed in serious jeopardy or behaviour which is likely to seriously limit or delay access to the use of community facilities'. A similar broad definition was adopted to define potential clients with learning disabilities presenting challenges as a result of mental health difficulties. That is, services were offered to individuals with psychiatric disorders which could not be managed or treated without additional specialist input by ordinary mental health services.

On the basis of these criteria, it was estimated that approximately 150 people would be regular users of the service, from a pool of around 750 Liverpool people presenting challenges (Kiernan, Qureshi and Alborz, 1989).

In order to make judgements on the acceptance or rejection of clients referred to the SSS, the following criteria were considered: the degree of the client's learning disabilities and other special needs; the severity of presenting challenges, as assessed by the potential for damage or injury; the urgency of the situation, including possible exclusion from ordinary settings and other services and the actual availability of SSS resources.

Desired client and service outcomes

The SSS aimed to achieve meaningful changes in clients' lives in line with the five accomplishments (O'Brien, 1987). In particular, the focus was on understanding the reasons for presenting difficulties, reducing the level of problems, enhancing clients' presence and participation in valued ordinary activities, improving personal competencies, and developing positive reputations for clients.

The SSS attempts to achieve the following short- and long-term service outcomes:

a) Provision of an effective emergency support service.
This involves the provision of a 24–hour, flexible crisis containment service to replace the use of acute admissions previously available in long-stay hospitals. The SSS attempts to prevent unnecessary admissions and reduce the length of appropriate admissions to non-institutional settings.

b) Accurate assessments of the reasons for challenges and the need for changing the person and/or environment.
The short-term goals for the SSS are focused on making specific changes in the person's behaviour or their natural environment, so as to prevent the occurrence of future problems.

Many problems reflect conflicts between the person and their environment. If this mis-match can be resolved, a reduction in the challenges may be possible. This involves the SSS changing the environment (e.g. physical changes at home or work, improving relationships with carers, developing a variety of functional and interesting activities) and/or changing the person's behaviour and competencies (e.g. teaching new skills and using specific therapies).

c) Short-term assistance in implementing interventions.
The SSS provides practical assistance and facilitates their implementation. This includes the provision of additional 'hands-on' staff time and support, specific or general training events, and regular support sessions to revise and refine interventions.

d) The maintenance and generalisation of positive intervention outcomes.
Services are often able to provide short-term intensive levels of support for small periods of time, and bring about positive short-term outcomes for clients, particularly with respect to reducing problems. The SSS aims to establish environments with naturally positive consequences for clients. Such real and meaningful outcomes for the client should be long-lasting and relevant to the individual's life (Meyer, Peck and Brown, 1990).

e) Enhancement of carer competencies.
SSS assists local carers in becoming more competent in their interactions with clients to prevent future difficulties and enhance coping.

f) Assisting the building of effective local support services.
A comprehensive support system should include: adequate numbers of supported living places; access to real work and integrated educational opportunities; options for regular, valued breaks from families, and social/ leisure support services.

The SSS therefore works to enable other local support services to build such a comprehensive support structure. Further, it enables local services to become more skilled at working with potential SSS clients, and so be less dependent on specialist services.

Organisational and personnel structure

The SSS is comprised of a Clinical Team and a team of Support workers. The structure is that of an 'Expert Model' (Bromstrom, 1975), with the Clinical Team as intervention specialists who direct the Support Team staff activities. Table 3.2 below provides the details of this staff group.

The Clinical Team includes a clinical psychologist, senior nurse manager, and deputy nurse manager and receives input from two psychiatrists. The team is directly accountable to the Clinical Director. It acts as the gatekeeper for referrals, negotiates the service input with carers and services, and organises the deployment of SSS staff and other resources. Each of these individuals acts as a 'case-carrier', which involves planning, supervising and monitoring all the activities of staff. To date, most of this work has been undertaken by the clinical psychologist and senior registrar.

Table 3.2 *Personnel structure of the SSS*

Clinical team		
Principal Clinical Pyschologist	Senior Nurse Manager	Psychiatrist Input (Consultant and Senior Registrar)
Scientific officer	Deputy Nurse Manager (G Grade)	

Support team	
Registered Nurses (6 × E Grade staff)	Support Workers (9 × B Grade staff)

Members of the Clinical Team offer a 24–hour on-call service. This has provided an immediate response to crisis situations and enabled rapid access to SSS staff and admission beds.

The Support Team is composed of six qualified nurses and nine unqualified support workers. Together, they provide the majority of the direct 'hands-on' support to clients, both in community settings and the admission facility. These staff work highly flexible hours, in a variety of situations, and are fully mobile in having direct use of cars for work duties. Staff undertake detailed assessments, provide direct support to clients in a range of settings, develop ideas for reports and recommendations, assist in the training of other staff and carers, and collect data on these activities. All these activities are supervised by the Clinical Team.

A scientific officer developed tools to monitor and evaluate the SSS activities, and has also provided some direct 'hands-on' support to clients and carers.

Staff training

Initially, members of the Clinical Team attended various external training events, which have subsequently influenced the organisation and delivery of SSS assessments and interventions. The most important of these are noted below:

- three national conferences on services responses to the needs of people with challenging behaviours (i.e. APT, 1990; BABP, 1990, and BIMH, 1988).

- IABA training workshops and courses on Non-Aversive Behaviour Modification, Maximising Staff Consistency, and Developing Assessments and Interventions for Severe Challenging Behaviours (LaVigna and Willis, 1991).
- training in Systematic Instruction workshops (TSI, 1990).

Subsequently, all the SSS staff participated in the Induction Training programme, involving a 12-day block of training workshops and a 6–week period of supervised client work.

The Support Team staff were introduced into their posts in a staggered fashion to enable smaller training groups and consequently more individualised attention, that is, three separate groups consisting of two registered nurses and three support workers received the Induction Training.

This Induction Training block was designed to provide: the rationale for the principles underlying the SSS model and activities; an information-base to guide staff actions; the time and initial opportunities to develop a number of basic assessment and intervention competencies. Most days involved a mixture of lectures, exercises, discussions, and role-plays.

As the majority of Support Team staff had been recruited from staff displaced from former posts at the long-stay hospital, the training focused on challenging previous institutional attitudes and practices. The staff were guided to understand and adopt the ordinary life model, and to develop a positive, non-aversive approach to working with challenging individuals.

Table 3.3 below provides the details of this induction training.
A 3–month follow-up evaluation day involved:

- Individual interviews with the Clinical Team: examining training   needs, helpfulness of supervision, current effectiveness of SSS working methods, and ideas for service changes.

Table 3.3   *Content of the 12-day induction training*

1	Values and social role valorisation
2	The 5 Accomplishments
3	The Personal Futures planning process
4	Defining the aims of the learning difficulty services
5	Aims of the SSS and mis-uses of normalisation
6	Understanding challenging behaviours
7	Gathering information and observing clients
8	Understanding psychiatric disorders
9	Understanding families and the Mental Health Act
10	Interviewing key social agents
11	Developing interventions and managing difficulties
12	SSS paperwork – record-keeping, completing assessments and developing a funtional analysis, staff activity sheets

- A written 20–item knowledge test, including 56 separate issues addressed during the induction and subsequent training.
- A role-play exercise assessing staff competencies in talking to people, gathering information and recording the key points.

This information was used to provide individual staff with feedback (acknowledging strengths and support needs), and also to refine the subsequent training and supervision methods. The results proved very positive and indicated that both the registered nurses and unqualified support workers had retained most of the information provided and utilised it effectively in clinical tasks.

The most important and 'real' training was provided 'on-the-job', through direct supervision and guidance at support meetings. For example, each member of the Support Team was originally assigned a client and completed a detailed assessment, under the supervision of a Clinical Team member. This included gathering information, composing draft summary reports and recommendations, presenting this information and implementing initial interventions. The weekly staff supervision meetings were vital to supplement the individual supervision sessions, and to allow opportunities to share with all the staff the broad range of interventions/support strategies the SSS employed.

Monitoring and evaluation methods

To date, the evaluation has primarily focused on process data (i.e. how the service operates). This involved collecting and analysing quantitative data on the deployment of staff time, referral information, and assessment outcomes. This focus on process variables was determined by the desire of the Clinical Team to understand:

- Who made demands on the SSS?
- Does the referral process function as originally designed?
- Is the SSS staff time used effectively and efficiently?

For this purpose, staff maintained detailed records of their activities (i.e. where they go, who with and what they do).

The weekly supervision meetings enable staff to gain an overview of SSS work, while at the same time providing opportunities for team support. Detailed minutes are kept on staff and client work objectives and progress. All this information is shared with the Clinical Director on a regular basis, and allows for discussion with him on service development issues.

Referrals to the SSS

It was decided to adopt a low profile initially in order to allow the SSS to gradually develop its working methods. The main publicity for the service, therefore, consisted of informal contacts with local services and low-profile briefings to Community Support Teams (CSTs).

Given the likelihood of prolonged and intensive involvement with individual clients, it was felt important that all potential clients were assessed by the Clinical Team to ensure that the following basic criteria were considered:

- severity of learning disability
- availability of SSS resources
- severity of the challenging behaviours.

All referrals therefore received an initial visit by a member of the Clinical Team, who collated this basic information to present at the Weekly Clinical Team meeting. Referrals were accepted or rejected on the basis of the factors outlined above and competing demands for on-going support to crisis referrals through the 'on-call' service.

Contrary to expectations, operationally most referrals did not come through the CSTs. Rather, a more open system operated with a range of sources for requests for SSS development. Table 3.4 below summarises this information for the 65 referrals from February to July 1991.

Table 3.4   *Sources of referral to SSS*

Community Support Teams (CSTs)		31
Care in the Community schemes		13
Social Services		7
Psychiatry		7
Miscellaneous		5
	Total	63
Accepted by SSS		55

Despite the fact that almost half the referrals to the SSS were not screened by prior CST involvement, the Clinical Team subsequently managed to liaise with the appropriate local CST after an initial visit for most clients. However, there remained approximately 25 per cent of clients who received no active CST involvement.

An analysis of the clients referred indicated that most clients still lived at home with their families (33 individuals) or in Care in the Community scheme homes (18 clients). Of the sixty-five clients referred to the SSS, thirty-seven individuals were noted as having mild learning disabilities and 28 clients had severe learning disabilities. All of the rejected referrals had no or minimal learning disabilities.

Fifteen individuals were referred at times of crisis, and seven individuals required admissions into the acute beds. Only four of these clients required extended input from the SSS (including one client who was sectioned under the Mental Health Act for 24 hours due to a perceived fire-risk). This suggests that a significant number of crisis situations were diffused through SSS input (usually within 30 minutes of receipt of a request for assistance) and avoided unnecessary admissions.

The challenges presented by clients referred to the SSS were analysed using the detailed referral information, and were subdivided into the five major categories of challenging behaviour described by McBrien and Felce (1990). The analysis indicated that most of the clients presented a variety of disruptive, dangerous and inappropriate behaviours, and of these individuals the majority (66%) also presented with accompanying aggressive behaviours directed at others.

The assessment and intervention process

A variety of approaches influenced the SSS assessment and intervention procedures including Carr *et al.* (1990); Brown (1991); Donnellan *et al.*, (1985); Durand (1990); Evans and Meyer (1985); O'Neil, *et al.* (1990); Lovett (1985); Lovett (1987) and McGee *et al.* (1987).

Like these authors, the SSS did not make use of any one technique or procedure for all clients. Rather, the focus was on introducing major lifestyle changes through: completing comprehensive assessments and functional analyses to understand the reasons for difficulties; developing multicomponent interventions with an emphasis on changing antecedents and setting events; a commitment to building the individual's competencies and avoiding aversive-control strategies (Horner *et al.*, 1990).

The SSS ensured that emergency containment strategies were distinguished from planned interventions. Any actions that intentionally caused clients pain, harm or a loss of dignity in order to avoid future challenges were not used as they were construed as aversive and unnecessary. However, some actions that were taken, which were designed to safely manage particularly challenging incidents, may inadvertently have been perceived as aversive by clients.

This distinction between employing planned punitive strategies and the use of 'unintentionally-aversive' safety-containment actions once all other possibilities had been explored, is important in the current aversive-non-aversive debate (Repp and Singh, 1990; see also Chapter 10). We have found that assuming a non-aversive position has not been incompatible with tackling the severe challenges SSS people have presented.

Assessments completed by staff involve: observations of clients in a range of challenging and non-challenging situations; interviews with clients, carers and other key social agents; reviews of written records and files. The intention was to thoroughly 'get to know' clients and assess all the possible factors that may have lead to the presenting challenges. Assessment reports included: detailed descriptions of the client; family history and relationships; current and past home situation; day services; health and medical histories; functional analysis of the presenting challenges; assessment of client's likes and dislikes; communication competencies; analysis of the carers'/services' ability to effectively support the client.

After these assessments were completed, an individualised, non-aversive Intervention Plan was developed for clients. This involved a number of possible actions, such as helping change the person's activities, teaching clients new skills, helping carers change their interaction styles, and strategies for safely managing difficult situations. The structure developed by LaVigna and Donnellan (1986) was used to generate these suggestions.

Where appropriate, practical 'hands-on' support was provided. This type of approach to assessing and working with individuals who present challenges is described in detail in Donnellan *et al.* (1988), and is being adopted by a number of similar services in the UK (e.g. Burchess, 1990).

Service activities

The different stages of service involvement are illustrated in Table 3.5 below.

An analysis of the activities SSS staff have undertaken was performed after six months to understand the ways in which resources were utilised. This indicates that the service has worked directly with clients (proactive and reactive interventions), worked alongside carers (training and support), and worked with the systems in which clients have been involved (re-designing services and activities).

The analysis indicates that:

- Assessments, reports and intervention plans have been developed and shared with key social agents for forty clients.
- Short-term 'hands-on' practical assistance by SSS staff has been offered to twenty-nine clients. This has included: support in implementing recommendations, modelling constructive ways of working with clients, and providing clients/carers with a break through the provision of accompanied, valued social opportunities.
- For 8 clients, training and support sessions have been offered to carers to assist the implementation of SSS recommendations. This has included: a number of training workshops for group home and day centre staff, regular support meetings and reviews to refine interventions, and family therapy sessions.
- Rapid emergency assessments and crisis management advice has been provided on twenty-five separate occasions. This was facilitated through the on-call service, accessed through the local hospital switchboard and SSS mobile phone and pager system. On twelve occasions carers required counselling or de-briefing.
- Rapid, short-term 'hands-on' staff time and support was provided via the on-call service on nine occasions. In order to facilitate this, two members of the Support Team were available on a short-term, stand-by basis 24 hours each day.

Table 3.5 *Stages of SSS involvement*

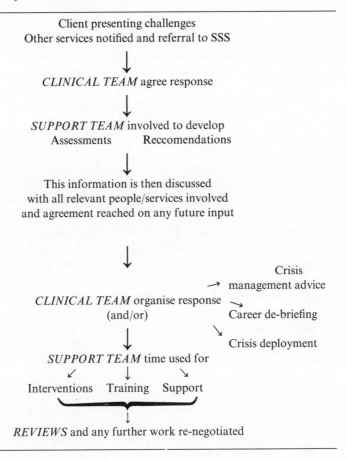

- Admissions were necessary for seven individuals. For three clients, a 1:1 staffing ratio was arranged, and on one occasion a client required 2:1 staffing support. The majority of stays (71%) lasted less than five weeks, with a pattern of one–two beds being occupied on most occasions. The median length of stay has been ten days. At present, it appears that one individual whose admission has lasted over thirteen weeks will require alternative long-term accomodation in a supported group home.
- 80% of the admission time has been taken up by support for individuals presenting challenges with underlying mental health difficulties, requiring medical and psychiatric interventions. The principle focus has been structured assessment in controlled environments, and the introduction of effective physical health interventions. It has also provided carers with a short-term break or respite. SSS staff have observed clients closely, assessed their mental state and behaviour,

noted any changes due to alterations in medication, and set the scene for an introduction to valued community activities.

CASE DESCRIPTIONS

Staff devoted on average 60 per cent of their available time to direct client-focused tasks. The following case descriptions illustrate the range of this input and provide some qualitative outcome information.

Sandra

She is a 30-year-old single woman with mild learning disabilities, who has been in institutional care from her early teens. She was previously identified as the most challenging client within the local long-stay hospital, and the viability of her move to the community had been questioned.

Throughout her adult life, she had presented a range of challenges. However, over the last year these had intensified to include severe self-injury and physical attacks on staff. The self-injurious behaviour consisted of insertions of a variety of objects into her vagina, eyes, ears, nostrils, and bladder, frequently requiring surgical removal. The most serious injury involved the creation and re-opening of a large wound in her thigh, causing the formation of a deep abscess and, threatening the need for amputation.

Sandra had been variously diagnosed as schizophrenic, psychopathic and epileptic. Although the clinical evidence for these are unclear, she was receiving large doses of psychotropic medication. She was referred to the SSS to assist with her move to the community. A detailed assessment revealed that most staff adopted an aversive approach aimed at punishing her for her actions, and failed to adopt a functional perspective in trying to understand the reasons for her behaviour. The Clinical Team then worked with staff to implement positive behaviour support plans (Horner *et al.*, 1990), advised on the staffing levels required for her future care and the type of home situation. Support was also provided in the selection of support staff, their induction training and on-going weekly supervision meetings. Another member of the SSS developed a system of data collection to analyse the changes in the presenting challenges. Finally, the staff team were provided with immediate crisis support during particularly challenging incidents.

Sandra has now been in her new home for over six months. The frequency and severity of her challenging behaviour has markedly reduced. The wound on her leg has fully healed, with the aid of surgery. The incidents of physical attacks on staff have reduced, together with an increase in her ability to tolerate demands. In line with these changes, the previous reliance on medication has been steadily reduced.

Recently, with the help of an incentive programme, she has been enabled to go to local shops independently. Sandra has also begun to attend an adult literacy course at college, and initiated discussions on the possibility of a future job working in a café.

Finally, she has begun to disclose incidents of sexual abuse throughout her life, which probably led to the initial problems in her childhood. Staff have been supported by the SSS to examine the implications of these issues, and the staff group will require on-going supervision and support to ensure staff consistency.

Phil

He is a 35-year-old single man with mild learning disabilities, living at home with his sister. He has a long history of serious physical and sexual assaults against his sister. These had brought him in contact with the courts on three occasions, where he received probation orders. Despite these assaults, he was seen as courteous and polite to others.

Previous interventions had been ineffective in reducing the frequency or severity of these assaults. The family had been strongly advised that Phil should be placed on a Guardianship Order, and move out of the family home. It was believed that the relationship with his sister was the major causal factor in the difficulties. However, this advice was ignored by the family and at the time of referral, he was awaiting a fourth appearance in court.

The referral to the SSS requested a detailed assessment, in order to allow the court to make an informed decision. A support worker was assigned to this task. However, within three weeks of this involvement, a crisis situation developed. Phil had assaulted his sister again and started a fire at home (probably accidentally), causing extensive damage to the first floor.

After an emergency assessment by the Clinical Team, he was admitted to an acute bed. During the admission, it became apparent that Phil was suffering with mental health difficulties, involving a paranoid delusional system extended to the staff and others closely involved in his care. This culminated in Phil physically threatening the support workers, and on one occasion he brandished a knife.

Interestingly, his sister was able to tell the Clinical Team that these actions were identical to the behaviour she had previously experienced directly before the assaults. As a result, he was initiated on anti-psychotic depot medication and within three weeks there was a considerable improvement in his mental state.

A detailed report was then prepared for the courts, and he was sentenced to a three-year probation order, with a condition of medical supervision.

Phil was then discharged home after a two-month admission. A new support worker was allocated to provide highly intensive support following discharge. This has continued, although the amount of time has been reduced to less than one day per week, over the course of four months. There have been no further assaults and his sister reports that he is 'more settled and content than he has been for years'.

There remains on-going liaison with the probation officer, social services and employment agencies. The SSS support worker has continued to monitor Phil's mental state, assisted in his return to voluntary work at a local sports centre, developed his self-confidence and facilitated a better relationship with his sister and other family members.

Paul

He is a 21-year-old young man with severe learning disabilities, who lives at home with his mother and younger half-brother. He also suffers with epilepsy and mild cerebral palsy. He has presented a number of challenging behaviours throughout his life, although these have almost exclusively been evident at home and only in the company of his mother. These challenges included playing loud music throughout the night, dismantling electrical sockets and other furnishings, damage to his home, and making 'excessive' demands on his mother, and verbal and physical attacks on her if these were unmet.

He had originally been referred to the local CST one year before the referral to the SSS. The CST had initially been successful in reducing some of these problems, through discussions with Paul and his mother which focused on helping her set reasonable limits and becoming more assertive as a parent.

The referral to the SSS came after Paul had severely physically attacked his mother and caused considerable damage to his home. Initially, his mother's confidence was severely shaken and support was needed to allow her to get some sleep. As a result, a SSS support worker spent four nights at their home to calm the situation. This was successful in containing the situation, and a detailed assessment was completed, together with specific recommendations for future CST work. This assessment noted that the problems reflected inconsistent and inappropriate mother-son interactions. The Clinical Team also agreed to supervise the re-introduction of previously successful interventions.

However, within two months another crisis referral was made to the SSS, after Paul had attempted to dismantle the main electricity meter, and only just escaped receiving a fatal shock. Due to the obvious risks, it was agreed to admit Paul for a short break to defuse the home situation and plan appropriate interventions. He was discharged home after three days with intensive SSS support, involving the deployment of male support workers from the time he returned home from the day centre until he went to bed after midnight. Their presence was sufficient to divert Paul from engaging in dangerous activities and the meter was secured to prevent further damage.

A structured incentive programme was then introduced to reduce the challenging behaviours, and reduce the support worker's time to a few hours social input on alternate evenings.

The crisis support offered by the SSS has enabled Paul to remain at home. He seems to have been successfully redirected to alternative activities, and thefocus of the interventions has returned to improving the interactions between Paul and his mother. He also appears to have benefited (by developing new competencies) from the social opportunities made available by the SSS staff time. There still remains a need to organise these activities and structure the relationship between Paul and his mother, and consider more meaningful day and evening leisure opportunities.

Charlie

He is a 27-year-old single man with severe learning disabilities and many of the problems associated with autism. After attending various special schools in Liverpool, he has attended the same local day centre for a number of years. During this time he has presented a number of challenging behaviours, including repeated question-asking, shouting, physical attacks to staff and clients, and property destruction. He had also repeatedly asked for a move from one area of the centre to another, and then back again. Following such requests being turned down, there had been two serious incidents involving Charlie hitting staff. At this point the SSS were asked for a detailed assessment and a recommended plan of action to tackle the challenges.

Within one week of this work being initiated, another incident occurred where Charlie hit a female member of staff. All the day centre staff then threatened industrial action, unless immediate action was taken to suspend him and others presenting challenging behaviours. They also insisted that he be severely reprimanded and punished if any future incidents occurred. The Clinical Team met with all the staff, and agreed to provide additional crisis support, as well as facilitating a training workshop and discussions with Social Services managers.

The assessment was then rapidly completed and guidelines developed for working with Charlie (both in terms of preventing and coping with challenges). It was apparent that the problems reflected the long-term use of aversive, consequence-control strategies both at home and at the day centre, together with a non-functional and uninteresting set of activities. The programme of day activities was then altered and written, practical suggestions for diffusing escalating situations were provided. The implementation of these changes was then monitored by the SSS, to ensure a high degree of staff consistency.

Through these antecedent-control strategies, the challenges presented by Charlie were rapidly eliminated. A subsequent staff training workshop enabled the day centre staff to build on this work and utilise similar ideas for other clients. As a result, the number of individuals suspended for challenging behaviours has been considerably reduced, together with a reduction in the use of punitive intervention strategies.

Since this work, there has been a sustained period of over six months without Charlie presenting any significant challenging behaviours, his relationship with his parents has improved, and the day centre activities have been extended: he has started a course in an integrated adult education class at a local college.

REVIEWING THE EXPERIENCE OF THE SPECIALIST SUPPORT SERVICE

Clinical issues

The SSS model has established a track record of successfully supporting people with learning disabilities and accompanying challenging behaviours/ mental health difficulties through the deployment of skilled staff time. However, it has proven important that clinical interventions have not been divorced from social support issues.

It is important to consider clients presenting challenges as 'people first', rather than collections of problems. Services must beware of the latter pathological perspective, and actively organise specialist services and staff to challenge such positions. This applies equally well to clients with mental health difficulties, whose long-term support needs will not be adequately addressed by purely health-focused, clinical interventions (Stark, Menolascino, Alberelli and Gray, 1988).

The wide range of support needs of individuals must not be underestimated simply because they have learning disabilities. Rather, services will need to adapt many traditional therapies and support strategies to develop clients' competencies and relationship skills (Meyer and Evans, 1989). Similar adaptations may be needed to adequately address medical complaints, physical illnesses and mental health difficulties (Department of Health Study Team, 1989).

No specific techniques or interventions have proved appropriate to working with the whole range of SSS clients. However, the commitment to a positive, constructional approach which avoids aversive interventions has been used in all client work (Berkman and Meyer, 1988).

It has also proven helpful that the Clinical Team has adopted an eclectic and 'open to most ideas' approach. The range of different multidisciplinary, clinical perspectives has been easy to blend, because all those involved have been willing to work together. Clearly, this important component is easier to prescribe than deliver when personality clashes occur.

Specialist services appear to need to include the following key support elements: rapid access to skilled clinical advice; making use of the removal of the client for a small period of time to a safe place to initiate clinical work; deployment of intensive skilled support to demonstrate alternative ways of working with the client. Special attention needs to be paid when organising and structuring fading strategies, to avoid unnecessary dependence on crisis support.

The large number of requests for support to clients with mild learning disabilities tends to demand assistance in dealing with mental health difficulties. The expertise and resources necessary for this includes mental state assessments; reviews of medication; acute admissions into learning disability and psychiatric services; developing personal and environmental stress-reduction strategies; on-going monitoring of symptoms; depot medication provision, and psycho-education work with families/staff (Stark *et al.*, 1988). In order to meet these demands there is clearly a need for increased specialist knowledge, skills and resources in the SSS, and liason with ordinary psychiatric services.

Service outcomes

The SSS model attempts to deliver a number of linked, but relatively independent outcomes. Some outcomes have clearly been easier to achieve than others. Although some degree of success was evident for all the defined objectives, this needs to be carefully examined if the SSS experience is going to be used to shape other local service initiatives (Routledge, 1990).

In terms of an effective emergency service, the SSS has been successful in providing a range of crisis responses including a highly accessible on-call service; emergency assessments and guidelines for the immediate containment of difficulties; advice and opportunities to de-brief carers experiencing acute problems; rapid deployment of 'hands-on' staff support to crisis situations, and as a last resort, admission beds. The SSS has offered a flexible service to clients which compares highly favourably in terms of cost and service quality with the previous hospital services. It has sucessfully 'met the challenge', without requiring a back-up hospital or large admission unit (Emerson *et al.*, 1987).

However, the continued need to support short-term admissions has exerted considerable pressure on the ability of the SSS to work in a planned way with clients. In some instances, this has resulted in the proactive assessments and interventions having to have lower priority than the emergency activities and support to the admissions. Also, the need to ensure that sufficient support was always available to undertake the latter activities, 'just in case', led to a wastage and under-utilisation of staff resources. Even so, this wastage was considerably less than that incurred by running a unit-based service for challenging individuals.

Subjectively, the assessments and interventions appear to have been successful on most occasions in reducing the referred challenges and difficulties. However, the lack of concrete data prevents an objective evaluation of the extent to which the clients acquired new competencies or improved their quality of life.

Service model, staffing and training

The model of the SSS as an adjunct to CST services has not worked as well as intended. On most occasions, the joint working actually lead to confusion and uncertainty on 'who did what'. On a wider level, the general notion of a generic, locality-based CST relating to a geographical patch has not proved to be the most efficient service delivery model in Liverpool. This has subsequently been replaced by the development of specialist, city-wide services based on the SSS model addressing a range of specialist clinical and service objectives (Learning Disabilities Directorate, 1991).

The SSS successfully adopted an expert model, with the Clinical Team clearly leading and directing the work of the Support Team staff. This model is important in ensuring a clear sense of purpose towards the challenging tasks the SSS undertakes. In particular, this required close collaboration between different professionals, especially the psychiatrists and clinical psychologists. It has already been argued that this successful partnership enabled the SSS to operate in a truly multidisciplinary fashion. In particular, it allowed the SSS to offer an integrated service to clients with learning disabilities presenting challenging behaviours or mental health difficulties. Often an unnecessary and inappropriate distinction is made in the services offered to these clients (Blunden and Allen, 1987).

The small size of the Clinical Team limited the quantity and range of clinical support offered by the SSS. It has become clear that additional professionals are needed including speech therapists, occupational therapists and clinically-orientated social workers, as well as more clinical psychologists and qualified nursing personnel.

Although the service has operated well through adopting a consensus, decision-making framework within the Clinical Team, at times the lack of a clear single line-management structure has confused the responsibilities for effective clinical interventions and resource-management (Emerson *et al.*, 1987).

Despite expectations to the contrary, there were considerable advantages apparent from recruiting staff who had long histories of working in devalued institutional services. In particular, those with 'direct contact' experience of challenging individuals appeared to respond positively to the new methods of working, and appeared very committed to achieving meaningful changes in clients' lives. Loyalty to this type of work is hard to create, but may be easier to shape with staff already desensitised to the hardships involved in working with challenging clients. The real challenge that remains is effective training, supervision and management arrangements (LaVigna and Willis, 1991; see also Chapter 6).

The training model implemented relied on the use of staff attending training events. Although this appears to have been crucial in fostering close team relationships, the provision of most of the information may have been better organised. One approach that has recently gained popularity is that of competency-based, criterion-referenced training programmes (Shaull, Willis and LaVigna, 1989), which are trainer-independent and clearly define the performances required of staff. This type of training would overcome the obvious problems arising when staff leave, and new staff need to be trained.

THE FUTURE SHAPE OF THE SSS – CONCLUDING REMARKS

This chapter has provided a detailed description of a team which offers a range of services to meet the specialist needs of people with learning difficulties and accompanying challenging behaviours/mental health difficulties. The early results suggest that it is possible to meet many of these needs within the context of a local community support service, where the option of utilising large admission units no longer exists.

The experience of the SSS suggests that such a local service should partially separate the two tasks of providing support in community settings and an emergency admission service. Although it remains essential that these two services should be linked, too strong an association may result in the effectiveness of both these valuable services being somewhat compromised.

However, the input of one (expanded) Clinical Team into both these areas appears advantageous. Clearly, the ability to accurately assess clients and then implement positive behaviour support strategies, requires skilled clinical direction.

Recently, it has also become apparent that the service may need to develop a small number of beds within existing local acute psychiatric services with effective professional support from the SSS to make this model work.

These lessons have been incorporated in the new service model, which includes a single line-management structure and 'separate-but-linked' community and acute admission service. The non-aversive assessment and intervention process has also been formalised, and an expanded Clinical Team has been developed to provide direct and indirect clinical interventions and support.

On the basis of the successful SSS intervention approaches, a number of new specialist community support services linked to the SSS have been developed, for example, staff teams to prevent exclusions of challenging individuals from local day centres and group homes, and specialist supported employment initiatives for challenging individuals.

The important issue for all local service providers is how to provide the necessary specialist support in non-stigmatising and unobtrusive ways, while still addressing clients' needs in positive ways. It is hoped that the information provided in this chapter will assist other local services in defining their particular response to meeting the complex support needs of clients with learning difficulties and additional challenging behaviours/mental health difficulties.

References

Ager, A. (1991), 'Effecting sustainable change in client behaviour: The role of the behaviour analysis of service environments' in B Remington (ed.), *The Challenge of Severe Mental Handicap: A Behaviour Analytic Approach* Wiley, Sussex.

APT (1990), Annual Conference on Challenging Behaviour, York.

BABP (1990), Spring Conference: Challenging Behaviour Symposium, Manchester.

Berkman, K. and Meyer, L. (1988), 'Alternative strategies and multiple outcomes in the remediation of severe self-injury: Going 'all out' nonaversively', *Journal of the Association for Persons with Severe Handicaps*, 13, 76–88.

BIMH (1988), Annual Conference, Manchester.

Blatt, B. (1987). The Conquest of Mental Retardation. Pro-Ed: Texas.

Blunden, R. and Allen, D. (1987), *Facing The Challenge: An Ordinary Life for People with Learning Difficulties and Challenging Behaviour*, King's Fund Centre, London.

Brandon, D. (1987), *Mutual Respect*, Hexagon, Manchester.

Bromstrom, R. (1975), *Developing Effective Training Styles*, Comcor, New York.

Brown F. (1991), 'Creative daily scheduling: A nonintrusive approach to challenging behaviors in community residences', *Journal of the Association for Persons with Severe Handicaps*, 16, 75–84.

Burchess, I. (1990), 'The Intensive Support Team: Discussion documents 1–3', Kidderminster Health Authority.

Carr, E., Robinson, S., Taylor, J. and Carlson, J. (1990), *Positive Approaches to the Treatment of Severe Behavior Problems in Persons with Developmental Disabilities: A Review and Analysis of Reinforcement and Stimulus-based Procedures*, TASH Monograph, Seattle.

Day, K. (1988), 'A hospital-based treatment programme for male mentally handicapped offenders', *British Journal of Psychiatry*, 153, 653–44.

Department of Health Study Team, (1989), *Services for Adults with Mental Handicap who are Mentally Ill, who have Behaviour Problems or who Offend*, DHSS, London.

Donnellan, A., LaVigna, G., Negri-Shoultz, N and Fassbender, L. L. (1988), *Progress Without Punishment: Effective Approaches for Learners with Behavior Problems*, Teachers College Press, New York.

Donnellan, A., LaVigna, G., Zambito, J. and Thvedt, J. (1985), 'A time-limited intensive intervention program model to support community placement for persons with severe behavior problems', *Journal of the Association for Persons with Severe Handicaps*, 10, 123–31.

Durand, V.M. (1990), *Severe Behavior Problems: A Functional Communication Training Approach*, Guilford Press, New York.

Emerson, E., Barrett, S., Bell, C., Cummings, R., McCool, C., Toogood, A. and Mansell, J. (1987), *Developing Services for People with Severe Learning Difficulties and Challenging Behaviours*, Institute of Social and Applied Psychology, University of Kent, Canterbury.

Emerson, E., Cambridge, P. and Harris, P. (1991), *Evaluating The Challenge: A Guide to Evaluating Services for People with Learning Difficulties and Challenging Behaviour*, King's Fund Centre, London.

Emerson, E. and McGill, P. (1989), 'Normalisation and applied behaviour analysis: values and technology in services for people with learning difficulties', *Behavioural Psychotherapy*, 17, 101–17.

Emerson, E., Toogood, A., Mansell, J., Barrett, S., Bell, C., Cummings, R. and McCool, C. (1987), 'Challenging behaviour and community services: 1. Introduction and overview', *Mental Handicap*, 15, 166–69.

Evans, I. (1987), 'Teaching personnel to use state-of-the-art nonaversive alternatives for dealing with problem behavior', unpublished paper prepared for the working conference entitled 'Preparing Personnel to Work with Persons who are Severely Handicapped: Focus on the Future', Peabody College, Vanderbilt University, Nashville, Tennessee, October 1983.

Evans, I. and Meyer, L. (1985), *An Educative Approach to Behavior Problems: A Practical Decision Model for Interventions with Severely Handicapped Learners*, Paul H. Brookes, Baltimore, MD.

Guess, D., Helmstetter, H., Turnbull, H., and Knowlton, S. (1987), *Use of Aversive Procedures with Persons who are Disabled: An Historical Review and Critical Analysis*, TASH Monograph, Seattle, WA.

Horner, R., Dunlap, G. and Koegel, R. (1988), *Generalization and Maintenance: Lifestyle Changes in Applied Settings*. Paul H. Brookes, Baltimore, MD.

Horner, R., Dunlap, G., Koegel, R., Carr, E., Sailor, W,. Anderson, J., Albin, R. and O'Neil, R. (1990), 'Toward a technology of 'nonaversive' behavior support', *Journal of the Association for Persons with Severe Handicaps*, 15, 125–32.

Keene, N. and Jones, H. (1986), 'Who needs hospital care?', *Mental Handicap*, 14, 101–03.

Kiernan, C. (1991), 'Professional ethics: Behaviour analysis and normalisation' in B. Remington (ed.), *The Challenge of Severe Mental Handicap: A behaviour analytic approach*, Wiley, Sussex.

Kiernan, C., Qureshi, H. and Alborz, A. (1989), 'Report to the Department of Health: Characteristics of people showing severe problem behaviour', HARC, Manchester.

King's Fund, (1988), *Information Exchange on Challenging Behaviour Services*, King's Fund Centre, London.

LaVigna, G. and Donnellan, A. (1986), *Alternatives to Punishment: Solving Behavior Problems with Nonaversive Strategies*, Irvington Press, New York.

LaVigna, G. and Willis, T. (1991), *Assessment and Analysis of Severe and Challenging Behavior*, IABA, Los Angeles.

LaVigna, G., Willis, T. and Sweitzer, M. (1990), *Maximising Staff Consistency*, IABA, Los Angeles, CA.

Learning Disabilities Directorate, (1991), *Description of Services*, Liverpool Health Authority.

Learning Difficulties Speciality (1990), *Operational Policy for the Specialist Support Service*, Liverpool Health Authority.

Lovett, H. (1985), *Cognitive Counselling with Persons with Special Needs*, Praeger, New York.

Lovett, H. (1987), 'Some considerations in providing services for people with mental and emotional handicaps: Human resource development implications', unpublished paper prepared for the Western Massachusetts Training Consortium Inc.

McBrien, J. and Felce, D. (1990), 'Challenging behaviour in people with severe or profound mental handicaps: A practical handbook on the behavioural approach', BIMH, Kidderminster.

McGee, J., Menolascino, F., Hobbs., D. and Menousek, P. (1987), *Gentle Teaching: A Nonaversive Approach for Helping Persons with Mental Retardation*, Springer, New York.

Meyer, L. and Evans, I. (1989), *Nonaversive Intervention for Behavior Problems: A Manual for Home and Community*, Paul H. Brookes, Baltimore, MD.

Meyer, L., Peck, C. and Brown, L. (1990), *Critical Issues in the Lives of People with Severe Disabilities*, Paul H Brookes, Baltimore, MD.

MRHA (1989), *A Framework for Living: A Strategy for Services for People with Learning Difficulties (Mental Handicap)*, Mersey Regional Health Authority.

O'Brien, J. (1987), 'A guide to personal futures planning' in G. T. Bellamy and B. Wilcox (eds.), *A Comprehensive Guide to the Activities Catalog: An Alternative Curriculum for Youth and Adults with Severe Disabilities*, Paul H. Brookes, Baltimore, MD.

O'Brien, J. and Lyle, C. (1987), *Framework for Accomplishment: A Workshop for People Developing Better Services*, Responsive Systems Associates, Decatur, GA.

O'Neil, R., Horner, R., Albin, R., Storey, K. and Sprague, J. (1990), *Functional Analysis of Problem Behavior: A Practical Assessment Guide*, Sycamore Publishing Company, Sycamore, IL.

Psychology Department, Learning Disabilities Directorate (1991), *The Personal Futures Planning Process Handbook*, Liverpool Health Authority/Social Services Department.

Psychology Department, Learning Disabilities Directorate, (1991), *The Assessment Collation Guide*, Liverpool Health Authority.

Repp, A. and Singh, N. (1990), *Perspectives on the Use of Nonaversive and Aversive Interventions for Persons with Developmental Disabilities*, Sycamore Publishing Company, Sycamore, IL.

Routledge, M. (1990), 'Services for people with mental handicap whose behaviour is a challenge to services. A review of the policy and service context in the seven districts covered by the HARC Behaviour Problems Project', University of Manchester HARC, Manchester.

Schaull, J., Willis, T. and LaVigna, G. (1989), *Criterion-Referenced, Competency-Based Training Program*, IABA, Los Angeles, CA.

Stark, J., Menolascino, F., Alberelli, M. and Gray, V. (eds.), (1988), *Mental Retardation and Mental Health: Classification, Diagnosis, Treatment, Services*, Springer-Verlag, New York.

Taylor, S., Biklen, D. and Knoll, J. (1987), *Community Integration for People with Severe Disabilities*, Teachers College Press, New York.

TSI (1991), *Training in Systematic Instruction Trainers Manual*, TSI Ltd, London.

Values Into Action (1990), Editorial, *VIA Newsletter*, Summer 61.

Developing services for people with severe learning disabilities and seriously challenging behaviours: South East Thames Regional Health Authority, 1985–1991

In 1985 the South East Thames Regional Health Authority established a Special Development Team to help facilitate the development of locally managed community-based services for people with severe learning disabilities and seriously challenging behaviours. In the following chapter we will attempt to describe the policy context and method of operation of this service, evaluate its performance against a number of criteria and identify some of the key issues arising from the first six years of this innovative project.

THE POLICY CONTEXT

The South East Thames Regional Health Authority (SETRHA) is responsible for the coordination of health care provided by fifteen District Health Authorities and the Special Health Authority (Maudsley and Bethlem Royal Hospitals) to 3.6 million people in the south east of England. The geographical area covered includes the south-east quadrant of Greater London, and the counties of Kent and East Sussex.

During the 1980s SETRHA embarked upon an ambitious plan of institutional reprovision centering upon the phase down and eventual closure of Darenth Park Hospital (Korman and Glennerster, 1985, 1990). Within this process, the role of the RHA was perceived to be facilitator of change through the coordination of planning and the establishment of financial mechanisms to enable the redistribution of the resources currently tied up in institutions. Examples of the latter included the development of a funding policy based upon 'dowry payments' and the provision of capital assistance for the purchase of ordinary housing stock. As a result of the success of these measures, several smaller institutions within the Region closed and the pace of the phase down of Darenth Park Hospital increased in the mid-1980s, leading to its eventual closure in 1988.

During the early stages of this programme, however, it came to be recognised that the resettlement of a number of individuals, those with 'special' needs, would present such a challenge to receiving services that additional RHA-led initiatives were considered appropriate. Such concerns were borne out by the experience of the hospital closure programme, which demonstrated the all too familiar pattern of receiving agencies reproviding services for the most able/least needy, leaving institutional services coping, with increasingly depleted resources, with an increasingly disabled population.

Existing policy options for those with special needs involved the development of subregional treatment and residential units for those clients whose needs were considered too complex or challenging for local services (South East Thames Regional Health Authority, 1979). Increasingly, however, such plans were seen as out of step with some of the more innovative developments occurring in leading districts within the Region, which had adopted an 'ordinary life' model (King's Fund, 1980) as a foundation for service development.

These developments were reflected in the appointment of a Regional Co-ordinator of Staff Training in 1983 and the subsequent organisation of training courses for professionals and managers on the development of staffed domestic housing for the residential care of people with serious disabilities (Mansell, 1988). The time was right, therefore, for the development of relatively radical proposals for those groups of clients who had until then, to all intents and purposes, been 'left out' of local service developments. Indeed, a subsequent review of the RHA's Special Needs Policy (South East Thames Regional Health Authority, 1985) proposed the development of three distinct initiatives in place of the existing plans for sub-regional units for people with special needs.

1. A Special Development Team (SDT) should be set up to provide expert assistance to District Health Authorities and other local agencies to help them provide services for people with severe learning disabilities and severely challenging behaviour.
2. A number of subregional facilities should be established to provide assessment and shortterm treatment for people with mild or moderate learning disabilities and challenging behaviours.
3. A Sensory Impairment Team should be established to provide expert assistance to District Health Authorities and other receiving agencies regarding the support of people with learning disabilities and sensory impairments.

These proposals were accepted by Regional and District officers, with the support of the Regional Nursing Officer being particularly crucial to its success, as it was for much of the hospital closure and reprovision process (Korman and Glennerster, 1990). In practice, however, they were not completely implemented. While the Special Development Team was established as a five-year project in 1985, only one assessment and treatment facility was established, the Mental Impairment Evaluation and Treatment Service at the Bethlem Royal Hospital (Murphy *et al.*, 1991; Murphy and Clare, 1991). A single Sensory Impairment Project Officer was appointed as a joint venture with the Royal National Institute for the Deaf and a pool of money was set aside at SETRHA to fund local projects on sensory impairment.

It is important to note that, from the outset, the Special Development Team and associated initiatives arose from and operated within a policy context dominated by institutional closure. As we shall see later, this context was to have important implications for the fate of the services jointly established by local agencies and the SDT.

THE SPECIAL DEVELOPMENT TEAM: A DESCRIPTION

The organisation and operation of the Special Development Team has been described in detail elsewhere (Cummings *et al.*, 1989; Emerson, 1990; Emerson *et al.*, 1987, 1988a, 1988b, 1989; McCool *et al.*, 1989; McGill *et al.*, 1991; Special Development Team, 1987, 1988, 1989; Toogood *et al.*, 1988). As a result, only the key features of the service will be described below.

The Special Development Team was set up as a five-year project (December 1985–December 1990) funded by the RHA out of approximately £1 million set aside within the Mental Handicap Funding Policy for 'special needs' initiatives. The team was based at the University of Kent, sharing accommodation with the RHA's Mental Handicap Staff Training Unit (Mansell *et al.*, 1987). Up until 1989 the Team was directly accountable to the Director of Administration, Personnel and Training (who was also the Regional Nursing Officer) within the RHA. On day-to-day matters, however, the Team was accountable to the Regional Co-ordinator of Staff Training (Mental Handicap), a post which was later to become the Directorship of the Centre for the Applied Psychology of Social Care at the University of Kent at Canterbury. From 1989 onwards, however, the Team was made fully accountable to the Director of the Centre for the Applied Psychology of Social Care at the University of Kent at Canterbury.

The SDT consisted of one Team Leader and five Team Members. All posts within the team were open to applicants from any professional background, all Team Members were solely accountable to the Team Leader and had identical job descriptions and roles. The SDT, therefore, was not a multi-disciplinary team, although, as it happened, it included individuals with backgrounds in clinical psychology, social work, nursing, teaching, and service management.

The SDT's remit was to help develop local services for clients within the Region who had severe or profound learning disabilities and presented severely challenging behaviour. Severely challenging behaviour was defined as 'behaviour of such an intensity, frequency or duration that the physical safety of the person or others is placed in serious jeopardy or behaviour which is likely to seriously limit or deny access to and use of ordinary community facilities' (Emerson *et al.*, 1988). The clients selected were those perceived as presenting the greatest challenge to the development of community services (see below). Formally the team's aims were defined as:

the provision of practical assistance to local health, educational and social services in the design and implementation of individualised model services over a five-year period for 38 people with a severe learning disability and seriously challenging behaviours; the provision of advice and information on a consultative basis to local services within the South East Thames Regional Health Authority area regarding the development of services for this client group in general.

Such a strategy was seen to fulfil a number of purposes. Firstly, by focusing upon the thirty-eight 'most challenging' individuals within the Region it was intended to provide additional practical support to local agencies in developing community-based services for their most difficult clients. The importance of such practical support was underscored by the difficult policy context within which local agencies were operating resulting from the RHA's aggressive deinstitutionalisation programme. Secondly, it was hoped that these local projects, as a result of the additional Regional input, would serve as demonstration projects through which local services would have the opportunity to develop policies, procedures and competencies which would be applicable to other services for people with serious disabilities within the locality. That is, it was hoped that the lessons learned from these demonstration projects would generalise across settings within localities. Thirdly, the strategy had an implicit objective of helping to demonstrate to local and national policy makers that well-planned community services provided the best option for all people with severe learning disabilities, including the most seriously behaviourally disordered. This latter objective was not, of course, a formally recognised aim of the Regional Health Authority but, rather, a key belief held by several of the key actors in these developments.

The SDT's mode of operation consisted of a four stage process involving case identification (Emerson *et al.*, 1987), the development of an individual service plan (Toogood *et al.*, 1988), support in commissioning services (Cummings *et al.*, 1989) and, finally, providing additional support to new services during their initial years of operation (Emerson *et al.*, 1989; McCool *et al.*, 1989).

Case identification

From the outset it was decided that the SDT would allocate its resources equitably among the fifteen District Health Authorities in the Region on an approximate per capita basis. Thus, each of the District Health Authorities was allocated two–four places on the SDT case-load depending upon the population base of the District. For each District a meeting was organised between the SDT and senior managers and professional staff of local agencies (health, social services and, occasionally, education) in order to identify potential clients. Typically a 'shortlist' of eight–ten potential clients were identified who were screened by the SDT and final decisions made in conjunction with local staff. The main criteria for selection or acceptance onto the Team's case-load were their level of ability (having a severe learning disability) and the severity of the challenge presented by their behaviour. Some clients were judged to be too able and the referring agency was directed on to the Regionally supported initiative for clients with mild learning disabilities the Mental Impairment Evaluation and Treatment Service (Murphy *et al.*, 1991; Murphy and Clare, 1991). Some referrals were judged to not display severely challenging behaviour. In such cases Regional policy was that local agencies needed to make their own arrangements to cope with such individuals without external assistance.

The SDT did not, therefore, operate an open referral system. The main reasons for this were concern regarding the number of referrals which such a system would generate; concern regarding the time-wasting screening of inappropriate or 'illegitimate' referrals, which did not have the backing of the responsible local agencies; and, most importantly, the desire to foster a sense of ownership among local senior managers and professionals in SDT-supported ventures by having them play a central early role in identifying the clients with whom the SDT would work.

As of the end of 1990 the SDT had accepted thirty-five referrals to develop services for clients in fourteen separate District Health Authorities. In the course of institutional reprovision there has been considerable diversity across the Region in who has taken the lead agency responsibility, and this is reflected in the SDT's case-load. Ten District Health Authorities have taken lead responsibility for twenty-four clients; three Local Authorities for nine clients; and one voluntary organisation (a housing association supported by the local authority) has taken responsibility for two clients.

Individual service planning

Following the acceptance of a client onto the Team's case-load a written individual service plan was developed as a collaborative venture between the SDT; managers and professional staff in the receiving services, and relatives, friends or advocates who could speak on behalf of the client themselves. The serious disabilities of the clients precluded their effective contribution to such an abstract process, although on many occasions they were present at meetings convened to develop this plan.

The individual service plan itself contained a detailed specification, including estimates of revenue and capital costs, of the support required to provide a high quality community-based service for the client. The processes involved in this task drew heavily upon the types of ethnographic group work advocated by Brost *et al.* (1982) and O'Brien (1987). As a result both the process and the final product were characterised by a strong emphasis upon normalisation related values and the use of mechanisms for providing support which appeared to combine effectiveness (in achieving the desired outcomes) with conformity to local social and cultural values. Thus, for example, all completed individual service plans advocated that the client live in ordinary domestic housing centrally located within the community so as to give ready access to as wide a range as possible of local facilities.

Attaining a balance between the use of 'ordinary means' and effectiveness proved problematic in many instances with regard to the proposed size of the residential component of the individual service plan. The majority of the clients accepted onto the case-load of the SDT showed intense aggressive behaviours which would, at times, require the immediate intervention of two or more members of staff to ensure the safety of the person and of others in the vicinity. This, in effect, dictated the staffing requirements of the proposed services, i.e. two–three staff on duty at any one time. It was clear, however, that such staffing ratios would be unnecessary for the vast majority of the time due to the low prevalence of such episodes. As a result, rather than develop an inefficient service in which the majority of staff were redundant at any one time, group living options were developed so that the 'redundant' staff time could be spent supporting other people with learning disabilities in the same residential setting. Thus, many individual service plans were based around houses for two–four people, not because of any belief in the desirability of group living *per se*, but simply resulting from pragmatic considerations relating to a necessary staffing establishment to provide a safe service. It should be noted, however, that, in the majority of instances, the group living situations were planned to be comprised of one person with seriously challenging behaviours living with one–three other people with learning disabilities but without either challenging behaviours or complex medical needs which might require the immediate attention of staff.

In addition to its staffing resources the team was able to help local agencies access Regional pump-priming monies to support the development of community services for this client group. A lump sum equivalent to £45,000 per client (1990 prices) was available, in addition to any existing dowry, to help with the initial revenue costs of services established by local agencies in collaboration with the Special Development Team. From 1986 onwards the RHA also made some capital monies available to further help this process and many of the projects which later developed used this capital to help purchase property. The possible use of these monies was identified within the individual service plan.

Once completed the individual service plan was submitted to senior managers of the responsible local agencies for their consideration. At the end of 1990, thirty-three individual service plans had been submitted to fourteen agencies within fourteen District Health Authorities.

Commissioning new services

If the responsible local agencies agreed with the proposals submitted in the form of an individual service plan, or negotiated a variation upon the plan with the SDT then the Team would provide additional support to the local agency in commissioning the new service. The tasks undertaken by the SDT at this stage included working with local managers and professionals in order to identify and purchase new property, recruit and train new staff, develop policies and procedures for the new service and help prepare the client for their move (Cummings *et al.*, 1989).

In mid-1991, of the thirty-three plans which had been submitted, nineteen had resulted in services being established by the SDT in conjunction with ten local agencies. The number of services established per year was: 1987(1), 1988(9), 1989(5), 1990(1) and 1991(3). Some of the characteristics of these services are described below in Table 4.1.

Supporting services

Once established the SDT provided additional professional support to the services during the first one–two years of their lives. While the supporting role played by the SDT varied across services, the types of activities undertaken at this point included advising upon the implementation of agreed policies and procedures, providing specialist advice concerning the analysis and treatment of the client's seriously challenging behaviours, staff training, progress chasing within the local agency and providing practical, informational and emotional support to local staff.

The services set up in conjunction with the SDT are managed by the responsible local agency, usually the District Health Authority. While they therefore fit in to existing management structures the SDT has endeavoured to encourage the development of additional structures to protect the services from threat. This has usually taken the form of setting up a Project Co-ordinating Group chaired by someone other than the home leader's line manager, e.g. the Principal Psychologist, and involving senior managers, client/family and SDT members, as well as the staff and managers involved in delivering the service. This group has usually met on a monthly basis, perhaps reducing to quarterly as time goes on.

While the other management and support arrangements depend ultimately on what is provided by the responsible agency, the SDT has encouraged the use of regular staff meetings and individual supervision and has often sought to build in staff training time to the initial staffing establishment.

Table 4.1 *Projects set up with the support of the Special Development Team*

Client characteristics[1]	Original living arrangements	Planned day service	Staffing establishment	Date opened	Current status	Overall revenue costs[2]
44 year old man severe self-injury and destructive behaviour.	4 bedroomed house shared with three others with mild/moderate learning disability and without seriously challenging behaviour,	No separate day service.	9 wte	21.6.88	Service relocated to a detached house after 1 year because of the amount of noise. Other arrangements still stand.	£140,00
26 year old woman, aggressive and destructive behaviour, extremely socially withdrawn	4 bedroomed detached house in residential area shared with three others with mild/moderate learning disability and without seriously challenging behaviour.	No separate day service.	9 wte	25.6.90	Original arrangements still stand.	£130,000
18 year old man, aggressive and destructive behaviour, severe non-compliance.	3 bedroomed detached house, shared with one other with severe learning disabilities and seriously challenging behaviour.	Local special school.	8.25 wte	29.4.91	Original arrangements still stand.	£120,000
17 year old man, aggressive and destructive behaviour.	3 bedroomed terraced house, shared with live-in member of staff and non-handicapped co-tenant.	10 hours home tutoring.	4.5 wte	23.10.88	In April 1991 client moved to the service immediately above, partly because of the isolation arising in a single-client service, partly because of a belief that now in a position to benefit from sharing, partly for logistic and financial reasons.	£60,000

Table 4.1   *cont.*

Client characteristics[1]	Original living arrangements	Planned day service	Staffing establishment	Date opened	Current status	Overall revenue costs[2]
30 year old man, aggressive and destructive behaviour	5 bedroomed bungalow in residential area, shared with two others with severe learning disabilities without seriously challenging behaviour.	No separate day service.	14.5 wte	1.7.91	Original arrangements still stand.	£210,000
39 year old woman, aggressive and obsessional behaviour	5 bedroomed detached house in residential area, shared with three others with severe learning disabilities without seriously challenging behaviour.	No separate day service.	10 wte	6.3.89	Client died of natural causes in January 1990.	£110,000
18 year old woman, self-injurious behaviour.	4 bedroomed detached house in residential area, shared with three others with severe learning disabilities without seriously challenging behaviour.	No separate day service.	13 wte	15.9.87	Original arrangements still stand though some of the co-tenants have changed.	£160,000
29 year old man, destructive and obsessional behaviour.	5 bedroomed detached house in residential area, shared with four others with severe learning disabilities, three of whom display challenging behaviour.	No separate day service.	14.6 wte	22.4.91	Original arrangements still stand.	£180,000

Table 4.1 *cont.*

Client characteristics[1]	Original living arrangements	Planned day service	Staffing establishment	Date opened	Current status	Overall revenue costs[2]
22 year old man, aggressive and anti-social behaviour.	3 bedroomed house, shared with one other with severe learning disabilities and seriously challenging behaviour (also an SDT client).	No separate day service.	10 wte	9.6.88	In April 1991 the placement was closed and the clients resettled to another, larger service in the District to save money.	£120,000
28 year old man, aggressive and destructive behaviour.	3 bedroomed house, shared with one other with severe learning disabilities and seriously challenging behaviour (also an SDT client).	No separate day service.	10 wte	9.6.88	In April 1991 the placement was closed and the clients resettled to another, larger service in the District to save money.	£120,000
31 year old man, aggressive and self-injurious behaviour.	3 bedroomed house (a 'staff' house on a campus development for 72 people – originally intented as an interim placement but the DHA was unable to obtain capital to go ahead with the property purchase), shared with two others with severe learning disabilites, one of whom displays seriously challenging behaviour (also an SDT client).	On-site day centre available.	10.5 wte	20.3.89	Original arrangements still stand.	£110,000

Table 4.1   *cont.*

Client characteristics[1]	Original living arrangements	Planned day service	Staffing establishment	Date opened	Current status	Overall revenue costs[2]
41 year old man, aggressive and destructive behaviour.	3 bedroomed detached bungalow in residential area, shared with two others with severe learning disabilities, one of whom displays seriously challenging behaviour.	No separate day service.	10.5 wte	20.3.89	Original arrangements still stand.	£110,000
24 year old man, self-injurious	3 bedroomed house (a 'staff house on a campus development for 72 people – originally intended as an interim placement but the DHA was unable to obtain captial to go ahead with property purchase), shared with two others with severe learning disabilities, one of whom displays seriously challenging behaviour (also an SDT client).	On-site day centre available.	10.5 wte	20.3.89	Original arrangements still stand.	£110,000
33 year old woman, aggressive behaviour.	1 bedroomed flat in a residential building in which a second flat occupied by four others with severe learning disabilities without seriously challenging behaviour.	No separate day service.	14 wte (supporting both flats)	5.10.88	In April 1990 the client was moved within the district, and subsequently out of the district because of difficulty in managing aggressive behaviour. With the support of the SDT a placement was	£70,000[3]

Table 4.1 *cont.*

Client characteristics[1]	Original living arrangements	Planned day service	Staffing establishment	Date opened	Current status	Overall revenue costs[2]
					reestablished in March 1991 in a single person flat on a campus development for 48 people within the District.	
22 year old man, aggressive and destructive behaviour.	5 bedroomed terraced house in residential area, shared with two others with mild learning disabilities without seriously challenging behaviour.	No separate day service.	10 wte	22.8.88	On 13.9.88, as a result of difficulty in managing aggressive behaviour, the client was moved to a large mental handicap hospital in another district where he remains to date.	£160,000
22 year old woman, aggressive behaviour.	3 bedroomed semi-detached house in residential area, shared with one other with severe learning disabilities.	No separate day service.	9 wte	27.11.89	Original arrangements still stand.	£140,000
33 year old woman, destructive and non-compliant behaviour.	4 bedroomed terraced house in residential area, shared with two others with severe learning disabilities without seriously challenging behaviours.	No separate day service.	10 wte	30.6.88	Original arrangements still stand.	£140,000
29 year old man, aggressive, destructive and sexually inappropriate behaviour.	2 bedroomed flat in residential area, living alone.	No separate day service.	7 wte	5.8.88	In September 1990 the client was moved to a staff flat in a local, small mental handicap hospital because of difficulty in managing his behaviour and threat of	£100,000

Table 4.1 *cont.*

Client characteristics[1]	Original living arrangements	Planned day service	Staffing establishment	Date opened	Current status	Overall revenue costs[2]
32 year old man, self-injurious and destructive behaviour.	3 bedroomed semi-detached house in residential area, shared with one other with severe learning disabilities without seriously challenging behaviours.	No separate day service.	10.5 wte	2.5.88	In October 1989 the client was moved to a similar but more accessible placement within the district because of a deterioration in mobility.	£150,000

Notes

1. All client ages as of date of opening of service.
2. Unless otherwise indicated revenue costs refer to the annual costs of providing the entire service, i.e. including co-tenants (where applicable) as well as the SDT client. Where current costs are not available the original cost of the service has been inflated at 8% per annum to produce an approximation to the current figure. All costs should be treated as approximate.
3. This refers to the cost of the single person flat only.

The support provided to the agency by the SDT is initially often very intensive. In the months before and immediately after the setting up of the service, one member of the team may be working on an almost fulltime basis with the service's staff, being involved in commissioning and staff training activities and then, perhaps most crucially, in working out 'on the ground' how to provide a good service to the individual client and how to overcome the many difficulties which inevitably arise. This period of work usually culminates with a report to the agency on the service at the end of the first six months. As well as being a description of what has happened, the report seeks to evaluate the success of the development to date and make recommendations to the agency concerning improvements.

As time goes on the support provided by the SDT has gradually reduced and become less direct, with advice and consultation being offered through the management and support structures which have been established. While the amount of support provided to individual projects has varied considerably, the aim has been to reduce involvement to the point where complete withdrawal can occur after eighteen months.

The current status of the nineteen services established to date is given above in Table 4.1. As can be seen of these nineteen services, thirteen have been sustained over periods of up to four years. Of the remaining six services: in one the client died of natural causes unrelated to their challenging behaviour; in the remaining five services clients have been relocated to larger, more institutional settings.

OUTCOMES

The impact of services for people with challenging behaviours can, of course, be judged against a number of criteria (Emerson *et al.*, 1991). The success of the STD will be considered here against the three criteria reflected in its manifest and latent objectives: the effectiveness of the provision of practical support to local agencies in the context of the Region's institutional reprovision programme; the impact of the services established upon the quality of life and challenging behaviours of service users, and the impact of the initiative upon general policies and procedures adopted by agencies for people with severe learning disabilities and challenging behaviours.

Supporting local agencies

As noted above, the STD was established as a RHA initiative to solve a particular planning problem within the context of a deinstitutionalisation or hospital reprovision programme: namely, to facilitate the resettlement of those individuals with a severe learning disability within the Region's existing institutions who presented the greatest challenge to local services (Korman and Glennerster, 1990).

The success of the Team in fulfilling this objective is reflected in a number of indicators reflecting the uptake of the Team's services by agencies within the RHA boundaries. As described in the preceding sections, within the first five years of the Team's operation it was involved with planning services with agencies within fourteen of the fifteen District Health Authorities within the Region. New services were subsequently established in conjunction with local agencies within eight of these fifteen DHAs. The local agencies taking lead responsibility for these local developments included seven District Health Authorities, one Social Services Department and one voluntary organisation.

While not reflecting a universal uptake, these indicators do suggest an acceptably high degree of uptake of the additional Regional support provided through the SDT when taken in context of a) the radical nature of the plans offered to local agencies; b) the high revenue costs associated with these plans; and c) the late establishment of the SDT in the context of the Darenth Park closure programme (Korman and Glennerster, 1990). It should, perhaps, be stressed that during the time leading up to the closure of Darenth Park Hospital in 1988, the notion that the most challenging people with severe learning disabilities could be provided for in small-scale community-based services was treated with considerable scepticism among the majority of local agencies. Against such a background the level of uptake of SDT sponsored services must be judged as being acceptably high.

However, while uptake proved acceptable, the attrition rate experienced by local projects was significant. As indicated above, of the nineteen longterm projects established six have since closed. There were a variety of reasons for closure.

● In two cases lead agency responsibility changed hands from the DHA to a not-for-profit organisation funded jointly by the DHA and the SSD. This organisation subsequently relocated the individuals to save money.
● In three cases the project closed because the lead agency (two different DHAs) felt that the client's behaviour could not continue to be managed within a community based setting. In one case the client was moved to a 'crisis intervention' placement on the periphery of a large hospital, where he remains after three years. In one case the client was relocated within the District to a small Mental Handicap hospital where he remains after one year. In the third case the client was relocated to a private psychiatric hospital and subsequently to a private placement but, with support from the SDT, returned to a newly developed placement in their home district.
● In one case the client died of a heart attack nine months after the project was established.

In addition, in three projects, the placement was maintained but only after a planned move within the district. We will return to the issue of project attrition below.

User outcomes

A number of approaches were taken to evaluate the impact of the services established in conjunction with the Special Development Team upon the quality of life and challenging behaviours of service users. These included both a formal evaluation of a sample of services, and strategies for the internal monitoring of service performance.

In addition to funding the establishment of the SDT, the South East Thames Regional Health Authority commissioned a formal evaluation of the Team's effectiveness. This evaluation examined the impact of services set up by local agencies in conjunction with the SDT upon the lifestyle and challenging behaviours of people moving out of long-stay hospital. The study, which is still ongoing, has focused upon the longitudinal monitoring of patterns of client and staff activity to provide indicators of client lifestyle, the quality of support provided within services and changes in challenging behaviours (Mansell and Beasley, 1989, 1990, 1991). Specifically, the study involves the collection of nonparticipant observational data using a momentary time sampling framework of a) client participation in domestic, recreational, vocational and educational activities; b) the nature of staff support being provided to the client; c) social interactions between clients and social acts directed towards staff by clients, and d) challenging behaviours exhibited by clients. In addition, information is collected on client medication, staffing levels and aspects of the physical environment in which clients are living.

While the full results of this study are forthcoming, preliminary analyses (Mansell and Beasley, 1989, 1990, 1991; McGill and Emerson, in press) indicate that as clients moved into the newly established services they received greater amounts of staff support and showed:

• marked overall increases in the amount of time spent in participation in ordinary domestic and recreational activities;
• no overall change in the minimal amount of time spent in formal educational or vocational activities;
• marked overall decreases in the amount of time spent engaged in stereotypic behaviours;
• no overall changes in the amount of time spent engaged in more serious challenging behaviours.

This overall pattern of results was also observed when the performance of the newly created SDT-sponsored services was compared against two major policy alternatives: the use of the traditional range of services typically available to a District Health Authority, including placement in the private sector (Mansell and Beasley, 1991); and the establishment of specialised staffed houses within which people with seriously challenging behaviours were congregated together (Emerson *et al.*, in press – a; McGill and Emerson, in press). These comparisons were made possible by a fortuitous combination of local developments.

Firstly, a number of clients on the SDT case-load who had been included in the formal evaluation did not, for a number of reasons (including delays in commissioning the new services and failure to agree plans with local agencies), move from their current institutional placements to SDT-sponsored services. As a result, it became possible to evaluate the impact of their move to a range of alternative placements including private psychiatric hospital, private residential care homes and congregate care staffed housing developments within the grounds of newly developed institutional services (Mansell and Beasley, 1991).

Secondly, within the Region an alternative model of service provision was advocated and subsequently developed by a group of District Health Authorities the reprovision of a hospital-based, medium term treatment facility in two highly resourced small staffed houses. This approach, advocated on the basis of cost and the special expertise available within the existing treatment unit, was considered to fall within the broad remit of RHA policy, given its use of small-scale ordinary housing. Quite fortuitously, four individuals who had been included in the SDT evaluation study moved into this alternative service, thus enabling a longitudinal component to be incorporated into the formal evaluation of this development in a second RHA-funded study, which employed identical measures to the existing SDT evaluation (Emerson *et al.*, in press – a).

As would be expected, the overall pattern of results as described above masks a considerable diversity of outcomes across individual services and service users. Thus while some of the new services achieved only modest increases in quality when compared against previous institutional placements, other services demonstrated substantial gains. Key variables which appeared to discriminate between successful and unsuccessful placements will be discussed below in the following section.

The failure of the formal evaluation to identify any overall trends in serious challenging behaviours is, of course, disappointing. These preliminary findings need to interpreted carefully, however, for a number of reasons:

- Firstly, the time sampling strategy employed is poor at estimating the percentage of time taken by low frequency behaviours and short duration behaviours (Saudargas and Zanolli, 1990). As has been pointed out (McGill and Emerson, in press), most seriously challenging behaviours are of low frequency and short duration.

- Secondly, the coding strategy employed fails to distinguish between different levels of intensity of similar behavioural topographies (Beasley *et al.*, 1989).

  Thus, for example, physical assault leading to serious injury and a non-injurious push would be coded in an identical manner. This observation highlights the care that needs to be taken in operationally defining challenging behaviours in observational research.

- Thirdly, marked improvements in staffing levels and aspects of the physical environments provided considerably greater opportunities for clients to exhibit challenging behaviours in the newly established services. Thus, for example, at a simple level there were more objects around to throw and more staff to hit.

- Finally, comparison of overall levels or rates of challenging behaviours across settings need to be evaluated in light of differences between settings in the rates of occurrence of known eliciting stimuli (Carr *et al.*, 1990). Thus, for example, if an individual's aggression is motivated by escape from social demands it would be possible to design a 'successful' intervention by simply ceasing to place any demands on the person. This did, in fact, happen to one SDT client who was moved from a community placement to a specialised treatment unit. Within the unit the person's aggression markedly reduced as did the amount of staff contact they received and the amount of time they spent engaged in constructive activities (Special Development Team, 1989). A more appropriate intervention, however, would be to provide the person with an alternative way of responding to unwanted demands. In the former example, intervention has proceeded through altering the overall probability of the challenging behaviour occurring by simply avoiding situations which are known to elicit it, but not, presumably, the conditional probability of it occurring in response to its eliciting stimuli. In the latter example, intervention would focus upon changing the conditional probability of the challenging behaviour occurring, ie. the probability it will occur given the occurrence of its eliciting stimuli. As Carr *et al.* (1990) point out information on the conditional probability is necessary for the proper interpretation of inter- vention effects. This point is of more than academic interest given that a) the motivational basis underlying the challenging behaviours shown by the majority of SDT clients appeared to be the escape or avoidance of either social demands, social interaction or social proximity (Emerson, 1990); b) the newly established services involved markedly higher rates of staff contact and social demands to participate in the activities characteristic of an 'ordinary life' than previous services (Mansell and Beasley, 1989, 1990, 1991).

In addition to the formal evaluation of user outcomes, a number of approaches have been taken to internal monitoring of the projects. These have included:

- the use of management information systems for the regular collection and review of data indicating service quality (e.g. participation in community activities, rates of challenging behaviours);
- the formal six-monthly review by the SDT on overall service quality;
- the establishment of local quality assurance processes, including Quality Action Groups around some of the projects.

In general these less formal approaches to evaluation have reinforced the findings described above. Clients are reported to be participating in a large and varied range of personal, domestic and community activities. Doubts have been expressed, however, about the quality and sustainability of these particular changes. In addition, considerable scope has been found for promoting more individual and active participation. Levels of challenging behaviour have generally been reported to be manageable, though, as time goes on and personnel change, even a continuing low level of serious disturbance can be difficult for services to tolerate and can lead to intermittent crises. The general picture is undoubtedly one of much higher quality than represented by most clients' previous experiences, but with many of the potential benefits of community living apparently still untapped.

One particular aspect of the service model associated with SDT sponsored projects frequently raises concern – the impact of sharing a service with someone with seriously challenging behaviours upon the quality of life of co-tenants. As noted above, the majority of services established by local services in conjunction with the SDT involved small group living arrangements for one person with severe learning disabilities and seriously challenging behaviours and one or more others who had a learning disability but did not have any seriously challenging behaviours, or complex medical needs.

While no information on this aspect of user outcomes was collected as part of the formal evaluation study, some informal observations may be made as a result of information collected from internal monitoring systems. In general, the possible picture of co-tenants living a vulnerable frightened existence has not been found. There have been very few reports of co-tenants being attacked or otherwise threatened. Undoubtedly, there have been times when they have been living in a fairly disturbed and disturbing environment, but their generally higher levels of ability or prior planning has often allowed them to retire from such situations to conditions of greater privacy within the house. Indeed, there is anecdotal evidence to suggest that co-tenants have benefitted from the higher staffing levels, 'structured programming' and external involvement with the projects.

It is interesting to note, however, that such concerns are rarely raised regarding services which congregate people with seriously challenging behaviours together in one setting. Surely, if people with learning disabilities have the right not to live with others who show challenging behaviour then this right must be extended to all people with learning disabilities, including people with challenging behaviours themselves. Thus, the ethical issue is one of whether it is appropriate for anyone to live/work in close proximity to someone with seriously challenging behaviours. Congregating together people with challenging behaviour does not provide a solution to this problem.

Dissemination

As we have indicated, in addition to its immediate practical objectives, the SDT had both manifest and latent aims regarding the dissemination of ideas, policies and procedures among local managers, professionals and other potential leaders. The impact of the SDT in this area is, of course, difficult to accurately assess. Some possible indicators of the extent to which the SDT (1) acted as a demonstration project itself and (2) successfully helped create local demonstration projects, are noted below.

At a broad level, the work of the SDT has been relatively extensively disseminated within the UK over the past five years through the publication of Annual Reports, a series of papers in a professional journal, presentations at local, national and international conferences and a limited number of visits to local projects by senior policy makers. Evidence for a limited impact of these activities upon the development of services for people with challenging behaviours in other localities is provided by the citation of materials in discussion papers produced by national organisations (e.g. Blunden and Allen, 1987; Department of Health, 1989) and the adoption, with appropriate modification, of selected aspects of the Team's operational policy by local initiatives (e.g. McBrien, in press). Indeed, the dissemination of the experience of the SDT does appear to have had some influence over the widespread adoption by many local agencies of the concept of peripatetic support teams for people with challenging behaviours. If nothing else, the Team appears to have unwittingly provided a standard definition of the term 'challenging behaviour'!

At a more local level, the work of the Special Development Team within the Region had an important impact upon the continuing debate regarding the need, or desirability, of specialised institutional provision for members of this client group. Indeed, the establishment of local 'ordinary life' services for some of the most challenging individuals within the region helped successfully to move the nature of the debate from consideration of the possibility of community for all to consideration of the viability of sustaining such a model in the current policy climate. That is, the experience of the SDT helped demonstrate what was possible and consequently debunk notions that 'ordinary life' type services were simply inapplicable to certain client groups. What it did not do, of course, was to demonstrate that this model could be sustained on a widespread basis.

Within specific localities it was hoped that the services established by the SDT would act as opportunities for local agencies to develop policies, procedures and competencies which could be generalised to other services for people with serious disabilities. Again, evaluating the success of the Team in achieving this objective has its obvious difficulties. In general, however, while there existed some notable exceptions there appeared to be little evidence of such spontaneous generalisation within local agencies. We will return to this issue later.

ISSUES: DETERMINANTS OF EFFECTIVENESS

The 'successes and failures' of the SDT during its first five years of operation raise a number of issues. In particular it is important to identify possible determinants of successes and, conversely, some of the reasons underlying the

Team's failures. It is, of course, not possible to isolate in any controlled way the operation of single variables upon the complex range of outcomes described above. The following discussion is, therefore, somewhat speculative.

The determinants of success and failure will be discussed below with respect to three dimensions of the Team's activities: the uptake and maintenance of services by local agencies; the quality of services provided, and the dissemination or generalisation of the lessons learned from these services.

Service uptake and maintenance

A number of factors appear to have been important in ensuring what we have argued to be a satisfactorily high uptake of the additional support provided by the SDT and the subsequent establishment of individually planned services in conjunction with local service agencies. The most important of these include (not necessarily in order of importance): the match between the concerns and values of local agencies and the service offered by the SDT; the political 'patronage' of the SDT by key senior managers; the resources which the Team and local agencies had at their disposal, and the consulting process used by the STD.

- *The match between the anxieties of local agencies and the remit of the Team* Probably the single most important factor determining the initial uptake of the services offered by the SDT was the close match between active organisational concerns and the remit of the Team. The Team was established in 1985 as the programme for the closure of Darenth Park Hospital was entering its final phase, a phase characterised by the need for receiving agencies to quickly establish local services for some of their most challenging clients while concurrently attempting to deal with the organisational consequences of rapid expansion. The appearance of a free 'expert' resource which would take some of the responsibility for planning and commissioning such services had obvious attractions. For those agencies in parts of the Region not directly involved in the Darenth closure establishment of joint services was of correspondingly lower priority. The importance of institutional closure in providing a facilitating context for the Teams' work is reflected in the timing of services opening. As we have noted above the modal year for service establishment was 1988, i.e. the year of the closure of Darenth Park.
- *The match between the value base of local service developments and the implicit values of the SDT* While not explicitly committed by its original remit to developing services based upon an 'ordinary life' model, it soon became apparent to local agencies that such a commitment in practice underlay the Team's activities. Not surprisingly, congruence between the values bases of the Team and local services helped facilitate joint working. It was not, however, a necessary and sufficient condition for uptake, as the Team was involved in establishing 'ordinary life' type services in conjunction with agencies committed to campus style developments and failed to achieve satisfactory joint working arrangements with

some agencies committed to 'ordinary life' values.

- *Political patronage* Throughout the successive stages of case identification, planning, commissioning and supporting services the Team benefitted substantially from its position as a high profile RHA initiative. The Team Leader, as an RHA officer, was directly accountable to the Regional Nursing Officer, who must be considered the key player in the development and implementation of the RHA's policies towards learning disabilities. In addition, the Team Leader was a member of key RHA and joint RHA–local agency committees concerned with policy formation and implementation. Both the actual and perceived access to such channels of influence undoubtably helped in facilitating effective joint working relationships in certain localities.

- *Resources* Not unexpectedly, the resources available to the Team and local services were influential in facilitating or hindering the establishment of local joint projects. The financial allocations made available to local agencies on top of the 'dowry' monies for joint ventures with the SDT were certainly influential in gaining the interest of local agencies. It is unlikely, however, that they played a major role in the decision to establish joint projects as the additional sum involved, a lump sum of £45,000 usually spread over three years, was relatively insignificant when taken in the context of the ongoing revenue costs of the projects themselves (see Table 4.1). More importantly, the resources available within local agencies for new ventures was a significant determinant of the capacity of local agencies to enter into joint working arrangements with the SDT. Thus, for example, while agencies receiving new monies as a result of the hospital reprovision programme were able to consider working with the SDT, local authorities (particularly inner London authorities) were undergoing a significant depletion of resources as a result of central government policies. Not surprisingly, such agencies did not feel able to seriously consider the new establishment of relatively expensive projects, even with the additional resources made available through the Team. The final aspect of resources which deserves consideration is the perceived importance of the staff resources and skills available to local agencies from within the SDT. In effect, the SDT supplied some local agencies with an experienced additional member of staff for a considerable period of time, a factor which certainly helped facilitate the planning, if not the uptake, of joint ventures.

  The overall impact of these factors was to maximise the probability of the SDT establishing joint projects with local agencies which were a) actively involved in hospital reprovision programmes; b) were committed at some key level in the organisation to an 'ordinary life' model of service development; and c) were likely to be influenced by the RHA. In practice this led to much of the Team's work being undertaken with District Health Authorities involved in the Darenth Park closure plan.

- *The consulting process* A number of aspects of the consulting process employed by the SDT appear to have been important in facilitating the uptake of service plans. These included:

  - The development of clear written contracts between the SDT and the referring agency, which appear to have been effective in reducing the possibilities of misunderstanding. In addition, their development has often proved to be a very helpful way of clarifying with the managers of the agency the nature of the task involved in developing and supporting such a service.

- The involvement, as far as possible, of all interested parties in the process of individual service planning appears to have been an effective mechanism for generating a sense of local ownership for the projects and establishing a momentum which appeared to help carry the projects through. The inclusion of senior agency managers (with access to and responsibility for the disposition of resources) in the individual service planning process, along with representatives of the agency currently providing a service, the client and their family or advocates, appeared to be particularly important in facilitating the transition of the project from plan to actuality. In effect, the early involvement of more senior managers helped establish powerful local commitment amongst key individuals who could exert considerable influence in local decision-making. Similarly, the individualisation of the planning process, i.e. the planning of a specific service for a known individual, appeared to be highly influential in strengthening local commitment and facilitating the acceptance of the plans. Firstly, individualisation, combined with ensuring as much contact as possible between participants in the planning process and the client, appeared to be a significant factor in generating local commitment to (and ownership of) the projects. Indeed, at one Regional committee this aspect of the Team's work was particularly criticised by a senior manager from one DHA, since tying plans to individuals made it much more difficult for them to turn down the proposals submitted by the local planning teams! Secondly, basing service plans on detailed individual assessment, including, for example, the use of analogue assessment techniques to identify the motivational dynamics underlying the person's challenging behaviours (Emerson, 1990), helped endow the plans with a professional or clinical credibility which agency managers in several instances found difficult to counter. The grounds of the debate concerning the appropriateness of aspects of the plan, for example, the client not living with others with challenging behaviours, was often conducted in terms of 'clinical' evidence regarding the appropriateness of this for the specific client, rather than issues of general principle. Thus, the individualisation of the process helped create a climate in which the local planning team had a virtual monopoly on access to key information relevant to the discussion of the proposal's appropriateness.

Thus the high rates of initial uptake of the services offered by the SDT and the relatively high rates of implementation of local projects appear to have been related to a number of background organisational factors and the characteristics of the consulting style employed. Notably, the topography and/or severity of the user's challenging behaviour was clearly unrelated to whether plans would be accepted. Somewhat ironically, however, these same factors may also have been implicated in the levels of attrition experienced by SDT-sponsored services. Firstly, it appears plausible to suggest that the power of the consulting process employed led to the establishment of some local projects which were in reality too fragile to be sustained in local circumstances. That is, the momentum generated by the process of individual service planning may have led to the acceptance of plans which were, in their context, too vulnerable to survive. Thus, while a less powerful planning and consulting strategy may have led to the establishment of fewer local projects, it may also have diminished the rates of attrition in the projects established.

More importantly, however, project attrition appeared to be directly related to the lack of comprehensiveness in local service systems, a common characteristic of often new and rapidly expanding service systems which have been established on the back of hospital reprovision programmes.

Mansell *et al.* (in press) identify the key components of a comprehensive service system for people with severe learning disabilities and challenging behaviours. These include the operation of effective systems for:

- the prevention and early identification of challenging behaviours;
- the provision of technical support (e.g. behavioural analysis and intervention, medical screening) and practical support (e.g. crisis intervention, emotional support to caregivers, flexible funding arrangements) to the settings in which people with challenging behaviours are living, learning, working and enjoying their leisure;
- the development of new placement options if the person's existing placement becomes either unacceptable or untenable.

The SDT initiative, of course, was clearly focused upon the latter component of this schema. In effect, the SDT was effective in establishing new placement options but did so in contexts characterised by serious deficiencies in the capacity of the local agency to provide effective practical and technical support to the placement once established. Deficiencies in the practical support of placements by managing agencies were particularly problematic in several instances. Thus, for example, failure to ensure adequate staffing levels and provide emotional support to care staff during a short-term crisis was directly responsible for the closure of one programme. At a broader level, of course, these problems point to deficiencies in the original planning process, which failed to pay sufficient attention to the characteristics of the organisational context within which services would have to operate.

These observations do, however, point to something of a dilemma. Should we establish potentially vulnerable services in inadequate contexts or focus instead on attempting to ameliorate some of the deficiencies in background service organisation? In choosing the former path we may be unwittingly providing confirming evidence for the advocates of institutional provision, who will be only too ready to seize the opportunities provided by service failure and consequent re-institutionalisation. In selecting the latter path we may be embarking upon an endless task while those people with the most serious disabilities remain waiting in the wings. Clearly, we need to do a bit of both. Considerable caution will need to be exercised, however, in pacing the process of developing new services for people with seriously challenging behaviours to ensure that sufficient safeguards are in place so that they can be sustained over time, regardless of the permanence of any 'hero-innovators' involved. The development of effective safeguards will require that close attention be given to developing a sense of ownership among senior managers, while at the same time increasing the costs of failure among this and similarly influential constituencies. Rapid service development which overstretches the capacity of local agencies to support new placements will inevitably lead to failure.

Service quality

Within the projects themselves a number of variables appeared to act as key determinants of service quality. These included the individualisation of service design; a structured approach to activity planning; maintaining appropriate levels of staff skills and resources; the avoidance of congregating people with challenging behaviours together.

- *Individualisation* Each service developed by local agencies with support from the SDT was designed around the perceived needs of a specific individual client (Toogood *et al.*, 1988). Service design was also, of course, informed by other matters including an ordinary life philosophy and resource constraints. While these common factors ensured a number of common features in the design of services (such as all being based on ordinary houses or flats), all services also evidenced many individually tailored features. This process of individual design has enabled the service to take account of important characteristics of the individual, which may have influenced the success or failure of the service. The kinds of features considered included the number and kind of other people with whom the person should live, the proximity involved in living arrangements (e.g. by providing the client with their own bedsitting room to which they could retire), the nature of the physical environment (including the need for soundproofing), and the number and kind of staff employed.

- *A structured, organised approach* All projects were encouraged to use detailed, often meticulous, approaches to planning and organising the service provided, including the development of a clear, agreed operational policy for the service (Cummings *et al.*, 1989; Mansell *et al.*, 1987; McCool *et al.*, 1989; McGill, in press). Starting from a process of individual programme planning, systematic strategies were devised to help involve the client in the activities generated in the process of everyday living. This was seen as of considerable value in its own right, as well as providing activities to which the client could be redirected in the event of challenging behaviour. As noted above, demands associated with the attempt to involve clients in activity had been identified as important triggers for the occurrence of the challenging behaviours shown by many clients. Consequently, it was considered very important to ensure that staff were prepared for and skilled in handling such behaviour in a way that minimised the degree to which it interfered with client participation in activity. Unfortunately, in several projects, a strong commitment by the staff group to those aspects of the service's value base which stress individual choice and the 'normality' of means to achieve change appeared to create conflicts with the implementation of a structured approach to activity planning. Such services were, in general, characterised by poorer performance on indicators of client participation.

- *Staff levels, support and training* The innovative and difficult nature of the services made it particularly important to both ensure adequate staffing levels and to ensure that all staff acquired the requisite skills to fulfil their responsibilities. Staff teams usually received two weeks of induction and orientation training prior to the service opening, followed by regular in-service training. Such 'on the job' training has proven vital to the successful implementation of approaches to engaging clients and managing their behaviour. It should be kept in mind, however, that providing staff with the requisite skills does not guarantee appropriate performance. Indeed, staff training *per se* appears to have little impact upon either staff performance or client quality of life unless it is appropriately tied to effective staff management procedures (Reid *et al.*, 1989). Ensuring adequate staff levels must be considered, like staff training, another necessary but far from sufficient determinant of service performance. As the safety nets of seclusion rooms and staff from other wards have not generally been available, high staffing levels have been necessary to ensure that any particularly difficult incidents can be managed without danger to clients, staff or members of the public. It should be noted, however, that the staffing ratios are not usually any greater than in alternative service models for comparable clients (cf. Emerson *et al.*, in press a). In addition to ensuring the numbers and skills of staff, services were also encouraged to develop a range of strategies for staff support. These included regular weekly or fortnightly staff meetings, staff supervision and individual performance review.

- *Avoiding congregating people with challenging behaviour* As far as possible the services planned for SDT clients deliberately sought not to have co-tenants who themselves displayed challenging behaviour. A number of considerations lay behind this trend. Firstly, for many individuals, evidence suggested that their challenging behaviours were exacerbated by the stressful nature of the social milieu characteristic of congregate care facilities. Secondly, it was considered that such a social environment would also present a significant impediment to ensuring effective staff performance, especially in maintaining respectful proactive interactions between caregivers and clients.

As noted above, the preliminary results from the evaluation of SDT-sponsored services also points to two areas of concern: the low levels of client engagement in formal educational or vocational activity (see also Special Development Team, 1988, 1989) and the apparent failure of the new services to bring about changes in the clients' seriously challenging behaviours.

The low levels of participation in educational and vocational activity reflect a number of issues. Most importantly, however, they reflect the scarcity of educational or vocational services in most localities that (a) would be willing to offer a service to SDT clients and (b) offered a type of service acceptable to local planning and co-ordinating groups. Thus, for example, in most localities the only external vocational or educational services which were accessible consisted of large, congregate care day centres, which were considered antithetical to the basic aims and objectives of SDT-sponsored services. As a result, early decisions were often taken to attempt to develop individualised job placements for SDT clients, supported from within the staffing establishment of the residential support team. While some isolated examples of success were evident, in general this strategy proved ill-founded through failing to take account of the time required and specialised knowledge and skills involved in establishing job placements.

As noted above, some caution needs to be exercised for methodological reasons regarding the interpretation of the formal evaluation results concerning changes in clients' challenging behaviours. In addition, these preliminary results tend to conflict with the informal judgements expressed by some of the local project co-ordinating groups. Nevertheless, some deficiencies are apparent in many of the local projects with regards to the implementation of technical approaches to the specific assessment and intervention of the client's challenging behaviours. The main reasons for this deficiency are twofold. Firstly, as indicated above, several services have developed an ethos to which technical intervention and structured approaches to user and staff activity planning are an anathema (Emerson *et al.*, in press – b; McGill, in press). Secondly, and more importantly, the initial support provided to local agencies by the SDT centred around the commissioning of practical aspects of the service and the development of general service procedures. Unfortunately, the opportunity costs of fulfilling this supporting role included, in many instances, the provision of the more technical types of support required to undertake a detailed analysis of the person's specific challenging behaviours.

Dissemination and generalisation

During the initial five years of the Team's operation there has been only limited evidence of the generalisation of competencies gained or procedures developed in the local joint projects to other services operated by the same agency. This issue is of some concern since it suggests either (a) local agencies had nothing to learn from the experience gained within SDT sponsored projects, or (b) a failure in organisational learning. If we assume the latter to be the case a number of factors appear to have been implicated in this failure to generalise new knowledge across settings. These included rapid staff turnover; weakness of agency co-ordination; the 'special' nature of the projects themselves.

During the period of rapid institutional closure in the SETRHA turnover in managerial and development staff within local agencies was considerable. Indeed, for several of the projects none of the managerial staff involved in supporting the project had been in post during the period of the project's planning. This rapid turnover had a number of adverse effects on dissemination. Firstly, many new managers simply had not spent sufficient time in SDT-sponsored services and other services in their locality to effectively facilitate generalisation. Secondly, many new staff appeared more concerned with making their own mark upon services, and hence establishing their authority, than with learning from the experience of others.

In addition, many local agencies were relatively new organisations facing the inevitable growing pains resulting from rapid expansion. As such, they were often very poorly equipped to detect and respond to variations in quality across residential settings. For many agencies and agency staff survival and the prevention of organisational collapse became their overriding concern. Within such a fraught climate dominated by rapid deinstitutionalisation, it is not perhaps surprising that little effective organisational learning occurred.

Finally, the special nature of the projects, as reflected in the 'special' nature of the clients and the involvement of external support, may have served to isolate them within the local agency. Thus, for example, any differences in operating procedures between SDT-sponsored and other services may have been simply attributed to the special needs of the service users. This tendency was likely to be exacerbated by the relatively well-resourced nature of STD-sponsored services in the context of local scarcity.

CONCLUDING COMMENTS

The establishment and the first five years' operation of the Special Development Team represents, in many ways, a unique social experiment. Indeed, it is unlikely that, with recent changes in national policy with regards to the organisation of health services and community care, the model exemplified by the STD as a regional initiative will be repeated. It is perhaps important, therefore to draw some general lessons from this experience, the most important of which are outlined below.

• High quality community living in which people's quality of life is transformed can be made a reality for even the most challenging people with severe learning disabilities. While for many this is simply to state the obvious, it should not be forgotten that there still exist many advocates of congregate institutional care.
• In making an ordinary life a reality for people who present serious challenges, and in sustaining this reality, a number of factors are important. These include the comprehensiveness of the local service system; an approach to service development based upon the strengths and needs of known individuals; the adoption by services of an organised, structured approach informed by pertinent social values; ensuring and effectively deploying sufficient resources in terms of staff and their skills. Client characteristics did not appear to play an important role in determining either service quality or the sustainability of service provision.
• Within current services these basic conditions are often absent. As a result those with the most seriously challenging behaviours remain vulnerable to being excluded from their communities, neglected and, at times, abused.

In general, the work of the SDT over the last five years has demonstrated that it is possible to develop and maintain, at least in the short term, individualised community-based services for people with severe learning disabilities and seriously challenging behaviours. It is clear, however, that such services are vulnerable to decay, both of quality and in terms of their very existence.

As described in the opening section, the SDT was established as a five-year project. Fortunately, the RHA has agreed to provided funding for an additional five years to continue and extend the work described above. The three major priorities for the future work of the Team will be:

- consolidation of existing achievements, by helping to maintain and improve the quality of those services which have been set up, and describing the process of individualised service development in a way that will be useful to others setting about the same task;
- extension of the model in further service development work, focusing on the needs of clients already in community residential services for individualised day and support services. It may also be important to seek to extend the model to the development of individualised housing services for clients whose problems are particularly difficult or whose circumstances are unusual;
- generalisation of achievements through the provision of training and consultancy to local agencies, to help them develop their competence to prevent and detect challenging behaviour, support people locally and manage crises effectively.

When drawing abstract conclusions about the success or failure of an innovation and attempting to identify general issues, it is easy to lose sight of the concrete, specific outcomes for individuals. We recently saw some photographs of one client, Sue, taken some seven months after she had moved into her new home. They show her walking on the beach, loading the washing machine, drinking tea in a café, pouring milk on her weetabix, and participating in many other ordinary, everyday activities. She is fully dressed and looks healthy – previously thin and almost emaciated, she has put on two and a half stones since coming out of hospital. When asked to comment on the changes her father wrote 'if it is possible, with only 9 months love, and house care, to see such improvement in health and behaviour, then I have only one question – why did it take 27 years of torment in an institution to achieve this?' (example adapted from McGill *et al.*, 1991). Of course, it did take more than love and care. It took the persistence and determination of senior officers in the face of strongly held beliefs that such clients would never be able to live outside hospital; it took the willingness of service planners to make the leap into the dark necessary to imagine the sort of lifestyle that Sue might have; it took the determination and skill of direct care workers and their managers to actually implement that vision, and it took the skill and knowledge of those supporting the service to solve the inevitable problems that arose. It happened, however, and provides an example that should not, must not be ignored. People with severe learning disabilities and the most seriously challenging behaviour can live in ordinary houses and can live lifestyles that bear no comparison to that found in institutional settings. In many ways this is a conclusion which no longer needs to be justified or 'proved'. It needs, instead, to be acted upon.

References

Beasley, F., Hewson, S. and Mansell, J. (1989), *MTS Handbook* (3rd ed.), CAPSC, University of Kent, Canterbury.
Blunden, R. and Allen, D. (1987), *Facing the Challenge: An Ordinary Life for People with Learning Difficulties and Challenging Behaviour*, King's Fund, London.
Brost, M., Johnson, T. Z., Wagner, L., and Deprey, R. K. (1982), *Getting to Know You: One Approach to Service Planning and Assessment for People with Disabilities*, Wisconsin Coalition for Advocacy, Madison, WI.
Carr, E. G., Robinson, S., Taylor, J. C. and Carlson, J. I. (1990), *Positive Approaches to the Treatment of Severe Behavior Problems in Persons with Developmental Disabilities*, The Association for Persons with Severe Handicaps, Seattle, WA.
Cummings, R., Emerson, E., Barrett, S., McCool, C., Toogood, A. and Hughes, H. (1989), 'Challenging behaviour and community services: 4. Establishing services', *Mental Handicap*, 17, 13–17.
Department of Health (1989), *Needs and Responses: Adults with a Mental Handicap and Behaviour Disturbance*, DoH Leaflets Unit, Stanmore, Middlesex.
Emerson, E. (1990), 'Designing individualised community based placements as alternatives to institutions for people with a severe mental handicap and severe problem behaviour', in W. Fraser, *Key Issues in Mental Retardation Research* (ed.), Routledge, London.
Emerson, E., Barrett, S., Bell, C., Cummings, R., McCool, C., Toogood, A. and Mansell, J. (1988a), *Developing Services for People with a Severe Learning Difficulties and Challenging Behaviours*, CAPSC, University of Kent, Canterbury.
Emerson, E., Beasley, F., Offord, G. and Mansell, J. (in press, a), 'Specialised housing for people with seriously challenging behaviours', *Journal of Mental Deficiency Research*.
Emerson, E., Cambridge, P. and Harris., P. (1991), *Evaluating the Challenge: A Guide to Evaluating Services for People with Learning Difficulties and Challenging Behaviour*, King's Fund, London.
Emerson, E., Cummings, R., Barrett, S., Hughes, H., McCool, C. and Toogood, A. (1988b), 'Challenging behaviour and community services: 2. Who are the people who challenge services?', *Mental Handicap*, 16, 16–19.
Emerson, E., Cummings, R., Hughes, H., Toogood, A., Barrett, S. and McCool, C. (1989), 'Challenging behaviour and community services: 6. Evaluation and overview', *Mental Handicap*, 17, 104–107.
Emerson, E., Hastings, R. and McGill, P. (in press – b), 'Values' in E. Emerson, P. McGill and J. Mansell, *Challenging Behaviours and Severe Learning Disabilities: Designing Quality Services* (eds.), Chapman and Hall, London.
Emerson, E., Toogood, A., Mansell, J., Barrett, S., Bell, C., Cummings, R. and McCool, C. (1987), 'Challenging behaviour and community services: 1. Introduction and overview', *Mental Handicap*, 15, 166–69.

King's Fund (1980), *An Ordinary Life: Comprehensive Locally-based Residential Services for Mentally Handicapped People*, King's Fund Centre, London.

Korman, N. and Glennerster, H. (1985), *Closing a Hospital: The Darenth Park Project*, Bedford Square Press, London.

Korman, N. and Glennerster, H. (1990), *Hospital Closure*, Open University Press: Milton Keynes.

Mansell, J. (1988), *Staffed Housing for People with Mental Handicaps: Achieving Widespread Dissemination*, South East Thames Regional Health Authority/ National Health Service Training Authority, Bexhill/Bristol.

Mansell, J., Brown, H., McGill, P., Hoskin, S., Lindley, P. and Emerson, E. (1987), *Bringing People Back Home: A Staff Training Initiative in Mental Handicap*, National Health Service Training Authority, Bristol.

Mansell, J. and Beasley, F. (1989), 'Small staffed homes for the severely mentally handicapped', in V. Cowie and V. J. Harten-Ash, (eds.), *Current Approaches: Mental Retardation*, Dupher Laboratories, Southampton.

Mansell, J. and Beasley, F. (1990), 'Evaluating the transfer to community care', in W. Fraser (ed.), *Key Issues in Mental Retardation Research*, Routledge, London.

Mansell, J. and Beasley, F. (1991), 'Staffed housing for people with seriously challenging behaviours', paper presented at the EABG Annual Conference, London.

Mansell, J., Felce, D., Jenkins, J., de Kock, U. and Toogood, S. (1987), *Developing Staffed Housing for People with Mental Handicaps*, Costello, Tunbridge Wells.

Mansell, J., McGill, P. and Emerson, E. (in press), 'Conceptualising service provision' in E. Emerson, P. McGill & J. Mansell (eds.), *Challenging Behaviours and Severe Learning Disabilities: Designing Quality Services*, Chapman and Hall, London.

McBrien, J. (in press), 'Support services', in E. Emerson, P. McGill and J. Mansell (eds.), *Challenging Behaviours and Severe Learning Disabilities: Designing Quality Services*, Chapman and Hall, London.

McCool, C., Barrett, S., Emerson, E., Toogood, S., Hughes, H. and Cummings, R. (1989), 'Challenging behaviour and community services: 5. Structuring staff and client activity', *Mental Handicap*, 17, 60–64.

McGill, P. (in press), 'Placement organisation', in E. Emerson, P. McGill and J. Mansell (eds.), *Challenging Behaviours and Severe Learning Disabilities: Designing Quality Services*, Chapman and Hall, London.

McGill, P., Hawkins, C. and Hughes, H. (1991), 'The Special Development Team, South East Thames' in D. Allen, R. Banks, S. Staite (eds.), *Meeting the Challenge: Some U.K. Perspectives on Services for People with Learning Difficulties and Challenging Behaviour*, King's Fund, London.

McGill, P. and Emerson, E. (in press), 'Residential services' in E. Emerson, P. McGill and J. Mansell (eds.), *Challenging Behaviours and Severe Learning Disabilities: Designing Quality Services*, Chapman and Hall, London.

Murphy, G. and Clare, I. (1991), 'MIETS: A service option for people with mild mental handicaps and challenging behaviour or psychiatric problems – 2. Assessment, treatment, and outcome for service users and service effectiveness', *Mental Handicap Research*, 4, 180–206.

Murphy, G., Holland, A., Fowler, P. and Reep, J. (1991), 'MIETS: A service option for people with mild mental handicaps and challenging behaviour or psychiatric problems – 1. Philosophy, service and service users', *Mental Handicap Research*, 4, 41–66.

O'Brien, J. (1987), 'A guide to lifestyle planning: using the *Activities Catalog* to integrate services and natural support systems' in G. T. Bellamy and B. Wilcox (eds.), *The Activities Catalog: An Alternative Curriculum for Youth and Adults with Severe Disabilities*, Paul H. Brookes, Baltimore, MD.

Reid, D.H., Parsons, M.B. and Green, C.W. (1989), 'Treating aberrant behavior through effective staff management: A developing technology', in E. Cipani (ed.), *The Treatment of Severe Behavior Disorders: Behavior Analysis Approaches* American Association on Mental Retardation, Washington, DC.

Saudargas, R.A. and Zanolli, K. (1990), 'Momentary time sampling as an estimate of percentage time: A field validation study', *Journal of Applied Behavior Analysis*, 23, 533–37.

South East Thames Regional Health Authority (1979), *Strategies and Guidelines for the Development of Services for Mentally Handicapped People.*

South East Thames Regional Health Authority (1985), *Mental Handicap Special Services,*

Special Development Team (1987), *Annual Report 1986*, CAPSC, University of Kent, Canterbury.

Special Development Team (1988), *Annual Report 1987*, CAPSC, University of Kent, Canterbury.

Special Development Team (1989), *Annual Report 1988*, CAPSC, University of Kent, Canterbury.

Toogood, A., Emerson, E., Hughes, H., Barrett, S., Cummings, R. and McCool, C. (1988), 'Challenging behaviour and community services: 3. Planning individualised services', *Mental Handicap*, 16, 16–19.

Evaluating services for people with challenging behaviour

The design of services for people with learning disabilities who have seriously challenging behaviour* has been brought into focus in recent years by a number of complementary developments. The strengthening of principles (DHSS, 1971; Wolfensberger, 1972; 1983; O'Brien and Tyne, 1981; Welsh Office, 1983) which set the accomplishment of positive client outcomes as the touchstone of service effectiveness has accentuated the plight of people with challenging behaviour. Detrimental consequences on the lives of such people include living in materially denuded environments; living with physical or psychotropic restraint; being open to exclusion from settings and opportunities taken for granted by the majority; being vulnerable to neglect and abuse, and being more likely to be avoided by others and experience institutional admission (Emerson, in press; de Paiva and Lowe, 1990; Brown and Craft, 1989). The growing catalogue of criticism of institutional residential provision has engendered a new emphasis on comprehensive community services capable of providing a decent quality of life in their own locality.

The current move to resettle people living in mental handicap hospitals and to close such facilities is concentrating attention on those with challenging behaviour, whom many see as a difficult group to maintain in the community. Despite the widespread acceptance of the general move to community integration for people with mental handicaps, non-institutional, community based services for those with severe challenging behaviour have remained contentious. Community services have not demonstrated the ability to cater

---

* A number of sources have found it useful to distinguish three categories of people with learning disabilities and challenging behaviour: those with severe or profound learning disabilities who display challenging behaviours as part of their characteristic daily activity; those, mostly people with mild learning disabilities, who have mental health problems, and those, again mostly people with mild learning disabilities, who are referred for treatment through the courts (DHSS, 1984; All Wales Advisory Panel, 1991). This paper explicitly excludes consideration of the latter group. Kiernan and Alborz (1991) provide a review of the literature relevant to this group.

for people with severe challenging behaviours. A higher proportion of people in institutions have challenging behaviour than live in the community (Kushlick and Cox, 1973; Oliver, Murphy and Corbett, 1987; Harris and Russell, 1989), and challenging behaviour continues to constitute a primary reason for hospital admission (Sutter, Mayeda, Call, Yanagi and Yee, 1980; All Wales Advisory Panel, 1991).

Uncertainty and inertia over the correct course of action has also arisen because staff working in hospitals have defended their expertise and the appropriateness of special provision for this group. Over many years challenging behaviour has been interpreted within hospital services as resulting from organic or psychiatric dysfunction. This leads to a definition of specialism which emphasises service characteristics associated with hospitals, psychopharmacological treatment and professional competencies possessed by psychiatrists and psychiatrically-trained nurses. The environment plays only a supporting role in the psychiatric account and, therefore, its importance is diminished. It follows that less is made of the adverse environmental comparison between institutional and ordinary domestic settings. On the contrary, centralisation is seen as facilitating the delivery of psychiatric expertise and therefore the importance given to these specialist skills may account for the continued advocacy of centralised or specialist provision.

Alternatively, the prevalence of challenging behaviours among people in institutions, coupled with the analysis of institutional impoverishment, has led other observers to see institutional conditions as a cause of underlying challenging behaviour. There has been an expectation or hope that the provision of more normative settings will lead to more usual patterns of activity and social interaction, which in turn will lead to an increase in appropriate behaviour and a concomitant decrease in inappropriate behaviour. Evaluation of pioneer attempts at the provision of community services has shown support for improvements occurring in these directions (see next section of this chapter). However, this work has also shown that community resettlement is not a panacea for challenging behaviour. Neither does it support the premise that such behaviour results from institutional conditions *per se* (see also Hill and Bruininks, 1984, and Eyman, Borthwick and Miller, 1981). The above simple view of the benefits of community care ignores non-environmental causes of challenging behaviour. It also fails to recognise that environmental conditions maintaining challenging behaviour, such as escape from demand, absence of appropriate stimulation or activity or inappropriately timed attention, can be equally common to both community and institutional settings. Hence, one should not expect challenging behaviour to disappear as a consequence of simple change in environment.

The change in objectives which underpin service design from custodial care to those of developmental growth and quality of life has occurred at a time when research on the aetiology and effective treatment of challenging behaviour has expanded considerably. Baumeister (1989) has recently summarised a number of aetiological theories, the diversity of which may be taken to challenge simple views of causation and maintenance. These can be loosely classified as factors concerned with the individual's physical and social environment and his or her internal status.

Environmental factors include level of stimulation and the occurrence of antecedent and consequent events which result in learning via operant conditioning. It has been suggested that each person seeks to achieve an optimum level of stimulation (Baumeister, 1978; Repp, Karsh, Deitz and Singh, in press). People with severe learning disabilities may use simple forms of behaviour, which manifest themselves as stereotypies, in order to alter levels of stimulation. The conditioning theory suggests that behaviours are learned or maintained as a result of the consequences for their occurrence: positive or negative reinforcement (Skinner, 1953). A specific conceptualisation of such conditioning is to be found in the communication hypothesis (Doss and Reichle, 1989), where the behaviour is viewed as 'an effective way in which the person has learned to communicate his/her needs to others' (Blunden and Allen, 1987).

As some forms of rhythmic or self-injurious behaviours occur in a percentage of all infants, notably during transition stages, their occurrence in people with learning disabilities can be seen as related to extreme delay in passing through developmental stages (eg. Kravitz and Boehm, 1962). Psychodynamic difficulties, such as incomplete ego development, early childhood trauma and guilt have also been discussed as underlying causes of challenging behaviour (see Baumeister and Rollings, 1976). Challenging behaviours have also been associated with psychiatric states, including mood disorders and psychotic illnesses. The diagnosis of these may be particular to individuals with mild learning disabilities, or, at least, to people with sufficient language so that interpretation rests on clinical signs other than the behaviour itself.

Particular organic conditions such as Lesch-Nyhan syndrome (Christie *et al.*, 1982) and possibly de Lange syndrome (Bryson *et al.*, 1971; but see Oliver, 1988), have also been associated with certain topographies of self-injurious behaviour, and there is also raised prevalence of self-injury in de la Tourette syndrome (Robertson, Trimble and Lees, 1989). Disturbance of neurotransmitters in some organic conditions has been suggested as a factor associated with self-injury (eg Cataldo and Harris, 1982). Neural dysfunctions such as frontal lobe seizures (Gedye, 1989) have also been examined. In addition to these main factors, Oliver and Head (1990) summarise other internal variables which have been identified as 'risk' elements in self-injury, including severity of learning disability (Oliver *et al.*, 1987) and communication and sensory deficits (Schroeder, Schroeder, Smith and Dallorf, 1978).

Even a brief overview such as this highlights the complexity of causal possibilities which assessment and treatment need to take into account.

Moreover, Blunden and Allen (1987) point out that there may be several causes and maintaining factors for an individual's challenging behaviour, as it can serve different functions in different contexts. Further, people with severe challenging behaviour typically exhibit several forms (Lowe, de Paiva and Felce, in press; Hoefkens and Allen, 1990), adding further to the complexity. Although there is a potential division of causal possibilities into internal and external factors, these may not be mutually exclusive. Oliver and Head (1990) propose a model for self-injurious behaviour which integrates operant conditioning and organic factors. Baumeister (1989) also draws attention to the complexity and interrelationships involved in challenging behaviour, suggesting that 'destructive acts' be conceptualised as 'biobehavioural processes where neurochemical and neurophysiological events are in dynamic transition with environmental and other behaviour'.

Increased understanding of challenging behaviour in relation to the environment and to specific organic conditions has led to a considerable treatment literature based primarily on behavioural psychology and medicine. While the expansion of the literature on successful resolution of challenging behaviour has increased optimism that people with such behaviour can be effectively helped and their place in ordinary society protected, the leap from research demonstration to routine service implementation is great . Steps in the transition certainly include i) the dissemination of knowledge about causal and treatment possibilities, ii) the development of technical proficiency in functional analysis and medical examination and the matching of treatment to the results of assessment, and iii) gaining correct and consistent implementation of a wide range of treatment approaches. This has to be achieved within a context of a diversely trained workforce, which is relatively poorly paid in its direct care grades and experiences an inevitable degree of turnover (de Kock *et al.*, 1987; Felce, Lowe and Beswick, in prep.). It also has to be achieved at a time of major organisational change by planners, development and training personnel preoccupied by the general shift from institution to community. As people with less severe handicaps and without behavioural difficulties have typically been the first to be resettled (DoH, 1989), experience of how to provide competent community services for those with severe challenging behaviour is not widely developed. Coupled with the generally low level of expertise in behavioural and other salient analysis and treatment approaches, the development of high quality community services remains a daunting challenge.

MECHANISMS FOR DEVELOPING SPECIALISM UNDER SCARCITY

It is widely recognised that the level of knowledge and expertise necessary for assessment of challenging behaviour is not generally available. Although institutions have provided care and treatment for people with severe learning disabilities and challenging behaviours for many decades, few would claim that typical institutional provision for this group would constitute a high quality service. Specialist settings within hospitals where people with challenging behaviours have been congregated are commonly known as 'back wards': containment rather than habilitation is accomplished and the basic requirements of a decent quality of life are frequently missing. Staff may well develop valuable skills in coping with challenging behaviour on a day to day basis, often under conditions of adversity. However, they generally have had little opportunity to develop skills concerned with establishing positive, individually oriented regimes or the implementation of behavioural programmes.

As a consequence, the shortage of skilled practitioners makes it difficult to realise developmental objectives for people with challenging behaviour and to promote their place in the community. If the requisite skills were prevalent, they could be represented in every service. One could then expect general competency to help effectively people with challenging behaviour, and all services to have the capacity to do so. However, currently, the inability of a service to cope with a person because of their challenging behaviour may cause administrative difficulties but few surprises. There is widespread recognition that the skills required constitute a specialism and, therefore, it is expected that individuals with challenging behaviour will be referred from mainstream to specialist settings where such skills are said to be exist.

The problem of developing comprehensive services where requisite skills are scarce has been met by a number of strategies. The first is specialisation, a means of concentrating specialism and limiting its availability to those who specially need it. The most long-standing formulation for specialist service delivery is the creation of specialist assessment and treatment units. The dedication of resources to a specific task may offer a number of advantages. It may be accompanied by a concentration of relevant expertise, clear operational policies and a collective identity that defines and accepts full ownership of the problem without recourse to further referral elsewhere. Specialist staff will readily gain casework experience. This growth in experience not only provides a greater tolerance of challenging behaviours and a reservoir of wisdom to apply to new challenges, but also makes the service more likely to become the focus of training, research and professional development.

Unfortunately, the development of experience and expertise compounds the differentiation of the specialist service from its more typical counterparts. The original need for specialisation is not only maintained, but strengthened. Demand for specialist services may intensify with the request for transfer of people out of mainstream services, which may be more readily defined as 'inappropriate placements'. The continued lack of competence and capacity in the mainstream service creates a barrier to the return of people from the specialist service. Even assuming that the specialist service has effected desirable behaviour change while the person was placed with it, treatment gains may not be maintained on discharge. Challenging behaviours may return if the original environment does not change its practices in line with the individual's requirements. This leads to the specialist service 'silting up', a frequently cited problem (Newman and Emerson, in press).

It is also difficult to distinguish how the design of specialist units differs from traditional hospital 'back wards' in some principal respects. Both congregate people with challenging behaviour together. Both have enhanced staffing and share the rhetoric of specialist competency with experience. Many current proposals for today's specialist units are part of plans for a continuing service on the sites of existing mental handicap hospitals, albeit reduced in size. The location of services, their design and the characteristics and professional backgrounds of staff will be similar to existing 'back wards'. Given this, it is particularly important to note the general absence of evidence concerning the effectiveness or quality of specialist units. Some papers on the subject remain purely descriptive with only anecdotal evidence of effect (e.g. Day, 1988). Others have attempted to deal with the considerable methodological problems involved in outcome assessment. Hoefkens and Allen (1990) conducted an evaluation of an intensive treatment unit, which served mainly people with mild or borderline learning difficulties and mental health problems. Deterioration in behaviour after discharge and a high readmission rate highlight the difficulties of producing enduring behaviour change. Emerson, Beasley, Offord and Mansell (in press) collected data on a new specialist unit for people with severe learning difficulties and challenging behaviour. Their study showed the specialist facility to be typical of previously evaluated institutional settings, providing low levels of stimulation and activity to the people who lived there.

A second general strategy to build competence and capacity in relation to challenging behaviour where skills and expertise are scarce, is to design a service model with clearly described procedures which can be replicated without requiring specially trained manpower. The first attempt to provide comprehensive local community-based services in Britain by the Wessex Regional Hospital Board may be thought of as an early but not very sophisticated example of this strategy. These services had a clear operational policy that they were to serve individuals irrespective of the severity of their challenging behaviour. There was a decided onus on them to cope with people with challenging behaviour. Guidance was also given on the nature of environmental regime to be established, which emphasised varied activity, small groups, close staff-service user relationships and respect for individual difference. Evaluation showed that the great majority of residents were maintained in these services, including those with challenging behaviour, and that improvement in quality compared to traditional hospitals occurred with respect to behavioural development, engagement in activity, staff interaction with residents and family involvement. However, a total of four out of 104 residents served by the settings evaluated were transferred back to traditional hospital settings because of their challenging behaviour (although not always following the wishes of staff and not necessarily resulting in improvements in behaviour or quality of life) (Felce, Kushlick and Smith, 1980).

Subsequent work in Wessex on the provision of ordinary housing services for people with severe or profound learning disabilities and the development of NIMROD, in Cardiff, constitute further examples of the approach to designing a service model which would prove effective at accommodating people with severe challenging behaviours. However, both of the more recent service initiatives developed further the guidance and induction training given to staff on how to establish the environmental milieu and how to identify and plan a response to individual needs. They used job-aids and handbooks as procedural guides for staff (see Felce, 1989; Lowe and de Paiva, in press), designed tailor-made training and followed a behavioural orientation to general environmental design and individual programming. The services accepted people with severe learning disabilities and multiple severely challenging behaviours (Felce, Lowe and de Paiva, in press). Evaluation showed significant improvements compared to more traditional services in behavioural development (Felce, de Kock, Thomas and Saxby, 1986; Lowe, de Paiva and Felce, in press), quality of daily life (Felce, 1989) and community integration (de Kock, Saxby, Thomas and Felce, 1988: Lowe and de Paiva, in press).

Both of the above developments were associated with research, not only in terms of evaluation but also in the researchers' involvement in the specification of the model and working procedures. In other words, the researchers acted as a specialist project design team for each of the novel service models. The work of the Special Development Team in the South East Thames Regional Health Authority in the late 1980s is an explicit example of the role of a specialist project team acting to establish mainstream service models capable of including those with the most challenging behaviours. Their remit drew on the success of the Wessex and NIMROD ordinary housing developments. It was to provide assistance to constituent health and local authorities to resettle a defined number of people with severe and profound learning difficulties identified as the most challenging from institutional to housing-based services (see Emerson and McGill, this volume). Their service design also drew heavily on behavioural psychology, the use of procedural guidance for staff and specific induction and training. The resulting services have been evaluated, again showing a beneficial comparison to traditionally available services (see McGill and Emerson, this volume; Beasley and Mansell, 1990).

Despite the success of these three service initiatives, their example has generally not been followed. The failure to replicate may be seen as the major disadvantage of this strategy to build more generally available specialist services without recourse to specialisation in admission or manpower policies. One can only speculate on the reasons for this. It is logical that the more complex the service prescription is, the more unlikely it will be that it will be followed precisely. Moreover, the service models described above emphasise the importance of factors other than those traditionally decided by planners in the planning process, such as how staff are trained and work from day to day. Replication would require a considerable change in managerial and planning behaviour and rapid assimilation of knowledge that is traditionally classified as clinical. A strong element in the service models was a commitment to the behavioural approach and the understanding and acceptance of this approach is not widespread, particularly amongst those planning services. In addition, it may be politically too difficult for planners and managers responsible for maintaining existing institutional services to make a commitment to comprehensive local services. The appeal of specialisation in service circles is still strong, both as an easy design solution and as a means of defending professional identities.

Service models to provide assistance to people living in the family home or for challenging behaviour in day services are less well developed, although NIMROD through its community support workers provided some response in this area. Relevant professional services, such as clinical psychology or community mental handicap teams, are again in short supply when the number of personnel in ratio to caseload is taken into account. Nor do such professionals generally have dedicated staff resources (as in the NIMROD community support workers), which they can deploy to help introduce and sustain treatment strategies in family homes or day services.

Specialist treatment units have been seen as a possible service response to people living elsewhere through a temporary admission for assessment and treatment. However, the proposition that effective treatment can be developed during a short stay in one environment and treatment gains maintained subsequently on discharge to another environment goes often unrealised (Bruhl *et al.*, 1982; Schroeder *et al.*, 1982; Newman and Emerson, in press; Hoefkens and Allen, 1990). Therefore, the proposal has recently gained ground that there should be specialist peripatetic support teams who can work with people with challenging behaviour wherever they live. This has come as a response to a general notion that it would be more advantageous to take services to the person and deliver treatment in the natural environment rather than removing the person to a specialist setting. It also recognises the high case-loads of existing professional services. In terms of the above distinction between a strategy of specialisation and a strategy of building service models where competency to cater for challenging behaviour is present in mainstream services, the proposal is a hybrid.

The potential remit for such teams could encompass the assistance-with-resettlement role of the Special Development Team, and their work in this respect would be as a project team to develop competent mainstream service models. A critical factor to their success in doing so will be whether they are established with a clear remit and the necessary managerial and financial backing, as the Kent team were. However, in their support role with respect to existing care settings, an expertise distinction between the specialist and mainstream services is established. This creates the potential for mainstream services to relinquish the ownership of the problem. Whereas it is possible for carers in mainstream settings to gain competence from association with the specialist workers, whether cross-fertilisation will occur will depend on the nature of the relationship, the status of the team, their management arrangements and powers, in short, what influence they can bring to bear on the setting (Durand and Kishi, 1987). Challenging behaviour teams would be in a strong position if mainstream services retain their willingness to continue to care for people with challenging behaviour, see the specialist services as helping them to do so, give them their full co-operation, become involved in the teams' work at an early stage and attempt to follow their advice. They may be in a weak position if failure to resolve or cope with challenging behaviour is ascribed only to the working of the team and not to the setting and the co-operation of the carers.

Problems analogous to the 'silting up' and the difficulties in generalising treatment gains discussed with respect to specialist units are also possible in the working of specialist support teams. If mainstream settings, professionals and carers remain intransigent to change and the adoption of effective strategies for environmental enrichment and behavioural development, then new referrals to the case-loads of specialist teams will grow without existing clients being discharged.

EVALUATING SPECIALIST CHALLENGING BEHAVIOUR SERVICES IN PRACTICE

Services for people with challenging behaviour were emphasised in Wales when they became one of the 'core priorities' for development in the mid-term review of the All-Wales Mental Handicap Strategy. Certain counties have responded to this policy initiative by establishing services which include a specialist peripatetic support team element. This has given rise to the opportunity to evaluate some of the questions surrounding their functioning. Agreement to evaluate the effectiveness of the work of teams in two counties was reached last year and the evaluation began about eight months ago. Although the underlying philosophy of both services is broadly similar (that services should be tailored to the needs of the individual and should promote access to normal patterns of life), there are major differences in their structure and resources.

Service A, established exclusively for adult clients, draws several elements together under a single manager, including: a) a pre-existing hospital-based specialist treatment unit; b) the provision of ring-fenced budgets to develop local community support arrangements including housing; c) a four-person peripatetic support team to provide hands on help and advice; d) a psychologist and clinical nurse specialist to design therapeutic interventions, to supervise the work of the support team, and to co-ordinate advice and help from other relevant therapists, including a psychiatric service for people with learning disabilities and mental illness. All elements are provided by the NHS but an open referral system, through an access panel comprising representatives from health, social services and the voluntary sector, means that the service is a potential resource to any client in the county.

Service B, offered to children and adult clients alike, relies exclusively on the operation of a peripatetic support team, under the management of a top grade clinical psychologist. The team comprises three senior members recruited from a variety of backgrounds, and three assistants as a pooled resource. The focus of the service is on direct work with clients, staff development and consultancy. It does not include any specialist treatment unit or additional budgets for service developments and its operational remit excludes taking clients with mental illness. A list of potential clients for the service was drawn up and initial priorities identified in consultation with all statutory agencies.

A number of specific questions are addressed in the evaluation which relate to the issues discussed in the previous section. The first aim is to investigate which people are referred as having severely challenging behaviour, and what factors might determine their being viewed as 'the most challenging'. The data on prevalence of particular problem behaviours suggests a greater number of potential clients than would generally be expected for case-loads of such intensive services. This implies that the people worked with by the specialist services are a selected group. The first set of questions then relate to the characteristics of the people served by the support teams, whether they differ from other people also seen as having challenging behaviour or, if not, whether there are main salient differences concerning the characteristics of settings.

The second research aim is to describe the behaviour of individuals in their natural environment prior to intervention, and to characterise broad environmental conditions such as activity programmes and the nature and frequency of staff interaction.

The third aim of the research is to evaluate the effectiveness of the two specialist services. This is being undertaken by reference to three outcome dimensions: first, whether the team intervention results in a change in the level of challenging behaviour; second, whether it maintains or extends adaptive behaviour, and, third, whether it enhances other aspects of the person's quality of life. As Blunden and Allen (1987) stress, these aspects should not be considered in isolation. However, they may be independent of each other; thus successful intervention may be judged in terms of growth in adaptive behaviour and quality of life even though the level of challenging behaviour goes unaltered.

THE EVALUATION DESIGN

All those individuals who are referred to both specialist services during a two-year period, from October 1990 to September 1992, are being included in the study. It is anticipated that the sample size achieved will be at least thirty. A random sample of people also identified as having severely challenging behaviour but who have not been referred to the specialist services will be taken in order to constitute a comparison group of similar size. The characteristics and experience of referred and non-referred clients will be compared.

The effectiveness of the specialist services' interventions will be evaluated using a case study approach. For each subject, where feasible, data will be collected before and after intervention on: a) the frequency and duration of maladaptive behaviours, b) the frequency and duration of adaptive behaviours, c) the relationship between behaviour and staff interaction, d) other aspects of the quality of experience of the person.

By paying attention to adaptive as well as maladaptive behaviours and by examining facets of the individual's quality of daily life, it is hoped to avoid possible interpretation pitfalls. Specifically, we wish to distinguish whether reduction of challenging behaviour, should it occur, has been achieved by suppressive means by removing environmental opportunities or whether it is associated with collateral improvements in opportunity, activity and quality of life.

MEASUREMENT

Characteristics of subjects and settings

Personal and setting profiles are being collected for each subject in the referred and non-referred samples, mainly by interview with primary carers. The personal profile comprises information on age, gender, dependency, social impairment, mental health status, sensory handicaps, adaptive behaviour, maladaptive behaviour, physical health status, medication and treatment history. The setting profile comprises information on type, size, characteristics of the physical environment, location, carer identities, carer numbers, carer training and carer morale and attitudes.

Dependency is rated by administration of the Social and Physical Incapacity and the Speech, Self-Help and Literacy Scales (Kushlick, Blunden and Cox, 1973). Social impairment is assessed using the Quality of Social Interaction Scale (Holmes, Shah and Wing, 1982). Adaptive behaviour is rated using the Adaptive Behavior Scale Part 1(ABS) (Nihira, Foster, Shellhaas and Leland, 1974), and maladaptive behaviour using the Aberrant Behavior Checklist (ABC) (Aman, Singh, Stewart and Field, 1985). Psychiatric diagnoses are abstracted from records and confirmed in consultation with the Consultant Psychiatrist. Mental health status is further measured by use of the Psychopathology Inventory for Mentally Retarded Adults (Informant Version) (PIMRA) (Matson, 1988).

Each setting is rated using the Characteristics of the Treatment Environment (Sutter and Mayeda, 1979). Carer morale is assessed by use of the Maslach Burnout Inventory for staff (Maslach and Jackson, 1981) and the Malaise Inventory (Rutter, Tizard and Whitmore, 1970) for family carers. The attitudes of staff are measured by administration of the Community-Oriented Programs Environment Scale (Moos, 1988).

The referred and non-referred samples will be contrasted to see the extent to which the nature of the behaviour, or other personal or setting characteristics, determine the person being described as presenting a severe challenge. Measures will also be administered after intervention to assess any change which may have occurred in subjects' reported adaptive and maladaptive behaviours or in such setting characteristics as carer morale and attitudes.

Observed behaviour

Direct observation of each subject is being undertaken to gain information on the frequency and cumulative duration of adaptive and maladaptive behaviours and on the nature and extent of carer:client interaction. Data are collected *in vivo* for at least three representative periods, each of usually three to four hours duration, until a stable and consistent pattern of behaviour is obtained. The observations are recorded using an Epson HX20 portable computer, which is programmed (Repp and Felce, 1990) for real-time multiple entry data capture allowing simultaneous collection of data on client and carer behaviour. While observational definitions of behaviour may be individualised, they generally include behaviours within the following categories:

Appropriate client engagement – engagement in a leisure, social, domestic, self help or educational activity, evidenced by some motor activity or attention to task or person.

Client disengagement – no engagement in activity, passive or unpurposeful.

Inappropriate client behaviour – including self-injury, violence to others, damage to property, inappropriate vocalisations, stereotypies, non-compliance, and anti-social behaviours such as spitting, public masturbation, inappropriate sexual overtures, undressing to the point of nakedness in public situations.

Staff behaviour – explicit or implicit instruction to perform an activity, demonstrating a task, physically assisting the client to perform a task, corrective instruction during an activity, positive feedback or praise, negative feedback or enforcing disengagement, helping the client (e.g. wiping face, dressing) without the client's active participation, collaborative activity (doing the same activity as the client), and other social interaction with the client.

Service intervention

The remit of both the specialist services is to develop an effective means of therapeutic intervention for people with severely challenging behaviour. This may involve a specific environmental change such as that brought about by the actions of the support teams (eg. through counselling staff, occasioning a greater range of activity or through a specific behaviour modification programme), a change in medication (as a result of advice from a therapeutic consultant) or a change in environment (such as in the resettlement of a client from hospital or, in one county, a transfer to the specialist treatment unit). The nature of each intervention for individual subjects will be abstracted from records and confirmed with the appropriate team member.

Quality of life

Direct observation of behaviour will explore environmental stimulation and extent of participation in activity. Other indicators of quality of life being used include the Index of Community Involvement and the Index of Participation in Domestic Tasks (Raynes and Sumpton, 1986), information on the range of activities participated in, and the extent of social contacts outside the service. Quality of setting is being assessed using the Characteristics of Treatment Environment and the Community Oriented Programs Environment Scales, as mentioned earlier.

Satisfaction with the specialist service input

An open-ended questionnaire has been designed for administration in each setting in the post-intervention phase. It will elicit information from primary carers and managers concerning their assessment of the effectiveness and contribution of the specialist services.

PRELIMINARY DATA

Data are presented for thirteen clients identified during the first six months of the study, eight referred to Service A and five to Service B (Table 5.1). Comparison subjects have yet to be identified and few of this initial group have moved through to post-intervention and follow-up. Comparative analysis on the nature of what constitutes severe challenging behaviour and assessment of the effectiveness of the challenging behaviour teams cannot as yet be reported. The data presented give a descriptive account of the characteristics and circumstances of the first clients included in the evaluation.

Table 5.1   *Characteristics of the sample at baseline*

	Team A (n = 8)	Team B (n = 5)	Total (n = 13)
Mean age (years)	32	28	30
age range	23–45	12–39	12–45
% male	50	40	46
% ambulant	100	80	92
% continent	75	20	54
% feeds, washes & dresses (self-help)	63	0	39
% speaks in sentences	75	20	54
% triad of social impairment	13	40	23
% in family home	13	20	15
% in hospital	62	60	62
% in community house	25	20	23
mean ABS score	164	75	130
mean ABC score	57	68	62
% with mental illness	63	20	46

Eight out of thirteen of the referred clients live in long stay mental handicap hospitals. Initially, the teams were to support five of these people in their resettlement. The focus in relation to the other three is on improving behaviour on the ward. Concrete plans for resettlement have emerged for three out of the five people targeted for resettlement, but difficulties have been encountered for the other two in gaining backing and resources to effect change. However, much of the team's work for one of these two clients has been in maintaining his day placement, which was in danger of being withdrawn. A further three of the referrals live in community-based residences. The focus of the team's work is to maintain their placements, which were in jeopardy at the time of referral. The remaining two people live in their family homes. For one, the team is being asked to help achieve successful resettlement and, for the other, team objectives are to support the parents to continue to care for their child (the only person under 18 years) and to support her special school placement.

Overall, most clients were ambulant, just over half were continent and could speak in sentences, and more than a third were competent in the self-help skills of washing, feeding and dressing. A quarter were assessed as having the triad of social impairments (Wing and Gould, 1979). The clients of Service B were of considerably higher dependency than those in Service A, and this was also reflected in the mean scores on the ABS obtained for the two groups. Mean scores on the ABC were 57 and 68 respectively for the people served by the two teams. Using the PIMRA, five of the Service A clients and one client in Service B were assessed as mentally ill.

Table 5.2 gives this information individual by individual. The SSL and ABS Scale ratings illustrate the differences in referral patterns between the two teams. Six out of the eight Service A clients were assessed as having independent self-help skills and able to speak in sentences. Four had ABS total scores associated with percentile ranks in the sixth decile or above, showing that they were of above average ability compared to the large sample of residential clients on whom the ABS standardised profiles were derived. A remaining three had ABS scores which yield percentile ranks in the third and fourth deciles. In contrast, none of the five Service B clients were assessed as having independent basic self-help skills and only one as speaking in sentences. Four of the five had ABS total scores with percentile ranks in the first decile. The triad of social impairments was found in three people all having low ABS total scores and assessed as unable to speak in sentences.

Table 5.2 also shows the number and topographies of challenging behaviour rated on the ABC at the highest level of problem (level 3). The ABC has five subscales: Irritability (15 items), Lethargy (16 items), Stereotypy (7 items), Hyperactivity (16 items), and Inappropriate Speech (4 items). In presenting the information in Table 5.2, we have subdivided the Irritability subscale into: Self-injury (3 items), Aggression (1 item), Temper (3 items), Screams/cries (4 items) and Irritable (4 items). We have also substituted 'Withdrawn' as the descriptor for the items in the Lethargy subscale. On average, each person had 11.5 items recorded at level 3 (range, 0–16). All bar one client showed a wide variety of challenging behaviours with an average of five of the nine categories of problem being present (range, 3–8, excluding S1).

It was not possible to gain direct access to one Service A client, and so Figure 5.1 presents the observational data obtained for twelve of the thirteen clients at baseline, in terms of engagement in purposeful activity, disengagement, inappropriate behaviour and interaction from staff. The shaded areas in the first bar chart indicate the proportion of engagement in social interaction. For all except S8, these data were collected within their residential settings, while the data for S8 represent time observed in school.

Engagement and disengagement varied greatly across individual clients. On average, clients spent about a third (mean, 35%; range, 5–79%) of the observed time engaged in some type of activity, just under half the time disengaged (mean, 46%; range, 17–89%) and approximately a fifth of the time (mean, 23%; range, 1–71%) engaging in inappropriate behaviours. Engagement was most commonly social interaction (mean, 10%; range, 1–23%), personal activity, mainly eating and drinking; (mean, 9%, range, 2–19%), and leisure activity, mainly watching television; (mean, 8%, range, 0–28%). Only a small proportion of the time observed was spent engaged in domestic activity (mean, 4%; range, 0–17%).

A variable pattern was also evident in the proportion of time clients were observed engaging in challenging behaviours. Many challenging behaviours are of brief duration and therefore may not be reflected well in a measure of the

Table 5.2 *Individual client characteristics*

Measure	Service A clients							
	1	2	3	4	5	6	7	*
SPI rating	SBI	SBD	SBD	SBD	SI	SBD	SBD	SBD
SSL rating	SH & Sp	Sp only	No SSL	SH & Sp	SH & Sp	SH & Sp	SH & Sp	SH & Sp
Social impairment	Sociable	Sociable	Triad	Sociable	Sociable	Sociable	Sociable	Sociable
Mental Illness	Yes	No	Yes	No	Yes	Yes	No	Yes
ABS score (percentile rank)	157 (35%)	195 (55%)	71 (8%)	137 (28%)	204 (60%)	188 (50%)	136 (24%)	218 (65%)
ABC score	13	51	82	67	41	80	56	64
LEVEL 3 BEHAVIOUR TYPES	NONE	SELF-INJURY (3) AGGRESSION (1) TEMPER TANTRUMS (3) IRRATABLE (2) WITHDRAWN (2) HYPERACTIVE (5)	SCREAMS (2) IRRITABLE (2) WITHDRAWN (9) HYPERACTIVE (2) INAPPROPRIATE SPEECH (3)	AGGRESSIVE (1) TEMPER TANTRUMS (3) WITHDRAWN (1) STEROTYPY (1) HYPERACTIVE (8) INAPPROPRIATE SPEECH (1)	TEMPER TANTRUMS (3) SCREAMS (1) HYPERACTIVE (5)	SELF-INJURY (1) AGGRESSIVE (1) TEMPER TANTRUMS (2) SCREAMS (1) IRRITABLE (3) WITHDRAWN (2) HYPERACTIVE (3) INAPPROPRIATE SPEECH (2)	SELF-INJURY (3) TEMPER TANTRUMS (3) SCREAMS (1) IRRATABLE (3) HYPERACTIVE (2)	AGGRESSIVE (1) TEMPER TANTRUMS (3) IRRITABLE (3) WITHDRAWN (1) HYPERACTIVE (3)

*Service A client for whom no observational data are available

SPI ratings: SBI = Severely behaviour disordered and Incontinent. SBD = Severely Behaviour Disordered only. SI = Severely Incontinent only. NA = Non Ambulant

SSL ratings: SH = Self-Help. Sp = Speech. No SSL = no speech, self help or literacy.

Table 5.2 cont.

Measure		Service B clients			
	8	9	10	11	12
SPI rating	SBD	SBI	SBD	SBI	NA
SSL rating	Sp only	No SSL	No SSL	No SSL	No SSL
Social impairment	Sociable	Sociable	Triad	Triad	Sociable
Menatl Illness	No	No	Yes	No	No
ABS score (percentile rank)	121 (35%)	75 (9%)	74 (7%)	52 (5%)	55 (7%)
ABC score	80	65	52	66	78
LEVEL 3 BEHAVIOUR TYPES	SELF-INJURY (1) AGGRESSIVE (1) TEMPER TANTRUMS (3) SCREAMS (3) IRRITABLE (2) HYPERACTIVE (4) INAPPROPRIATE SPEECH (1)	SELF-INJURY (3) TEMPER TANTRUMS (1) SCREAMS (1) IRRITABLE (1) WITHDRAWN (1) STEREOTYPY (5) HYPERACTIVE (3)	SELF-INJURY (1) AGGRESSIVE (1) WITHDRAWN (2) HYPERACTIVE (3)	SCREAMS (1) IRRITABLE (1) WITHDRAWN (2) HYPERACTIVE (3) INAPPROPRIATE SPEECH (1)	SELF-IJURY (3) AGGRESSIVE (1) SCREAMS (1) IRRITABLE (1) STEREOTYPY (1) HYPERACTIVE (3)

*Service A client for whom no observational data are available
SPI ratings: SBI = Severely behaviour disordered and Incontinent. SBD = Severely Behaviour Disordered only. SI = Severely Incontinent only. NA = Non Ambulant
SSL ratings: SH = Self-Help. Sp = Speech. No SSL = no speech, self help or literacy.

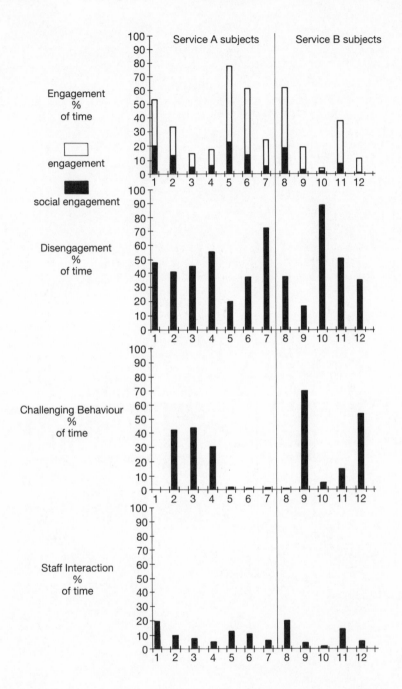

5.1 Observed client and staff behaviour

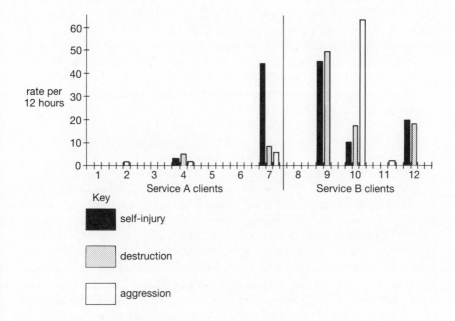

5.2 Incidence of self-injurious, destructive and aggressive behaviours

percentage time that they filled. For five subjects, challenging behaviour barely registered, and, for a further two, it was observed for only a small proportion of the time. For the remaining five, however, challenging behaviour occupied a considerable proportion of the observation periods (range, 31%–71%). Such challenging behaviours mainly comprised stereotypic movements and vocalisations, with self-restraint ocurring much of the time for one subject. Self-injury, aggression and destructive behaviours occupied little time. However, they did occur appreciably in four clients, three of whom were part of the case-load of Service B. Figure 5.2 shows the frequencies of these behaviours in terms of rates per 12 hour period.

Staff interaction also varied across clients but with a more restricted range (5–21%). A high proportion (87% overall) was in the form of general conversation. Only Subjects 8 and 11 received any appreciable instruction or assistance to participate in purposeful activity.

Analysis of the variation in engagement levels seems to implicate the ability levels of the clients, nature of the environment and nature of staff interaction. Much of the engagement can be attributed to the clients' abilities to occupy themselves. There appears to be a direct relationship between the higher engagement levels observed (see S1, S2, S5, S6 and S8) and independent ability as reflected in high ABS percentile ranks. These people also had the highest social engagement and staff spent the highest proportions of time conversing with them. With the exception of Subject 11, those individuals with low ABS scores received generally lower levels of interaction from staff and were engaged for less than one fifth or one tenth of the time. Overall, the correlation between engagement levels and total ABS scores was significant at $p < 0.01$ (Pearson $r = 0.67$).

The engagement levels of three subjects (1, 8 and 11) were higher than the general pattern of engagement against ABS scores would indicate. Subjects 1 and 11 lived in ordinary housing schemes and may have benefitted from increased opportunity arising out of the better material environment. In the case of Subject 11, staff were also more directive in their interaction and gave a greater level of assistance and instruction, which seems to be reflected in higher client engagement. This may also be said for Subject 8. The data cover part of her school day during which there was not only a more organised activity structure but, again, staff interactions included a higher proportion of prompts and direct help. It is also relevant that Subject 5, who was busy for most of the time, as well as being extremely able, lived on a new hospital unit with a good material environment. Otherwise, clients typically lived in poor hospital suroundings with few activity opportunities and were given little help from staff to fill their time constructively. Overall, the environment contributed little to the welfare of all but a few of the subjects.

A multiple regression was carried out to investigate how well a linear function of ability (as measured by total ABS score), extent of staff help (as measured by the proportion of time clients received instruction, prompts and physical guidance), and environment (as indicated by a dichotomous variable where 1 was scored for clients in materially enriched settings and 0 was scored for materially barren settings) could explain the variation in engagement. Variables were entered in the above order and all contributed significantly to the explanation of engagement levels. ABS score accounted for 40 per cent of the variance ($F = 8.36$, $p < 0.02$), ABS and staff help accounted for 69 per cent of the variance (change in $F = 10.58$, $p < 0.01$), and all three variables accounted for 91 per cent of the variance (change in $F = 23.33$, $p < 0.002$).

DISCUSSION

Clearly, we are still at a very early stage in this research and little can be said definitively about the main questions concerning the nature of challenging behaviour or the effectiveness of specialist team activity. Two main impressions can be gained from the information collated so far. First, there is considerable variation within and between the client groups identified in the two counties as having severely challenging behaviour and, second, teams are generally working with clients whose current environments are contributing little to the establishment of appropriate behaviour and full occupation.

The clients served by the two teams are almost two separate groups, although to some extent this is to be expected from the differences in operational policy. Service A clients are more able and a higher proportion have mental illness. Service B clients are predominantly individuals with the most severe or profound learning disabilities. Although the ABC showed the two groups to be similar in level and variety of challenging behaviour, direct observation showed that Service B clients exhibited higher frequency self-injurious, aggressive or destructive behaviours. This distinction conforms to a more general one within the category 'severely challenging'. A person may be challenging either because they exhibit inappropriate behaviours as part of their everyday pattern of responding or because what they do has a dramatic effect or creates serious concern, even if done only episodically. The former may be more prevalent among people with more severe disabilities and the latter may be of greater significance among people with higher abilities, for whom the diagnosis of mental illness can be more certain.

The diversity within the client group has implications for the required competencies of specialist services. That 'severely challenging behaviour' is not a unitary phenomenon is a fact that may need to be reflected in the debate about, and design of, appropriate services. If the argument regarding the need for specialism is sound, then the wide spread in the characteristics, behaviours and underlying pathology of people with challenging behaviours does not necessarily make it logical to conceive of a single area of specialism. The scope for variation in target clients as well as therapeutic orientation and working methods is considerable. The notion that a single additional resource, such as a specialist support team, is an adequate planning response to meet the problem may well prove to be an oversimplification.

A high proportion of the referred clients currently live in settings which do very little to encourage appropriate behaviour. This situation presents the challenging behaviour services with a number of dilemmas. First, the poor quality of regime and the resulting poor quality of life of the person may prompt the conclusion that the person would benefit from moving to a better setting, typically well-staffed small community residence. The challenging behaviour service may not have the direct managerial and service planning powers to effect such a change. Even if they do, such a change takes many months to achieve, and leaves the team with the question of what to do for the person in the interim. This latter problem is one example of a more general second dilemma of how much effort to put into trying to change poor quality hospital settings through environmental redesign, staff training or through the introduction of specific programmes of action. Considerable attempts have been made to reform such environments in the last few decades with attempts to make settings more 'domestic', to increase staff interaction with clients and to get the implementation of various therapeutic approaches. However, the experience has been mainly one of failure, with reforms failing to stick.

Third, it is not clear that specialist input is required in every instance of severely challenging behaviour for successful resettlement to be achieved. The earlier attempts in Wessex and by NIMROD to establish service models to which people with severely challenging behaviour could be resettled with no prior preparation or extraordinary subsequent support resulted in a high proportion of transferred residents remaining in the community (see Lowe, de Paiva and Felce, in press). One consequence of involving a specialist challenging behaviour service from the start is that it will never be known whether such individuals could not have been resettled successfully without such specialist intervention. In these circumstances it will often not be possible to gauge whether the service input affected outcome and there will be no way of establishing whether resources were well used or ill deployed.

This latter issue concerns the interface between mainstream and specialist services and whether the presence of the second encourages underachievement by the first. It is difficult to be always able to distinguish the genuine need for help of a well organised, competently managed, skilled mainstream setting from the request for support of a poorly established and run facility. The example of Subject 1, who presents virtually no challenging behaviour either as seen by direct observation or as assessed on the ABC, shows that specialist services can face problems in defining the boundaries of their role. This problem can be particularly acute where placement breakdown is anticipated and the referral gains priority in order to prevent institutional admission.

In conclusion, it is premature to draw too much from what are only the beginnings of a two-year research project. However, the discussion of the nature of specialism and some of the preliminary indications from the data suggest that challenging behaviour support teams, like other services, will face a number of issues which may limit their effectiveness in practice. The specialist peripatetic support team has become a popular formulation and there is a common view that such teams are a more desirable option than specialist units. Notwithstanding this, evaluation is important. Research is required not only on the general effectiveness of challenging behaviour services but also on significant elements of service design, such as what training specialist staff should have, what working methods are effective and what ways of understanding and responding to challenging behaviour prove most useful.

References

All Wales Advisory Panel (1991), *Challenges and Responses. A report on services in support of adults with mental handicaps with exceptionally challenging behaviours, mental illness or who offend*, Welsh Office, Cardiff.

Aman, M. G., Singh, N. N., Stewart, A. W. and Field, C. J. (1985), 'The Aberrant Behavior Checklist: A behavior rating scale for the assessment of treatment effects', *American Journal of Mental Deficiency*, 89, 485–91.

Baumeister, A. A. (1978), 'Origins and controls of stereotyped movements' in C. E. Meyers (ed.), *Quality of Life in Severely and Profoundly Mentally Retarded People: Research Foundations for Improvement*, American Association on Mental Deficiency, Washington DC.

Baumeister, A. A. (1989), 'Etiologies of self-injurious and destructive behavior', *Proceedings of the Consensus Conference on the Treatment of Severe Behavior Problems and Developmental Disabilities*, National Institutes of Health, Bethesda, MD.

Baumeister, A. A. and Rollings, J. P. (1976), 'Self-injurious behavior', in Ellis (ed.), *International Review of Research in Mental Retardation*, Academic Press, New York.

Beasley, F. and Mansell, J. (1990), 'Severe mental handicap and problem behaviour: Evaluating transfer from institutions to community care' in W. I. Fraser (ed.) *Key Issues in Mental Retardation Research. Proceedings of the Eighth Congress of the International Association for the Scientific Study of Mental Deficiency, 1988*, Routledge, London.

Blunden, R. and Allen, D. (eds.) (1987), *Facing the Challenge: An Ordinary Life for People with Learning Difficulties*, King Edward's Hospital Fund for London, London.

Brown, H. and Craft, A. (eds.) (1989), *Thinking the Unthinkable: Papers on Sexual Abuse and People with Learning Difficulties*, FPA Education Unit, London.

Bruhl, H. H., Fielding, L., Joyce, M., Peters, W. and Weisler, N. (1982), 'Thirty month demonstration project for treatment of self-injurious behavior in severely retarded individuals', in J. H. Hollis and C. E. Meyers (eds.), *Life-Threatening Behavior: Analysis and Intervention*, American Association on Mental Deficiency, Washington, DC.

Bryson, Y., Sakati, N., Nyhan, W. L. and Fish, C. H. (1971), 'Self-mutilative behavior in the Cornelia de Lange syndrome', *American Journal of Mental Deficiency*, 76, 319–24.

Cataldo, M. F. and Harris, J. H. (1982), 'The biological basis for self-injury in the mentally retarded', *Analysis and Intervention in Developmental Disabilities*, 2, 21–39.

Christie, R., Bay, C., Kaufman, I.A., Bakay, B., Borden, M. and Nyhan, W. L. (1982), 'Lesch-Nyhan disease: clinical experience with nineteen patients', *Developmental Medicine and Child Neurology*, 24, 293–306.

Day, K. (1988), 'A hospital-based treatment programme for male mentally handicapped offenders', *British Journal of Psychiatry*, 153, 635–44.

de Kock, U., Felce, D., Saxby, H. and Thomas, M. (1987), 'Staff turnover in a small home service: a study of facilities for adults with severe and profound mental handicaps', *Mental Handicap*, 15, 97–101.

de Kock, U., Saxby, H., Thomas, M. and Felce, D. (1988), 'Community and family contact: an evaluation of small community homes for adults', *Mental Handicap Research*, 1, 127–40.

de Paiva, S. and Lowe, K. (1990), *The Evaluation of NIMROD, a community-based service for people with mental handicap: the incidence of problem behaviours*, Mental Handicap in Wales Applied Research Unit, Cardiff.

Department of Health (1989), *Needs and Responses*, Department of Health Leaflets Unit, Stanmore.

Department of Health and Social Security (DHSS) (1971), *Better Services for the Mentally Handicapped*, HMSO, London.

Department of Health and Social Security (DHSS) (1984), *Helping Mentally Handicapped People with Special Problems*, HMSO, London.

Doss, S. and Reichle, J. (1989), 'Establishing communicative alternatives to the emission of socially motivated excess behavior: a review', *The Journal of the Association for Persons with Severe Handicaps*, 14, 101–112.

Durand, V. M. and Kishi, G. (1987), 'Reducing severe problem behavior among persons with dual sensory impairments: an evaluation of a technical assistance model', *Journal of the Association for Persons with Severe Handicaps*, 12, 2–10.

Emerson, E. B. (in press), 'The challenge of severe self-injurious behaviour' in J. P. Fryns and T. Kempeneers-Foulon (eds.), *Scientific Progress in Mental Retardation*.

Emerson, E., Beasley, F., Offord, G. and Mansell, J. (in press), 'Hospital based supported housing for people with seriously challenging behaviours', *Mental Handicap Research*.

Eyman, R. K., Borthwick, S. A. and Miller, C. (1981), 'Trends in maladaptive behavior of mentally retarded persons placed in community and institutional settings', *American Journal of Mental Deficiency*, 85, 473–77.

Felce, D. (1989), *Staffed housing for adults with severe or profound mental handicaps, The Andover Project*, BIMH Publications, Kidderminster.

Felce, D., de Kock, U., Thomas, M. and Saxby, H. (1986), 'Change in adaptive behaviour of severely and profoundly mentally handicapped adults in different residential settings', *British Journal of Psychology*, 77, 484–501.

Felce, D., Kushlick, A. and Smith, J. (1980), 'An overview of the research on alternative residential facilities for the severely mentally handicapped in Wessex', *Advances in Behaviour Research and Therapy*, 3, 1–4.

Felce, D., Lowe, K. and Beswick, J. (in prep), 'Staff turnover in ordinary housing for people with severe or profound mental handicaps'.

Felce, D., Lowe, K. and de Paiva, S. (in press), 'Ordinary housing for people with severe mental handicaps and challenging behaviours', in E. Emerson, P. McGill and J. Mansell (eds.), *Severe Learning Disabilities and Challenging Behaviour: Designing Quality Services*, Chapman Hall, London.

Gedye, A. (1989), 'Extreme self-injury attributed to frontal lobe seizures', *American Journal on Mental Retardation*, 94, 20–6.

Harris, P. and Russell, O. (1989), *The Prevalence of Agressive Behaviour among People with Learning Difficulties (Mental Handicap) in a Single Health District: Interim Report*, Norah Fry Research Centre, University of Bristol.

Hill, B. K. and Bruininks, R. H. (1984), 'Maladaptive behavior of mentally retarded individuals in residential facilities', *American Journal of Mental Deficiency*, 88, 380–87.

Hoefkens, A. and Allen, D. (1990), 'Evaluation of a special behaviour unit for people with mental handicaps and challenging behaviour', *Journal of Mental Deficiency Research*, 34, 213–28.

Holmes, N., Shah, A. and Wing, L. (1982), 'The Disability Assessment Schedule: A brief screening device for use with the mentally retarded', *Psychological Medicine*, 2, 879–90.

Kiernan, C. and Alborz, A. (1991), *People with Mental Handicap who Offend*, Hester Adrian Research Centre, University of Manchester, Manchester.

Kravitz, H. and Boehm, J. J. (1962), 'Rhythmic habit patterns in infancy: their sequence, age of onset and significance', *Child Development*, 33, 43–56.

Kushlick, A., Blunden, R. and Cox, G. (1973), 'A method of rating behaviour characteristics for use in large-scale surveys of mental handicap', *Psychological Medicine*, 3, 466–78.

Kushlick, A. and Cox, G. R. (1973), 'The epidemiology of mental handicap', *Developmental Medicine and Child Neurology*, 15, 748–59.

Lowe, K. and de Paiva, S. (in press), *NIMROD – An Overview: A Summary Report of a Five Year Research Study*, Welsh Office, Cardiff.

Lowe, K., de Paiva, S. and Felce, D. (in press), 'Effects of a community-based service on adaptive and maladaptive behaviors: a longitudinal study', *American Journal on Mental Retardation*.

Maslach, C. and Jackson, S. E. (1981), 'The measurement of experienced burnout', *Journal of Occupational Behaviour*, 2, 99–113.

Matson, J. (1988), *The Psychopathology Instrument for Mentally Retarded Adults*, International Diagnostic Systems Inc., Louisiana.

Moos, R. H. (1988), *Community-Oriented Programs Environment Scale Manual*, Consulting Psychologists Press, California.

Newman, I. and Emerson, E. (in press), 'Specialised Treatment Units for People with Challenging Behaviours', *Mental Handicap*.

Nihira, K., Foster, R., Shellhaas, M. and Leland, H. (1974), *AAMD Adaptive Behavior Scale for Children and Adults*, American Association on Mental Deficiency, Washington DC.

O'Brien, J. and Tyne, A. (1981), *The Principle of Normalisation: A Foundation for Effective Services*, Campaign for the Mentally Handicapped, London.

Oliver, C. (1988), 'Self-injurious behaviour in people with a mental handicap', *Current Opinion in Psychiatry*, 1; 567–71.

Oliver, C. and Head, D. (1990), 'Self-injurious behavior in people with learning disabilities: determinants and interventions', *International Review of Psychiatry*, 892, 101–16.

Oliver, C., Murphy, G. H. and Corbett, J. A. (1987), 'Self-injurious behaviour in people with mental handicap: a total population study', *Journal of Mental Deficiency Research*, 31, 147–62.

Raynes, N. V. and Sumpton, R. C. (1986), *Follow-up Study of 448 People who are Mentally Handicapped: Final Report to the DHSS*, University of Manchester, Department of Social Policy, Manchester.

Repp, A. C. and Felce, D. (1990), 'A micro-computer system used for evaluative and experimental behavioural research in mental handicap', *Mental Handicap Research*, 3, 21–32.

Repp, A. C., Karsh, K. G., Deitz, D. E. D. and Singh, N. N. (in press), 'A study of the homeostatic level of stereotypic and other motor movements of persons with mental retardation', *Journal of Mental Deficiency Research*.

Robertson, M. M., Trimble, M. R. and Lees, A. J. (1989), 'Self-injurious behaviour and the Gilles de la Tourette syndrome: a clinical study and review of the literature', *Psychological Medicine*, 19, 611–25.

Rutter, M., Tizard, J. and Whitmore, K. (1970), *Education, Health and Behaviour*, Heinemann, London.

Schroeder, S., Schroeder, C., Rojahn, J. and Mulick, J. (1982), 'Analysis of self-injurious behaviour: its development and management', in J. L. Matson and J. R. McCartney (eds.), *Handbook of Behavior Modification for the Mentally Retarded*, Plenum Press, New York.

Schroeder, S.R., Schroeder, C. S., Smith, B. and Dalldorf, J. (1978), 'Prevalence of self-injurious behaviour in a large state facility for the retarded: a three year follow-up study', *Journal of Autism and Childhood Schizophrenia*, 8, 261–69.

Skinner, B. F. (1953), *Science and Human Behavior*, Free Press, New York.

Sutter, P., Mayeda, T., Call, T., Yanagi, G. and Yee, S. (1980), 'Comparison of successful and unsuccessful community-placed mentally retarded persons', *American Journal of Mental Deficiency*, 85, 262–67.

Sutter, P. and Mayeda, T. (1979), *Characteristics of the Treatment Environment: MR/ DD Community Home Manual*, Los Angeles Neuropsychiatric Institute Research Group, Lanterman State Hospital, California.

Welsh Office (1983), *All Wales Strategy for the Development of Services for Mentally Handicapped People*, Welsh Office, Cardiff.

Wing, L. and Gould, J. (1979), 'Severe impairments of social interaction and associated abnormalities in children: Epidemiology and classification', *Journal of Autism and Developmental Disorders*, 9, 11–29.

Wolfensberger, W. (1972), *The Principle of Normalisation in Human Services*, National Institute on Mental Retardation, Toronto.

Wolfensberger, W. (1983), 'Social role valorisation: A proposed new term for the principle of normalisation', *Mental Retardation*, 21, 234–39.

Staff issues: training, support and management

This chapter covers staff training and management in relation to challenging behaviour. Training, support and management should be inextricably interlinked in order to obtain an effective service for people with learning disabilities and challenging behaviour. The Collins Concise Dictionary defines training as 'the process of bringing a person, etc., to an agreed standard of proficiency, etc., by practice and instruction'. However, Reid *et al.* (1989) emphasised that training, although necessary, is *not* sufficient to improve staff performance. Longer term management factors are, according to the authors, also necessary for maintenance of that performance and, in addition, are crucial in staff support and minimising staff stress.

The issues covered in this chapter are wide-ranging and therefore the aim is to stimulate thought rather than offer detailed, comprehensive analysis.

DEFINING SERVICE AIMS

In a needs-led service, staff are frequently taught what should be accomplished for the service users. For example, the 'five accomplishments' (O'Brien, 1987) already mentioned in chapter 3, are frequently used as service aims. Nevertheless, in practice hands-on staff are not always clear when a person with learning disabilities should, for example, have free choice, when they should adapt their behaviour to the needs of the group, when there should be compromise or when it would be preferable for the person to move to another setting where their needs correspond more closely to the prevailing norms.

Challenging behaviour may occur unnecessarily because of this lack of clarity. For instance, there may be conflict because one member of staff gives a person freedom of choice where another does not. Staff may disagree about what are acceptable ways in which they and the individual can communicate anger or dissatisfaction. Lack of clarity in regard to objectives can generate anxiety in staff and in individuals, which may make it more likely that challenging behaviour will occur. Achieving agreement amongst staff and service users on the specific application of, say, the five accomplishments is a complex and time-consuming process.

The situation is compounded if a large number of staff are involved and there is high staff turnover, since different people may have different opinions and perceptions of the aims of the service and how to translate these into practice. In consequence, small organisations, or ones where power is devolved to the bottom, can be more efficient (Raynes *et al.*, 1979).

TRAINING

Defining which skills are necessary to meet the aims of the service

The British Institute of Mental Handicap (BIMH) and the Central Council for Education and Training in Social Work (CCETSW) (*A Guide to Training Resources*, 1989) give a useful overview of the skills necessary when working in a service for people with learning disabilities (see list below for a brief summary). The greater the staffs' general and expert knowledge and ability, the greater their power to prevent challenging behaviour. For example, a person will be less likely to create conflict as a result of boredom if staff have the ability to teach them activities which they find interesting. In another situation, carers may need to be aware of how to position a physically disabled person in their wheelchair. This may make it less likely that, due to pain and discomfort, the person will show challenging behaviour.

Summary of skills needed for working with people with learning disabilities

1. *Societal issues*: knowledge of how people with learning disabilities are viewed as members of society and the sociological consequences.
2. *Systemic issues*: knowledge of how services are designed and organised to promote desirable experiences and outcomes for their users:
   a planning and managing services, e.g. quality assurance etc.
   b working with service users, e.g. individual plans, assessment, goal planning, skills teaching, working with challenging behaviour, counselling, communication and group dynamics, working with families, advocacy and representation, establishing opportunities and participation.
3. *Individual issues*: how to relate/interact in desirable ways with service users. Physical and sensory development, physical and mental health, home life, social life, community life, work life, making choices and stating opinions, making adjustments to change, and grief and bereavement.

It is apparent from this list that it may be necessary for staff to have a very wide range of competencies in order to attend to the needs of the person and prevent unnecessary challenges. The more relevant knowledge staff have, the less likely it is that situations will develop to crisis point where specialist help is required. It is not practical for all staff to be trained in all the above competencies, particularly if staff turnover is high, but it is vital for people in first-line managerial positions to have enough training and experience to effectively supervise staff.

I have listed below a range of skills which I consider pertinent to working with people with learning disabilities and challenging behaviour. Because of differences in service philosophy and treatment methods employed in different districts, not all the skills will be accepted as necessary by everyone working in the field.

Range of skills and knowledge necessary for working with people with learning disabilities and challenging behaviour

* The skills mentioned in the summary above.
* A knowledge of a wide range of possible causes and relevant short-term and long-term interventions for challenging behaviour, tied to a detailed knowledge of the individual.
* Sophisticated behavioural techniques.
* Psychological therapies based on cognitive and emotional change.
* Diffusing agitation and coping with physical assault.
* Staff stress management and support techniques.

The skills listed here are a 'personal selection' as there is a dearth of literature to draw from. There is a particular lack of research and training in dealing with anxiety, depression and schizophrenia in people with learning disabilities. Further, there are three skills areas which I consider to be crucial but poorly researched. I will describe these in some detail. They are: (1) The identification of a person's needs on a day-to-day basis; (2) Improvement of the quality of interaction between staff and individuals with learning disabilities and (3) Self-awareness and self-control in staff.

1 Identifying a person's needs on a day-to-day basis

It is encouraging that in recent years there has been a greater awareness of individuals' needs and of the importance of 'fitting the system to the person' rather than vice-versa, with regular reviews and in-depth assessment becoming more usual.

There is a necessity for staff to *routinely* identify a person's needs. Hands-on carers need to be constantly asking themselves whether or not the individual in their charge is content, bored, sad or in pain. It is not sufficient to wait six months for an in-depth review, or for a visiting 'specialist' to identify needs as a result of a crisis developing. Assessment and prevention should occur wherever possible on a daily basis. This is essential whether or not the person signals their distress or displeasure with challenging behaviour.

And yet sometimes it is not easy to identify the cause of a person's distress, particularly if the individual cannot or does not communicate their feelings. It often requires a certain amount of knowledge of learning disabilities in general and of the person in particular, in addition to the ability to 'weigh the evidence'. What is the evidence for or against a guess that the individual is bored, what is the evidence for or against a guess that they are in pain? How can these guesses be tested? If staff could weigh and test evidence, they would not need to resort to helpless declarations that the person is 'attention seeking', and they would have greater power to intervene appropriately. For a detailed discussion of the uses of functional analysis, see Chapter 7.

As a first training step, it is essential for staff to be aware of and able to identify a wide range of possible causes of challenging behaviour (Carr and Durand, 1985; Donnellan *et al.*, 1984; Lally, 1988, 1989; Lister and Rapley, in press). However, there is a need for further research and training regarding the ways in which staff can routinely carry out such assessments.

2 Improving the quality of personal interactions

There is also a need for further research on ways to improve the quality of the interaction between the person with learning disabilities and other people, to make the relationship more *mutually* rewarding. The importance of this is recognised in other fields, for instance marital therapy (Jacobson and Margolin, 1979) and family therapy (Walrond-Skinner, 1977). Although there is now great concern to improve the quality of relationships in the learning disability field, there is not always enough emphasis on the need for interactions to be mutually enjoyable.

Studies show that staff often have very low rates of interaction with service-users, and such interaction which does occur may disproportionately favour clients who are more independent and are perceived by staff as attractive, likeable and intellectually competent (Dailey *et al.*, 1974; Grant and Moores, 1977). At the same time, lack of staff attention can lead to challenging behaviour (Durand and Carr, 1987, 1991). Challenging behaviour may therefore be associated with situations where staff do not interact enough with the person because for them the quality of the interaction is not intrinsically rewarding. As Holborn (1990) points out, the advantage of making a situation enjoyable and interesting in itself (rather than solely relying on managerial factors such as external praise or money) is that the 'reward' is always immediate.

Quality of interaction may be improved by:

• staff and clients (including peers and individuals in the community) sharing activities that both enjoy;
• staff and others learning to interact with clients in ways that give them pleasure (the work of Clegg, 1990 is interesting in this regard). If clients react by showing pleasure, staff may themselves find the situation more rewarding;

- teaching the person to act in ways that will give others pleasure (e.g. being helpful);

In all cases, the enjoyable aspects of the situation for *both* the person and staff should be considered. In practice, this requires good management and organisation.

To strengthen the process, staff could be given an external reward for attempting to make relationships with people with learning disabilities more mutually enjoyable. In some work settings, improved skills are related to promotion. The ability to make quality relationships could be counted as a competency necessary for upgrading.

3 Self-awareness and self-control in staff

How can staff help people to be aware of and control feelings of jealousy, inadequacy, fear, dislike and anger (all of which may cause challenging behaviour) if they have not learned to master (and I do not mean merely suppress) these feelings themselves? The topic is relevant to staff stress and support and so, in addition to the following discussion, will be addressed further in the end section of this chapter (see p. 153).

There is some evidence that emotional warmth in carers is correlated with low levels of behaviour problems. Patterson and Stouthamer-Loeber (1984) found that firm consistent discipline given in an atmosphere of warmth and positive involvement was influential in bringing about positive change in delinquents. It is not always clear which is cause and which effect. Quine (quoted by Wertheimer, 1991) found that carers felt warmer towards a child when they had learned to control the child's behaviour, but it is possible that lack of warmth exacerbates maladaptive behaviour, which in turn exacerbates lack of warmth.

It may be particularly important that staff show warmth to people who have suffered from a lack of consistent caring. They may sometimes feel too resentful at an individual's behaviour to give the warm feeling that is required. More research is needed to identify strategies that will enable staff to overcome negative feelings, to implement interventions warmly and effectively and to do so consistently for long periods of time.

What are the best methods of learning skills?

Reid *et al.* (1989) surveyed over 120 research studies evaluating training and management. Methods of learning include:

- verbal information (e.g. a classroom lecture). This is often ineffective on its own;
- written information;
- being shown what to do, in a real situation or using video or role-play;
- practising the task and being given feedback on how to do it. This is very effective, although time-consuming.

Using all components is the most effective strategy, particularly if the trainee is motivated by praise for correct performance (Reid *et al.*, 1989). However, there is a need for more studies on how to teach people to generalise what they have learned to other situations.

In practice, staff are often regarded as 'trained' when they have merely received information, although this is shown to be ineffective in ensuring that they attain an agreed standard of proficiency (e.g. Gardner, 1972). Staff may state that they enjoyed a course or understood the content, but this does not mean that they can put their knowledge into practice. Carers may not be shown what to do or given practice and feedback on the task. Consequently, they do not receive the most powerful method of training and there is no way of ensuring that the trainee has mastered the component skills. When 'on-the-job' methods of training are used, they may be regarded as 'management' or 'hands-on supervision', since the training role is usually carried out by a manager. It cannot be emphasised enough that good training does not consist of arranging a series of lectures or an induction course – it involves ensuring that trainees can carry out what is required in practice.

Ideally, there should be a list of skills that are generally necessary for the work. Training should be given as required and staff observed to reach a certain standard of proficiency on each of the skills listed, before they are left unsupervised.

The effectiveness of any training course will depend on which teaching procedures are used. The problem with short workshops is that there is rarely the opportunity to practice to a criterion of proficiency; there is also the possibility with sophisticated behavioural courses that trainees will not thoroughly understand the principles taught, and as a consequence will misapply them. Even longer courses, including qualification courses, often do not give the trainee opportunity to practice skills with direct, immediate feedback from an instructor, and yet training may be ineffective without this component. Again, it has been found that paper tests may bear no relation to performance in practice (e.g. Watson and Uzell, 1980), and so a qualification based on such tests may sometimes give a misleading impression of a person's ability. Ideally, a trainee should be observed in real-life situations in which they are required to demonstrate an understanding of the knowledge taught and to apply this knowledge to a variety of circumstances.

In reality, of course, many staff have received no training at all. Hogg and Mittler (1987) pointed out that the majority of residential care staff employed by local authorities are unqualified. As mentioned above, challenging behaviour may occur directly as a result of lack of knowledge. Problems may build up to crisis point in situations where staff are not sufficiently experienced to prevent them, although in practice staff will frequently apply a large amount of intelligence and ingenuity to the difficult situation they find themselves in. A number of qualified people may then be called in to deal with the crisis. The problem may not at this stage be easily dealt with, since staff are now expected to learn a considerable amount in a short time, when they themselves are under stress. The situation is equivalent to calling in a driving instructor only when the novice has crashed the car.

The need for trained first-line supervisors

It would be too time-consuming to train very thoroughly every member of staff, particularly since there are a very wide range of competencies that are needed. It would be more cost-effective to thoroughly instruct those in the best position to train and supervise others by showing them what to do, giving them feedback and motivating them. A national survey of directors of social services, nursing and nurse education indicated that the greatest priority should be given to training first-line managers (Radford, 1988). Reid *et al.* (1989) strongly recommend that the person responsible for training staff should be the day-to-day supervisor of the staff. This strategy was effectively adopted by the Special Development Team that was set up in the South East Thames Region to help people with severe learning disabilities and challenging behaviour (see Chapter 4). The project leaders in staffed housing were given intensive training by highly qualified professionals and were then in a position to supervise and instruct unqualified support staff (Cummings *et al.*, 1989).

The effectiveness of this approach is entirely dependent on the ability of the supervisor to spend time teaching staff by directly observing them. First-line managers who are based mainly in an office will be unlikely to be successful, since 'teaching by talking' is the method most likely to fail. Teaching managerial staff time-management and hiring clerical staff for routine jobs will facilitate more 'on-the-job' instruction and supervision.

It is also essential at the planning stage to decide what skills are most important for staff to learn, since thorough, effective training is time-consuming. What is most important will vary with the individual needs of the client group.

In addition to giving advice, or helping during crises, specialists should give intensive training to supervisors. The 'pyramidal' approach has already been shown to be very effective with the EDY (Education for the Developmentally Young) behavioural techniques course. By 1985 3,000 staff were trained nationally to a criterion, using a very effective package of techniques, including the use of performance feedback (Farrell, 1985). Eighty educational psychologists and twenty educational advisors were initially trained by a small team and they themselves trained others, mainly teachers. The rationale for this was:

Crisis intervention may assist with the problems of one child for a short period but is likely at the same time to undermine the confidence of the teaching staff in their own ability to deal with problems. Ways are needed to provide 'hands-on' staff with the expertise to meet disabilities as they arise (McBrien and Foxen, 1987, p. 410).

In another example of pyramidal training, Page *et al.* (1982) trained three supervisors, who then trained 45 direct care staff working with people with learning disabilities. Would staff be more motivated to learn if a career structure was tied in to the acquisition of relevant skills? A possible model might be that qualified individuals (eg. members of a challenging behaviour team) train hands-on supervisors. These supervisors need to train a certain number of hands-on staff in order to be promoted. These hands-on staff receive promotion to supervisor as a result of reaching criteria in specified skills.

It would be highly desirable if the National Vocational Qualifications (now being developed for hands-on staff in Social Services) included basic competencies in preventing and dealing with challenging behaviour.

Good initial selection may lessen the necessity for extensive training. This is a very important consideration when a considerable amount of knowledge is necessary to perform a job. Clear service aims and good organisation, resulting in good staff and client motivation and stress prevention, may also reduce the need for training.

Sharing skills

Douglas (1985) contrasts two styles of teaching: an expert handing down knowledge to passive learners, as opposed to a two-way process where people share ideas with each other and problem-solve. Problems can arise, however; care staff may not be aware that personal experiences have biased them and may not realise the value of expert knowledge, arrived at through carefully controlled research. The 'expert' may not realise that the knowledge they are imparting needs to be modified to fit the particular circumstances.

One or more people may possess a range of skills for dealing with the challenging behaviour of an individual, but there is no mechanism for them to pass on their skills to others. This may occur because the person has not analysed what they are doing, or does not know how to pass on the skills, because others disagree with their approach, or because there is a lack of opportunity for people to meet and plan. This seems an unnecessary waste of resources. There should be more evaluation of what people are doing *correctly*, and then opportunity and motivation for others working with the individual to learn these methods.

One of the encouraging advances in the last few years has been the development of packages of care based on good team assessment and a thorough knowledge of the individual. The King's Fund Centre (Blunden and Allen, 1987) has played a useful role in promoting and publicising this approach. Staff training in this context can occur in relation to the individual case.

Training in practice

Formal training may occur as a prerequisite of a qualification (social work, psychology, nursing etc.) or post-qualification, including the thorough, mainly behavioural courses recently set up at the universities of Manchester and Kent specifically for people working with people with learning disabilities and challenging behaviour. Formal training may occur at local or regional level, with initiatives run by individuals or teams within Health, Social Service, voluntary or private bodies. Training may aim to reach systematically a very wide number of people on a national basis, for example, the EDY behavioural techniques course. Lectures, workshops and short courses are organised by the BIMH, the British Association for Behavioural Psychotherapy and the King's Fund Centre, amongst others. A list of organisations offering training and development is listed in the BIMH guide (1989). In the future, staff in social services will be expected to acquire National Vocational Qualifications. However, I understand that the competencies in regard to challenging behaviour and learning disabilities have not yet been identified.

The usefulness of any course should be assessed in a critical spirit and in relation to the points made earlier. Does it cover the skills required? What opportunity is there for learning through practice and feedback, rather than 'chalk and talk'? Does it cover issues of generalisation and maintenance related to the setting in which the trainee will be working?

In addition to formal courses, it is desirable for systems to be set up within a service to ensure that the skills that people possess are passed on to other people within and between settings and over time.

MANAGEMENT

In this section, staff management will be considered in general and in relation to challenging behaviour. Management is defined in this context as 'the process of organising systems and motivating staff to ensure that the aims of the services are met'. There may be a need within a service for more training on basic management skills. It should not be assumed that staff are born with the ability to organise their time well and to set priorities.

Styles of leadership

A classic study by Lewin *et al.* (1939) compared autocratic, democratic and *laissez-faire* styles of leadership with children (the children were not labelled as having learning disabilities). The autocratic leaders told the boys what to do and sometimes praised or blamed them. Democratic leaders led discussions and allowed the boys to make their own decisions, and when praising would say why. *Laissez-faire* leaders only offered help when asked to do so and offered no praise or blame.

Boys were less aggressive and attention-seeking when led democratically rather than autocratically. Although slightly less work was done than with the autocrat, the democratically-led boys did not stop working when the leader left the room. By contrast, the *laissez-faire* groups accomplished very little.

Later studies in industry support the Lewin *et al.* (1939) findings. In one study reported in Hardy and Heyes (1979) the management style of a factory was changed from autocratic to democratic. After two years of the democratic style of leadership the absentee rate had been cut by half and the amount of goods per week had risen by a third. The implications of these studies are particularly pertinent to the management of staff working on their own with people with challenging behaviour in the community. They do not receive constant supervision and therefore need to be self-motivated.

A study by Johnson *et al.* (1991) of students, attributes good maintenance of procedures to participative management over five years. Blunden and Evans (1988) attributed good intervention maintenance partly to participative management, but state that this finding is only suggestive. There is a need for studies which contrast styles of management in a controlled way in the field of learning disabilities.

Nevertheless, there is sufficient evidence from industrial research (Hardy and Heyes, 1979) to make it worthwhile to consider the possible implications for the field of learning disabilities and challenging behaviour. It would appear that it is more effective for staff to participate in decision-making. However, this should occur within the framework of the overall aims of the service, as in a factory where, whichever style of management is used, the major aim is to manufacture certain products. It is worth emphasising at this point that democracy does *not* mean that staff can do what they like. Once decisions have been agreed upon, they should be implemented consistently. It would seem most efficient to delegate authority down the line to those who are in daily, direct contact with clients. Raynes *et al.* (1979) found that this approach resulted in better motivated staff and better outcomes for clients. Felce *et al.* (1985) stressed the importance of delegating decision-making and control to staff in small homes. This may have been one factor in the maintenance of improved quality of life for the residents of these houses (Saxby *et al.*, 1988).

It would appear that there should be minimal interference from higher management except to ensure that the overall aims of the service are being adhered to, and that there is a clear knowledge beforehand of the aims of the service and the risks people are allowed to take.

Behavioural methods of management

It is frequently assumed that behavioural methods can only be applied in an authoritarian way. Reid *et al.* (1989) state that very few studies identified whether behaviour management procedures were acceptable to staff or not. Behavioural methods were reported to be more effective than a more *laissez-*

faire management approach, but a more democratic style may have improved performance still further. Seys and Duker (1988) found that appointing a staff member to organise daily meetings, give feedback and prompt self-recording increased the amount of time staff spent training clients from ten minutes per group (not per person!) to twenty minutes per group. This is not likely to have made a great impact on the quality of life of an individual person within the group, but is an improvement nevertheless. Reid *et al.* (1989) do cite a few studies where staff self-managed their own activities (e.g. Burg *et al.*, 1979) but state that there is a need for more research. With increased interest in the social validity of interventions (see vol. 24 of the *Journal of Applied Behavioral Analysis* (1991) for a series of articles on this topic), staff satisfaction with interventions is now regarded as very important. Since staff satisfaction may be related to the degree of their participation in decision-making, it is important to involve care staff in the planning of any structured intervention.

The basic tenet behind the behavioural studies described in Reid *et al* is sound – management does not consist of merely telling people what to do or even discussing it with them. It is ensuring that they know how to do it, do not forget how and when to do it, and are motivated to do it. An essential first step is to have clear specific aims. Using a democratic approach may make management even more effective.

The procedures Reid *et al.* (1989) describe include:

Defining what has to be done
Monitoring what has to be done
Giving the member of staff instructions and
    organising goal planning procedures
Showing the individual what to do
Giving them feedback and motivating them to do it.

They cite many studies where there has been an improvement in staff performance as a result of these methods, which often combine training and management.

Parsons *et al.* (1989) outline a systematic procedure introduced in an institution which was threatened with closure if staff did not improve the amount of active treatment with clients. (In the USA there have been intensified efforts by regulatory agencies to encourage more comprehensive treatment services in living units.) Methods included structuring service-user leisure time, room management, staff training involving performance feedback by the supervisor, monitoring and feedback on what staff were doing at least weekly. The area director reviewed the written observations of the supervisor. The experimenter was responsible for supervising the area director. Active treatment increased from 20 per cent to 38 per cent after intervention and was maintained in different facilities from nine to fifteen months. This was a system that ensured that the people at the top of the organisation could check that the people at the bottom were doing what they were supposed to be doing.

Blunden and Evans (1988) report that a hierarchical management and reporting system appears to have been a significant factor in the maintenance after six years of relatively high levels of staff-client interaction during a one-hour daily activity period. However, they report that other less tangible features such as 'ownership' and 'commitment' by key staff also appear to have been important. Ward staff spoke of it as 'their project'. The senior charge nurse on the ward when the original research was conducted had identified strongly with the project and had published an account of it in the nursing press. Although he later transferred to another ward, most staff reported that his enthusiasm was a major factor in good maintenance.

All the procedures described by Reid *et al.* (1989) could be carried out in a participatory way: for instance, staff and service-users' could define what is to be done and how, with the service-users ideas feeding back into the overall aims of the organisation. Staff could self-monitor and reward, although with the caveat that what is done should be evaluated for effectiveness.

Reid *et al.* do not mention the use of intrinsic reinforcement (e.g. Haywood and Switzky, 1986), that is, attempting to make tasks more intrinsically interesting and enjoyable for staff so that they are more motivated to carry them out. The studies Reid *et al.* describe rely on the use of extrinsic reinforcement, where staff are rewarded by praise, money, etc. It seems probable that the more staff participate in the design and management of their tasks, the more they will choose tasks and methods which are more intrinsically satisfying for them, so lessening the need for extrinsic reinforcement.

Holborn (1990) points out the disadvantages of a system which is solely authoritarian and where staff are mainly reinforced extrinsically. He argues that in the USA: '. . . despite the pervasive philosophy of normalisation and the more recent emphasis on "quality assurance", service provisions in today's Medicaid-funded residential environment has become more regulation oriented and less person oriented. The newest enemy of people . . . is the very system designed to protect and ensure quality of life' (p. 89).

He states that there are a great number of rules which staff are required to follow, and argues that this produces excessive documentation to 'prove' that policies are being implemented and services are being provided. If these rules are not followed, this can lead to the termination of programme funding. Holborn concludes that this aversive consequence can lead to 'subversive' behaviours, such as falsifying data. He points out that intrinsic reinforcement is immediate, whilst the extrinsic reinforcement that is the result of rule-following is often delayed and may be inconsistent. Intrinsic reinforcement is therefore more likely to be effective. He advocates an increase in the opportunity for staff to be motivated intrinsically by what they do and (like Hayes *et al.*, 1986) suggests a reduction in the number of specific rules, with extrinsic reinforcement of more general rules being encouraged.

It appears that it is probably most effective to use both intrinsic and extrinsic methods, reserving the latter (particularly ones which are likely to be powerful, such as pay and promotion prospects) to ensure that the main aims of the service are adhered to. In the Johnson *et al.* (1991) study cited above, some external supervision and reinforcement in the form of prompts, spot checks and contingent rent reductions were used to encourage students to perform household chores. However, there was little need for further supervision over the five-year maintenance period. In other words, participative processes may decrease the need for intensive supervision (as Lewin *et al.* showed as early as 1939).

In addition to management processes which maximise staff motivation from day to day, there should be planning and recording systems in place (e.g. individual plans, teaching programmes, records of the day-to-day organ-isation of client activity) to ensure stability of performance over time, even with staff turnover. Supervisors can train new staff to implement these systems. Saxby *et al.* (1988) studied the maintenance of staff and client activity in two small community houses for adults with severe or profound learning disabilities. They attributed the impressively high level of service-user time (44% and 46%) spent in appropriate behaviour, even after several years, to systematic staff procedures which emphasised the planning and monitoring of resident activity throughout the day (Felce and de Kock, 1983).

STAFF STRESS AND SUPPORT

There are many definitions of stress. Woolfolk and Richardson (1979) defined stress as 'a perception of threat or expectation of future discomfort that arouses, alerts or otherwise activates the organism'.

They state that the arousal that is most often linked to stress is that of the fight-or-flight response. This is a basic, animal reaction, where hormones automatically set off reactions in the body (e.g. a stronger heart beat) which make it easier for an animal to either fight or run away in a dangerous situation. Because of our animal roots, human beings still tend to react automatically in this way to threat.

The Lazarus model (Folkman, 1984) defines stress in terms of the perceived ability to cope 'Stress is a relationship between the person and the environment that is appraised by the person as taxing or exceeding his or her resources and as endangering his or her well-being' (p. 840). Human beings can control their automatic tendencies to 'fight or flight' and can decrease stress by problem solving, by dealing with the cause of the stress. Both definitions cited above emphasise the importance of cognitive factors. Individuals will not feel stressed if they do not perceive a situation as threatening. Stress is sometimes associated with depression, in addition to arousal. For instance, the Malaise Inventory (Rutter *et al.* 1970), which taps depression, anxiety and psychosomatic concerns, has been used as a measure of stress (Byrne *et al.*, 1988).

Any of these factors may affect staff behaviour – whether an event is perceived as threatening or pleasantly exciting, whether the person is aroused to fight or avoid, whether they are depressed or whether they have the resources to cope productively with the situation, in a crisis or over time. However, due to the number of different definitions and the different means of measurement (generally speaking stress has been measured by self-report only, without measuring physiological reactions and without behavioural data) the conclusions reached in this section will be suggestive only.

Relationship of stress to challenging behaviour

It is worth noting that behaviour that is not initially seen as challenging, may do so if staff experience a build-up of stress in other areas of work. Individual behaviour which is defined as challenging by staff may in this situation best be seen as an indicator that staff management needs attention. On the other hand, staff may cope very well initially with seriously aggressive behaviour and yet if there is a build-up of stress in other areas of their work they may no longer be able to cope. Again, staff stress needs to be attended to, in order that they can continue coping and carrying out interventions with the individual. If a member of staff is undergoing considerable stress at home, they may need to work in less challenging situations until the situation is resolved.

Allen *et al.* (1990) found that hospital staff related behaviour problems to stress. Increased stress in parents is related to child behaviour problems (Byrne *et al.* 1988). Stoneman and Crapps (1988) found that greater stress was associated with fostered individuals who showed maladaptive behaviour. It is not clear from these studies whether the stress exacerbates the behaviour problems, the problems cause the stress or both, but it seems likely to be both, since:

1. Arousal can lead to an increased tendency to the 'fight' reaction. Carers may become more irritable and more likely to enter into conflict with service-users, which (particularly if the person is showing aggressive behaviour) is likely to escalate rather than ameliorate the situation.
2. Reducing behaviour problems may reduce stress – Quine (quoted in Wertheimer, 1991) noted that helping parents control their child's sleeping problems decreased stress.

Since stress in staff may intensify conflict with service-users, and since certain management styles have been associated with aggression, effective training and management are vital prerequisites for a challenging behaviour service.

Burn-out

Burn-out has been defined by Pines (1982) as the last stage of stress, a state of total exhaustion caused by working with people in emotionally demanding situations. Lazarus and Cohen (1978) report that stress appears to be a necessary condition for burn-out to occur, and although many workers experience job stress and do not burn out, none burn out without experiencing job stress.

Burn-out is correlated with poor physical health, sleeplessness, increased consumption of alcohol, headaches, backaches, stomach aches, nervousness, hopelessness and loss of idealism (Pines, 1982). As always, however, it is important to remember that a correlation does not indicate which factor is cause and which effect. Do people find it harder to cope if they are in poor physical health, does stress cause poor physical health or both? Maslach and Jackson (1981) found that the burn-out syndrome had three aspects 1) emotional exhaustion, 2) negative attitudes towards clients: 'the loss of concern for the people with whom one is working, . . . in which the professional no longer has any positive feelings, sympathy, or respect for clients or patients', 3) loss of feeling of accomplishment in the job. Burn-out has been related to absenteeism and turnover (Caton *et al.*, 1988).

It is obvious that stress in staff should be reduced long before it reaches the burn-out stage, both for the sake of the people themselves and because of the consequent negative effects on service-users.

Knapp *et al.* (1989), in their report on the staffing of twenty-eight community care projects, found that 21 per cent of staff turnover was due to stress, dissatisfaction or conflict. When staff leave, it is necessary to hire and train new staff. Since this is expensive, and can lead to a gap in services for a period, staff turnover due to stress should be minimised.

What creates stress?

Holt (1982) found that work stress was related to exclusion from decision-making, role ambiguity and role conflict, poor use of skills and abilities and demands the worker could not meet. Stressful events in the workers' personal life lowered resistance to occupational stress.

Although there is no clear evidence in the literature that the support of colleagues and supervisors reduces stress, high support has been correlated with lack of conflict, lack of role ambiguity, job security, the use of skills and participation in decision-making (Pinneau, 1975). In a study of child-abuse projects, the strongest predictor of burn-out was lack of leadership (Armstrong, 1979). Lack of support and structure was related to burn-out in new professionals in a public service agency (Cherniss, 1980).

It appears that stress is reduced if staff are clear about what they are supposed to do, have the skills to do it, and take part in participative decision-making.

Zastrow (1984) examined organisational and individual strategies for the reduction of stress. Organisational strategies ranged from case-load reduction, time away from pressure, limiting hours of stressful work, balancing stressful and non-stressful tasks, increased training, a pleasant working environment and a greater variety of work. Individual management strategies included time management through planning and prioritising goals (Lakein, 1973).

In the field of learning disabilities, major stressors identified have been inadequate staffing levels, lack of time, resources, training and management support (Allen *et al.*, 1990; Potts and Halliday, 1988; Fleming and Stenfert Kroese (1990); Thomson, 1987; Ward, 1989). Allen *et al.* (1990) found that in the community 'being left to cope alone with a poorly understood role accounted for much of the stress in the houses'. Disturbed nights followed by day shifts also increased stress. They found that house managers needed support from second-line managers. Fleming and Stenfert Kroese (in press) found that although staff in the community were able to take service-users out during the daytime, evening outings were very rare. This was due to low staff levels, and lack of transport facilities. Evenings, therefore, tended to be stressful as group homes were lacking in space and the member of staff was usually working alone for a long period of time. Thomson (1987) reported that staff found that most stress was created by the policies of the institution/agency, and the difference between what they could do and what they wanted to do. She noted that 'getting the work done' decreased stress.

Caton *et al.* (1988) found that there was a significant relationship between emotional exhaustion and under-utilisation of staff members' skills and abilities. However, it was not clear whether people were under-utilising their abilities because of exhaustion and/or that they were burnt out because their skills were going to waste.

Staff training and stress

Allen *et al.* (1990) emphasise strongly the importance of staff training. Ward (1989) and Stenfert Kroese and Fleming (1992) identify insufficient training in teaching new skills to clients as a source of stress. Ward (1989) reported that staff were also stressed by insufficient training in dealing with challenging behaviour.

Stoneman and Crapps (1988) discovered that foster parents who received training after accepting residents with learning disabilities into their home reported less client-related stress than did those without training.

Crawford (1990) emphasises the importance of training in giving staff support and makes the eminently sensible suggestion that training should be based on a task analysis of each person's job.

Changing perception and reducing arousal to decrease stress

In addition to these factors, stress may also be modified by changing a person's perception of a situation and by lowering their arousal level. These strategies are supplements to, and should not be used as substitutes for, addressing the cause of the distress.

In some cases it may be relatively simple to change people's perception of a situation: for instance, to explain that a person with Gilles de la Tourette syndrome is not swearing with malicious intent but is reacting involuntarily.

At other times, it may be more difficult to change the way in which staff interpret and react to events and they may need specific support or training. Cognitive-behavioural strategies have been widely used to help people control their emotions (anxiety, anger and depression), by changing their perceptions of their circumstances and thereby reducing arousal level, for example, decreasing anxiety by controlling fearful thoughts, relaxation, meditation, and a gradual approach to the feared situation (Beck *et al.*, 1979; Marks, 1981; Novaco, 1979). Zastrow (1984) suggests the use of cognitive therapy, relaxation, exercise, hobbies, and humour to alleviate stress. Humour and exercise decrease stress in staff working with people with learning diffiulties (Thomson, 1987). It would be interesting to know what makes people able to use positive constructive humour in stressful situations – is it related to degree of stress, to their understanding of the service-users' predicament, the degree to which staff feel able to cope or the general approach of the group of people with whom they work? What is it that allows one person when they are attacked to understand the point of view of the attacker and defuse their feelings with humour whilst another person feels offended, resentful and less willing to help the service-user in the future? The use of humour may also have negative results – clients may be made to feel 'devalued' by staff's humorous comments. It is important that staff are made aware of the distinction between shared hunour and 'abusive' humour.

Ideally, staff working with people with challenging behaviour should have the opportunity to learn these adaptive techniques. Mere 'book learning' or lectures will be unlikely to be effective. It is necessary for training to include a practice and feedback element. Staff will then be enabled to control their own stress; if they do not do this they may behave in counterproductive ways which the service-user may copy. Effective staff selection at hands-on and first line manager level is desirable to lessen the need for long, intensive training. An essential quality of someone working in the field is the willingness to look at their own behaviour and to learn to change it if necessary.

Support networks and teamwork

Byrne *et al.* (1988) review a substantial body of research which indicates that the support provided by one's social network can protect people from the harmful effects of stress (e.g. Gottlieb, 1981; Haggerty, 1980). Support networks act in three ways to protect against the harmful effects of stress and influence psychological well-being: they provide practical help and information, emotional empathy and understanding (Crnic *et al.*, 1983). Thomson (1987) found that staff working with people with learning disabilities believe that informal support to colleagues is the most helpful factor in alleviating stress. However, Stenfert Kroese and Fleming (1992) report that positive monitoring (Porterfield, 1987), quality circles and quality action groups (IDC, 1986) are rarely available for community-based residential workers.

I would also emphasise the importance of good teamwork. It seems desirable to promote co-operation rather than competition between colleagues, and to ensure that staff support each other in stressful situations rather than vent their frustration on each other, on the service-user or on management. The supervisor and management systems which reward co-operation can play a vital role in building a supportive team, particularly if individuals within the team have learnt to control (rather than merely deny) their own feelings, through informal support and, if necessary, training in the cognitive-behavioural strategies alluded to above.

CONCLUSION

The major problems currently facing services for people with learning disabilities and challenging behaviours are a lack of resources (Radford, 1988), the constant state of flux in services due to constant and rapid change of ideas, high staff turnover, differing aims and methods within and between Health and Social Services, and the amount of time spent on putting into practice the 'Care in the Community' principles.

And yet I am recommending more time spent on training and 'hands-on' management, since extensive knowledge and experience are needed, at least at the level where supervisors can directly observe untrained staff.

Time and money spent on training and management can be an eficient use of resources if this investment prevents crises occurring which absorb even more time and money. All too often, the opposite happens: staff are too busy attending to a constant series of crises to spend the time on the planning and training which would have helped them prevent the crises in the first place.

It is vital not to waste resources. Money spent on training will be wasted if staff already know what they are taught – it may be more important that they are motivated by good management to apply their knowledge (Ziarnik and Bernstein, 1982). Numerous investigations show that training is necessary but not sufficient (Adams *et al.*, 1980; Cullen, 1987; Edwards and Bergman, 1982; Gardner, 1972). Effective management is essential before and after training, to ensure that staff are motivated to pursue the aims of the service.

It may well be an effective use of resources to invest some challenging behaviour money in each district to train at least two first-line supervisors thoroughly (using the expertise already available locally, as well as external courses).

These staff should be selected for possessing a range of vital skills so that training needs to be less intensive. Competencies selected or trained should include management skills, organisation and recording, teaching and motivation, prevention of challenging behaviour, quality interaction and self-awareness and control.

These first-line managers should then have time and opportunity to train staff by direct 'on the job' supervision, and they should have clear ideas about how specifically to implement the overall aims of the service, as they will manage most efficiently without much time spent consulting with higher management. They should be rewarded by pay and promotion for fulfilling the aims well.

Wherever possible, there should be advocates for the people with learning disabilities, since they will not be able to state their case as persuasively as staff. Settings should be run democratically to be most intrinsically satisfying to both clients and staff. Co-operation rather than competition with other personnel in the setting and the service should be rewarded. Recording procedures (Felce and de Kock, 1983) should be in place to ensure that activities are carried out consistently over time even with staff turnover.

It is desirable to minimise the intrusiveness of training and supervision in the home of a person with learning disabilities. Allen *et al.* (1990) make the point that highly structured or detailed supervision may 'institutionalise' staff houses in the community. They report that workers in these settings generally wish to have a high degree of independence from supervision. On the other hand, they found that staff felt stressed being left to cope on their own with little feedback in a poorly understood role. It cannot be assumed that care staff have the ability or motivation to perform their job well, or that aims can be achieved without a degree of organisation. Allen *et al.* (1990) recommend intensive induction training before members of staff commence working in community homes. This may be worthwhile – if effective teaching methods, including opportunities for practice and feedback, are used – but again, staff will need further training and management in the 'real-life' setting.

References

Adams, G. L., Tallon, R. J. and Rimell, P. (1980), 'A comparison of lecture versus role-playing in the training of the use of positive reinforcement', *Journal of Organizational Behavior Management*, 2 (3), 205–12.

Allen, P., Pahl, J. and Quine, L. (1990), *Care Staff in Transition: The Impact on Staff of Changing Services for People with Mental Handicaps*, HMSO, London.

Armstrong, K. L. (1979), 'How to avoid burn-out: a study of the relationship between burn-out and worker; organisational and management characteristics in 11 child abuse and neglect projects', *Child Abuse and Neglect*, 3, 145–49.

Beck, A. T., Rush, A. J., Shaw, B. F. and Emery, G. (1979), *Cognitive Therapy of Depression*, Guilford, New York.

Bersani, H. R. and Heifetz, L. J. (1985), 'Perceived stress and satisfaction of direct-care staff members in community residences for mentally retarded adults', *American Journal of Mental Deficiency*, 90, 289–95.

BIMH and CCETSW (1989), *A Guide to Training Resources in Mental Handicap* (1st ed.), Kidderminster.

Brechin, A. and Swain, J. (1987), *Changing Relationships*, Harper and Rowe, London.

Blunden, R. and Allen, D. (1987), *Facing the Challenge: An Ordinary Life for People with Learning Difficulties and Challenging Behaviour*, Kings Fund, London.

Blunden, R. and Evans, G. (1988), 'Long-term maintenance of staff and resident behaviour in a hospital ward for adults with mental handicaps: report of a six year follow-up', *Mental Handicap Research*, 1, 115–26.

Burg, M. M., Reid, D. H. and Lattimore, J. (1979), 'Use of a self-recording and supervision program to change institutional staff behavior', *Journal of Applied Behavior Analysis*, 12, 363–75.

Byrne, E. A., Cunningham, C. C. and Sloper, P. (1988), *Families and their children with Down's Syndrome: One Feature in Common*, Routledge, London.

Carr, E. and Durand, V.M. (1985), 'Reducing behavior problems through functional communication training', *Journal of Applied Behavior Analysis*, 18, 111–26.

Caton, D. J., Grossnickle, W. F., Cope, J. G., Long, T. E. and Mitchell, C. C. (1988), Burn-out and stress among employees at a state institution for mentally retarded persons', *American Journal on Mental Retardation*, 93, 300–04.

Cherniss, C. (1980), *Staff Burn-out – Job Stress in the Human Services*, Sage Publications, Beverley Hills, CA.

Clegg, J. (1990), 'Interactions between staff and adults with profound intellectual disabilities', paper presented at the British Institute of Mental Handicap Conference, York.

Crawford, J. V. (1990), 'Maintaining staff morale: the value of a staff training and support network', *Mental Handicap*, 18, 48–51.

Crnic, K. A., Greenberg, M., Ragozin, A., Robinson, N. and Basham, R. (1983), 'Effects of stress and social support on mothers of premature and full term infants', *Child Development*, 54, 209–17.

Cullen, C. (1987), 'Nurse training and institutional constraints', in J. Hogg and P. Mittler (eds.), *Staff Training in Mental Handicap*, Croom Helm, London.

Cummings, R., Emerson, E., Barrett., McCool, C., Toogood, A. and Hughes, H. (1989), 'Challenging behaviour and community services: 4, Establishing services', *Mental Handicap*, 17, 13–16.

Dailey, W. F., Allen, G. J., Chinsky, J. M. and Veit, S. M. (1974), 'Attendant behavior and attitudes towards institutionalized children', *American Journal of Mental Deficiency*, 78, 586–91.

Donnellan, A. M., Mirenda, P. L., Mesaros, R. A. and Fassbender, L. L. (1984), 'Analyzing the communicative functions of aberrant behavior', *Journal of the Association for the Severely Handicapped*, 9 (3), 201–12.

Douglas, R. (1985), *The Manager as Trainer*, (A resource pack developed on behalf of the Local Government Training Board at the National Institute for Social Work), Local Government Management Board, Luton.

Durand, V. M. and Carr, E. G. (1987), 'Social influences on "self-stimulatory" behavior: analysis and treatment application', *Journal of Applied Behavior Analysis*, 20, 119–32.

Durand, V. M. and Carr, E. G. (1991), 'Functional communication training to reduce challenging behavior: Maintenance and application in new settings', *Journal of Applied Behavior Analysis*, 24, 251–64.

Edwards, G. and Bergman, J. S. (1982), 'Evaluation of a feeding training program for caregivers of individuals who are severely physically handicapped', *Journal of the Association for the Severely Handicapped*, 7, 93–101.

Farrell, P. (1985), EDY: *Its Impact on Staff Training in Mental Handicap*, Manchester University Press, Manchester.

Felce, D. and de Kock, U. (1983), *Planning Client Activity: A Handbook*, Health Care Evaluation Research Team, Southampton University, Southampton.

Felce, D., De Kock, U., Saxby, H. and Thomas, M. (1985), *Small Homes for Severely and Profoundly Mentally Handicapped Adults*, final report for the DHSS.

Fleming, I. and Stenfert Kroese, B. (1990), *Evaluation of a community care project for people with learning disabilities*, Journal of Mental Deficiency Research, 34, 451–64.

Folkman, S. (1984), 'Personal control and stress and coping processes: a theoretical analysis', *Journal of Personality and Social Psychology*, 46, 839–52.

Gardner. J. M. (1972), 'Teaching behavior modification to non-professionals', *Journal of Applied Behavior Analysis*, 5, 517–21.

Gottlieb, B. H. (ed.) (1981), *Social Networks and Social Support*, Sage, Beverly Hills, CA.

Grant, G. W. B. and Moores, B. (1977), 'Resident characteristics and staff behavior in two hospitals for mentally retarded adults', *American Journal of Mental Deficiency*, 82, 259–65.

Greenberg, M., Ragozin, A., Robinson, N. and Basham, R. (1983), 'Effects of stress and social support on mothers of premature and full term infants', *Child Development*, 54, 209–17.

Haggerty, R. J. (1980), 'Life stress, illness and social supports', *Developmental Medicine and Child Neurology*, 22, 391–400.

Hardy, M. and Heyes, S. (1979), *Beginning Psychology*, Weidenfeld and Nicolson, London.

Hayes, S. C., Brownstein, A. J., Haas, J. R. and Greenway, D. E. (1986), 'Instructions, multiple schedules, and extinction: distinguishing rule-governed from schedule-controlled behavior', *Journal of the Experimental Analysis of Behavior*, 46, 137–47.

Haywood, H. C. and Switzky, H. N. (1986), 'Intrinsic motivation and behavior effectiveness in retarded persons' in N. R. Ellis and N. W. Bray (eds.), *International Review of Research in Mental Retardation*, 14, 1–46, Academic Press: London.

Hogg, J. and Mittler, P. (1987), *Staff Training in Mental Handicap*, Croom Helm, London.

Holborn, C. S. (1990), 'Rules: the new institutions', *Mental Retardation*, 28, 89–94.

Holt, R. (1982), 'Occupational stress', in L. Goldberger and S. Breznitz (eds.), *Handbook of Stress: Theoretical and Clinical Aspects*, Free Press, New York, pp. 419–44.

Independent Development Council for People with Mental Handicap (1986). *Pursuing Quality. How Good are your Local Services for People with Mental Handicap?*, King's Fund Centre, London.

Jacobson, N. S. and Margolin, G. (1979), *Marital Therapy*, Brunner Mazel, New York.

Johnson, S. P., Welsh, T. M., Miller, L. K. and Altus, D. E. (1991), 'Participatory management: maintaining staff performance in a university housing cooperative', *Journal of Applied Behavior Analysis*, 24, 119–27.

Knapp, M., Cambridge, P. and Thomason, C. (1989), *Final Report of an Evaluation of the Care in the Community Initiative*, PSSRU, Kent.

Lakein, A. (1973), *How to Get Control of Your Time and Your Life*, Signet, New York.

Lally, J. (1988), 'When anger is a cry for help', *Community Living*, 2, 16–17.

Lally, J. (1989), 'Evaluation of a checklist used to identify possible reasons for aggressive behavior', British Psychological Society conference paper, London.

Lazarus, R. S. and Cohen, J. B. (1978), 'Environmental stress', in I. Altman and J. F. Wohlvill (eds.), *Human Behavior and the Environment: Current Theory and Research*, Plenum, New York.

Lewin, K., Lippett, R. and White, R. K. (1939), 'Patterns of aggressive behavior in experimentally created social climates', *Journal of Social Psychology*, 10, 271–99.

Lister, T. M. and Rapley, M., *Insight into Challenges*, Barnardos (in press).

McBrien, J.A. and Foxen, T.H. (1987) A pyramid model of staff training in behavioral methods: the EDY project' in J. Hogg and P. Mittler (eds.), *Staff Training in Mental Handicap*, Manchester University Press, Manchester.

McCubbin, H.I. and Thompson, A.I. (1987), *Family Assessment Inventories for Research and Practice*, University of Wisconsin, Madison, WI.

Marks, I. M. (1981), *Cure and Care of Neuroses: Theory and Practice of Behavioral Psychotherapy*, Wiley, New York.

Maslach, C. and Jackson, S. E. (1981), T'he measurement of experienced burn-out', *Journal of Occupational Behavior*, 2, 99–113.

Novaco, R. W. (1979), 'The cognitive regulation of anger and stress', in P. C. Kendall and S. D. Hollon (eds.), *Cognitive-behavioral Interventions*, Academic Press, New York.

O'Brien, J. (1987), 'A guide to personal futures planning', in G. T. Bellamy and B. Wilcox (eds.), *A Comprehensive Guide to the Activities Catalog: An Alternative Curriculum for Youth and Adults with Severe Disabilities*, Paul H. Brookes, Baltimore, MD.

Page, T. J., Iwata, B. A. and Reid, D. (1982), 'Pyramidal training: a large-scale application with institutional staff', *Journal of Applied Behavior Analysis*, 15, 335–51.

Parsons, M., Cash, V. B. and Reid, D. (1989), 'Improving residential treatment services: implementation and norm-referenced evaluation of a comprehensive managment system', *Journal of Applied Behavior Analysis*, 22, 143–56.

Parsons, M. B., Schepis, M. M., Reid, D. H., McCarn, J. E. and Green, C. W. (1987), 'Expanding the impact of behavioral staff management: a large-scale, long-term application in schools serving severely handicapped students', *Journal of Applied Behavior Analysis*, 20, 139–50.

Patterson, G. R. and Stouthamer-Loeber, M. (1984), 'The correlation of family management practices and delinquency', *Child Development*, 55, 1299–1307.

Pines, A. M. (1982), 'Changing organisations', in W. S. Paine (ed.), *Job stress and Burnout: Research, Theory and Intervention Perspectives*, Sage Publications, Beverley Hills, CA.

Pinneau, S. R. (1975), 'Effects of social support on psychological and physiological strains', Ph.D. thesis, University of Michigan, Ann Arbor, MI.

Porterfield, J. (1987), *Positive Monitoring*, BIMH Publications, Kidderminster.

Potts, M. and Halliday, S. (1988), 'Hostel to house – measuring the effects of change', paper presented at the DCP Birthday Conference, York.

Radford, N. (1988), 'Be prepared', *Nursing Times*, 84 (1), 66.

Raynes, N., Pratt, M. and Roses, S. (1979), *Organisational Structure and the Care of the Mentally Retarded*, Croom Helm, London.

Reid, D. H., Parsons, M. B. and Green, C. W. (1989), *Staff Management in Human Services*, Charles C. Thomas, IL.

Reid, D. H., Parsons, M. B., McCarn, J. E., Green, C. W., Phillips, J. F and Schepis, M. M. (1985), 'Providing a more appropriate education for severely handicapped persons: increasing and validating functional classroom tasks', *Journal of Applied Behavior Analysis*, 18, 289–301.

Rutter, M., Tizard, J. and Whitmore, K. (1970), *Education, Health and Behavior*, Longman, London.

Saxby, H., Felce, D., Harman, M. and Repp, A. (1988), 'The maintenance of client activity and staff-client interaction in small community houses for severely and profoundly mentally handicapped adults: a two year follow-up', *Behavioral Psychotherapy*, 16, 189–206.

Seys, D. and Duker, P. (1988), 'Effects of staff management on the quality of residential care for mentally retarded individuals', *American Journal on Mental Retardation*, 93, 290–99.

Shoemaker, J. and Reid, D. H. (1980), 'Decreasing chronic absenteeism among institutional staff: effects of a low-cost attendance program', *Journal of Organizational Behavior Management*, 2(4), 317–28.

Stenfert Kroese, B. K. and Fleming, I. (1992), 'Staff attitudes and working conditions in community-based group homes of people with learning difficulties', *Mental Handicap Research*, 5, 82–91.

Stoneman, Z. and Crapps, J. M. (1988), 'Correlates of stress, perceived competence and depression among family care providers', *American Journal on Mental Retardation*, 93, 166–73.

Thomson, S. (1987), 'Stress in staff working with mentally handicapped people', in R. Payne and J. Firth-Cozens (eds.), *Stress in Health Professionals*, John Wiley and Sons, Chichester.

Walrond-Skinner, S. (1977), *Family Therapy*, 2nd edn, London, Routledge and Kegan Paul, London, Boston and Henley.

Ward, L. (1989), ' "An ordinary life": the early views and experiences of residential staff in the Wells Road Service', *Mental Handicap*, 17, 6–9.

Watson, L. S. and Uzell, R. (1980), 'A program for teaching behavior modification skills to institutional staff', *Applied Research in Mental Retardation*, 1, 41–53.

Wertheimer, A. (1991), 'Stopping a long day's journey into night', *Search*, 9, May, 29–32.

Woolfolk, R. L. and Richardson, F. C. (1979), *Stress, Sanity and Survival*, Futura Publications, London.

Zastrow, C. (1984), 'Understanding and preventing burn-out', *British Journal of Social Work*, 14, 141–55.

Ziarnik, J. P. and Bernstein, G. S. (1982), 'A critical examination of the effect of inservice training on staff performance', *Mental Retardation*, 20, 109–14.

Intervention issues

The application of functional analysis in the treatment of challenging behaviour

The aim of this chapter is to make explicit the rationale for conducting a functional analysis. It also outlines the current methods available for performing such an analysis, along with the strengths and weaknesses associated with each method. The clinical implications of functional analysis are explored and case examples provided to demonstrate how functional data can be used to guide intervention decisions.

INTRODUCTION

Psychological assessment has been defined as the 'systematic use of a variety of special techniques in order to better understand a given individual, group or social ecology' (McReynolds, 1968). Behaviourists believe that people's behaviours are influenced by events which precede and follow them. Therefore, in order to achieve an understanding of how people behave, the functional relationships between the behaviour, its antecedents and its consequences must be investigated and described. This then is the role of functional analysis (Kiernan, 1974). The primary concern of clinicians working with people who display challenging behaviour is not usually the understanding of behaviour *per se*, but the devising and implementing of effective interventions to decrease such behaviours. This urgency for intervention at the expense of understanding appears to have led to the demise of functional analysis (Oliver and Head, 1990). Whilst it is easy to understand how protracted periods of assessment can appear unethical in the eyes of those who view the need for intervention as paramount, it is the aim of this chapter to show that such an omission is, in fact, a false economy. If the aim of clinicians is to produce long-lasting, generalisable change with the least intrusive, non-aversive behavioural method then a thorough understanding of the behaviour is a crucial first step.

The stimuli which trigger and maintain challenging behaviour in people with learning difficulties are not completely understood but models are being constructed which attempt to describe the complex ways that potential stimuli may interact, to both 'cause' and maintain such behaviour. These integrated models have moved away from viewing behaviours as having a unitary cause but instead stress the interaction between 'risk' factors, i.e. those which predispose individuals to develop challenging behaviours; 'onset' factors, i.e. those which are associated with the first occurrence of the challenging behaviour and operant, 'process' factors which reinforce and so maintain the behaviour. Oliver and Head (1990) have described such a model for the development and maintenance of self-injurious behaviour (SIB) in people with learning disabilities and Clare *et al.* (in press) have investigated similar processes to help explain fire-setting among people with learning disabilities.

In essence these models propose that people with learning disabilities may be predisposed to develop challenging behaviour for a number of reasons. For example, the reliable association found between Lesch-Nyhan syndrome and SIB (Christie *et al.*, 1982) indicates a direct organic contribution to the behaviour. Similarly, the increased rates of behavioural difficulties among children with language problems (Richman *et al*, 1982) and social impairments (Wing, 1987) suggest that such deficits also have a predisposing role. Without adequate communication skills, achieving effective interaction with the environment becomes unreliable. Subtle attempts at communication such as raising a hand or calling out may be missed entirely or misinterpreted by care staff. Challenging behaviours may provide the only effective method available for individuals to get their needs met. Challenging behaviours, almost by definition, are guaranteed to provoke a response from carers. Indeed, carers are much more likely to respond to undesirable behaviours than appropriate behaviours (Felce *et al.*, 1987). In this way the factors which predispose individuals to develop challenging behaviour can interact with the strategies which carers employ to respond to the problem behaviours, making the occurrence of challenging behaviour even more likely. Management strategies involve the presentation of valued stimuli, for example, attention, distraction in the form of food, drink or alternative occupation and restraining devices, or they may involve the removal of aversive stimuli, such as the termination of a demand or social situation. The actions of carers can therefore unwittingly serve to either positively or negatively reinforce the very behaviour they are designed to reduce.

One of the least understood elements of these integrated models of challenging behaviour is the range of onset factors. Minor illnesses such as ear infections have been recorded as leading to self-injurious head banging (DeLissovoy, 1963), but the events leading to the first act of any challenging behaviour are generally poorly documented. Despite this gap in the models, the implications of viewing challenging behaviour as the result of an interaction between a potential multiplicity of predisposing onset and maintenance influences are clear. Firstly, a formal functional analysis is required to aid understanding of the processes which trigger and maintain the challenging behaviour. Secondly, if it is accepted that challenging behaviour can fulfil certain needs for people by compensating for communication skills deficits, then emphasis must be given to teaching alternative, socially acceptable skills which will serve the same function as the challenging behaviour. It is therefore argued that a skills-building element should form an integral part of any intervention designed to decrease challenging behaviour.

Let us consider what would happen if the first of these requirements was not met. It is often assumed that social attention is the primary maintaining factor for many challenging behaviours. If this assumption is carried through to its logical treatment conclusions, it would be expected that some form of time-out from social attention or social extinction would comprise part of the intervention package for the challenging behaviour, along with a skills-building component aimed at enhancing socially acceptable 'attention getting skills'. Such an intervention strategy may well prove to be effective, but only if the original assumption regarding the maintaining variable was correct. If the behaviour was in fact maintained by self-stimulatory feedback, as may occur with a stereotypy or self-injurious behaviour, then it would be predicted that such intervention would have no impact on the levels of the behaviour. If social avoidance or social escape were maintaining the behaviour, it would be predicted that a time-out strategy would actually increase the behaviour and the skills-building component would be completely redundant. In this latter example, failure to understand the behaviour prior to the implementation of the time-out intervention would result in the behaviour being rewarded each time it occurred. With the former example, the contingencies maintaining the behaviour would remain untouched by the behaviour programme, leaving the behaviour also unchanged. Unless an objective analysis is made of the variables which maintain challenging behaviour, illogical decisions will be made in the devising of intervention strategies. Such decision-making errors would then compromise the potential effectiveness of behavioural programmes. Functional analysis not only aims to identify the maintaining variables of a behaviour but also the potential predisposing and onset factors. Such a thorough assessment increases the treatment options available to clinicians by suggesting possible preventative strategies and antecedent manipulation strategies as well as consequent manipulation strategies.

The second requirement for the implementation of effective interventions is the understanding of challenging behaviour in terms of it serving an adaptive purpose for the individual, such as gaining pleasant stimuli or terminating and avoiding unpleasant stimuli. If this is ignored the focus of behavioural interventions becomes simply the eradication of challenging behaviour in isolation from the building of appropriate and socially acceptable skills. Such an orientation not only promotes the use of punitive and aversive interventions (see Chapter 10) but also bodes ill for the long-term maintenance of behaviour change (Murphy and Wilson, 1981). If the 'need' to display the behaviour remains, and no alternative skills are taught to meet that need, then it is likely that the challenging behaviour will re-emerge once the aversive consequence is terminated. Teaching a socially appropriate behaviour which allows the individual to interact effectively with his or her environment (Carr and Durand, 1985) hopefully reduces the need to engage in challenging behaviour. Subsequently, the likelihood that inappropriate behaviour will re-emerge in the long term is reduced and the influence of predisposing factors in the development of challenging behaviour is minimised.

In summary, the role of functional analysis in helping to understand behaviour is crucial to the development of logical intervention strategies aimed at both reducing the challenging behaviour and increasing appropriate skills, which are functionally equivalent to the undesirable behaviour.

METHODS OF CARRYING OUT A FUNCTIONAL ANALYSIS

Having discussed the importance of employing functional analysis in any intervention aimed at the amelioration of problem behaviours, we move on to consider the different methods which have been developed to carry out this assessment.

At present there are five broad categories of methodology which may be employed, either singly or in combination, to assess the functional relationships between a behaviour and its social environment. However, there is no consensus regarding the necessary and sufficient operations which constitute the completion of a functional analysis (Lundervold and Bourland, 1988). Each method will be discussed in terms of the amount and quality of the information which it generates and the practicalities of its application in a clinical setting.

Interview techniques

The most popular technique for conducting a functional analysis for challenging behaviour in clinical practice is to interview the client's parents, carers or teacher. The interview will seek to determine antecedents and consequences to the target behaviour and will also obtain information on broader setting events, e.g. location, noise levels, and individual characteristics, e.g. epilepsy, sensory impairments, which may influence the occurrence of the behaviour. This method relies on the interviewing skills of the practitioner coupled with the observational skills of the informant. The reliability and validity of the answers given will be influenced by the subjective interpretation and selective recall of the behaviour by the informant. Apart from checklists, which are discussed later in this section, it is surprising to note that there have been no attempts to develop standardised interview schedules for determining the functional relationships between challenging behaviours and their social environment. A structured interview format with proven reliability and validity would be an extremely useful tool for practitioners working in this area. Interviews enable practitioners to sample across large time periods while remaining a quick and easy method of collecting information. This method of carrying out a functional analysis is likely to continue to remain a popular option, especially for low frequency behaviour or behaviour which occurs in very specific settings.

ABC charts

The second method for devising a functional analysis of a challenging behaviour is to use Antecedent-Behaviour-Consequence (ABC) charts to record the chain of events associated with the target behaviour. Carers are asked to note down every incident of behaviour occurrence over an extended time period in order to establish a baseline record. In completing an ABC chart, the respondent provides information on antecedents (what has happened before the target behaviour), the behaviour itself and the consequences (what happened afterwards). In order to facilitate a meaningful interpretation of the data it is important to ensure that all occurrences of the target behaviour are recorded and that behaviour descriptions are clearly specified, e.g. 'banged his head on the carpet and cried for five minutes', rather than 'had a temper tantrum'. There is considerable variation in the level of complexity and detail required by different ABC charts but there have been no evaluations of the treatment efficacy of different formats. For high frequency behaviour, e.g. behaviour which occurs at a rate of more than once per hour, this method of conducting a functional analysis may not be practical. One way of overcoming this problem would be to record only the first incident of the target behaviour which occurred in each hour of the day. This is a more objective method of collecting data on ABC chains as it is less likely to be influenced by the carer or parent's selective memory of the event and their interpretation of its meaning. However, the interpretation of results obtained from ABC charts rests on an assumption about the relationships within this chain. While the antecedents and consequences identified by this method have a temporal association with the behaviour there may not be a functional relationship between them.

Natural observations

Direct observation of a client's behaviour in his or her domestic, educational and/or work environment is another commonly used method for carrying out a functional analysis. Edelson, Taubman and Lovaas (1983) employed this method when assessing a group of twenty children exhibiting challenging behaviour. By randomly sampling each child's behaviour at different times on different days, they found that for nineteen of the twenty children, there was an association between staff's presentation of demands, social denials and verbal punishments and a subsequent increase in the rate of challenging behaviour.

However, in their analyses Edelson *et al.* (1983) collapsed demands, social denials and verbal punishment into one category, thus obscuring the identification of a possible function for each child's difficult behaviour, and failed to record the consequent events which followed each episode of difficult behaviour. The results of this study provided only half the picture by revealing a temporal association between challenging behaviour and certain social antecedents but giving very little information about possible functions of the behaviour for each child. Using a continuous recording method rather than a time-sampling technique is clearly preferable to interval time-sampling when seeking to establish the complete antecedents-behaviour-consequences cycle, and is not difficult to achieve with the use of a video recorder or lap-top microcomputer.

This method of conducting a functional analysis depends on the practitioner's clinical skills in correctly identifying the qualitative and quantitative properties of the behaviours in question. Natural observations can be both time-consuming and tedious for behaviours which are not of high frequency. Observer reactivity, that is, the extent to which staff or parents alter their behaviour as a direct result of the presence of an observer, is a difficult variable to measure but it is a potential influence which must be considered when interpreting the results of a functional analysis undertaken by this method.

Analogue observations

A more recently established method of determining the function of a challenging behaviour for a given individual is to create a number of analogue conditions (artificially created environments) in order to test systematically the validity of different hypotheses as explanations for an individual's challenging behaviour. This method, which has been developed by psychologists working with individuals who show self-injurious behaviour (Iwata *et al.*, 1982; Carr and Durand, 1985), involves the manipulation of environmental events to observe their effects on the frequency of occurrence of the challenging behaviour. The aim is to determine which reinforcers are operating to maintain the behaviour in the individual's natural environment. The four analogue conditions employed by Iwata *et al.* (1982) comprised Social Disapproval (easy task, social attention contingent on occurrence of self-injurious behaviour), Academic Demand (difficult task, withdrawal of social attention contingent on self-injurious behaviour), Unstructured Play (easy task, social attention contingent on non-occurrence of self-injurious behaviour) and Alone (no task, no social attention). Six of the nine children who participated in this study showed higher levels of self-injury associated with particular stimulus conditions, indicating that their challenging behaviour was a function of specific environmental characteristics. However, three children did not show differential rates of self-injurious behaviour across the four conditions.

Analogue methodology has undoubtedly contributed to the understanding of some categories of challenging behaviour, and recent research has begun to investigate its predictive validity by examining the efficacy of treatment interventions derived from this method (e.g. Durand and Carr, 1987). However, there are a number of limitations with regard to the information which is generated by this method and the practicalities of using analogue environments in a clinical setting. The use of analogue observations may be a time-consuming and non-productive investigation for approximately one third of individuals (Iwata *et al.* 1982, Sturmey, Carlsen, Crisp and Newton, 1988). This may be because the small number of experimental environments set up to test a specific hypothesis sample only a small subset of the social environments which may be experienced by an individual with learning difficulties. This may lead to a number of problems when interpreting the data. First, an analogue condition which represents, for example, Social Disapproval, may not provide an accurate representation of an individual's experience of this event in his or her daily life and may lead to erroneous inferences regarding the function of a particular behaviour. Second, an individual may not experience one or more of the analogue conditions, perhaps due to environmental deprivation and low staffing levels or to staff's efforts to minimise the frequency of a challenging behaviour by avoiding circumstances which seem to lead to its occurrence.

Carrying out a functional analysis of an individual's behaviour using analogue observations may be difficult to achieve in a clinical setting where accommodation and resources are limited. This technique also demands trained staff to undertake the assessment and is only applicable for challenging behaviour of high frequency. Before using analogue observations to assess the functional significance of challenging behaviour, especially self-injurious behaviour, practitioners need to consider the ethical implications of employing an assessment technique which may provoke high rates of the target behaviour and result in client distress. For high frequency behaviour which has generalised to a large number of settings it may be more useful to test proposed hypotheses by attempting to create a social environment where low rates of the behaviour occur.

Motivation Assessment Scale

Finally, the most recent contribution to functional analysis methodology has been the development of a number of informant questionnaires. The Motivation Assessment Scale (MAS) developed by Durand and Crimmins (1988) has received the most attention from researchers in this field. This assessment device is a sixteen-item questionnaire which seeks to evaluate the relative influence of an individual's desire for social attention, tangible rewards, escape from non-preferred activities and sensory stimulation on problem behaviour. The reliability and validity of this instrument have been described (Durand and Crimmins, 1988), although both can be criticised. Firstly, there is no description of the population of children who were used in the standardisation process in terms of their ages, cognitive abilities, etc. Secondly, in calculating the inter-rater reliability of the measure, the researchers quoted percentage agreement figures for individual items which were not corrected for chance using the Kappa Co-efficient and which were surprisingly low, ranging from 0·26 to 0·79, even without this correction. There is no mention of whether items of low inter-rater reliability were subsequently revised or excluded from the measure. Finally, validity was assessed by comparing MAS scores with the results obtained from other methods of carrying out a functional analysis rather than investigating the ability of the MAS to predict treatment effectiveness.

With regard to the information yielded by the MAS, the scores obtained following its administration certainly give clues as to the broad set of motivating factors which may be maintaining the behaviour, and assist in prompting staff and parents to systematically analyse how environmental factors might be influencing the client's behaviour. However, the MAS is unlikely to give a sufficiently detailed functional analysis which could lead straight on to an intervention plan. Bird, Dores, Moniz and Robinson (1989) used the MAS together with direct observations to carry out a functional analysis of self-injury and physical aggression in two single case studies. Functional communication training proved successful in decreasing the levels of these behaviours.

In using the MAS in the clinical setting, further practical difficulties arise. Firstly, the seven-point rating scale for behaviour frequency is problematic when raters attempt to distinguish between the meanings of 'almost never' and 'seldom'.

Secondly, the set of questions do not have universal applicability to all problem behaviours, for example, the items for rating sensory stimulation are not meaningful when considering physical aggression. Thirdly, it is difficult to ensure that the rater is interpreting each item correctly and considering the frequency with which the behaviour occurs in relation to the setting description, rather than the frequency with which the setting condition occurs in relation to the behaviour. The MAS seeks to determine the functional significance of a behaviour by investigating how frequently it occurs in response to particular social environments. Fourthly, the accuracy of the responses to some MAS items which ask about functional communication must be questioned when applied to individuals with profound learning difficulties. Finally, staff and parents sometimes experience difficulty in perceiving and understanding the difference between similarly rated items on the checklist, especially if previously they have not considered the potential influence of environmental events on the individual's behaviour.

Discussion

It is extremely important for clinicians to be aware of the reliability and validity of the methods and measures which they are using if meaningful interpretations are to be made. Somewhat surprisingly, researchers have failed to investigate the predictive validity of any of the methods described in this section and therefore we do not know which method is most likely to result in a favourable therapeutic outcome for any given set of circumstances. Furthermore, there has been only one study which has investigated the reliability of these different methodologies by measuring the level of agreement in determining functions for behaviours when provided with the same set of client referrals. This investigation, described by Oliver (1988), used clinical interviews, observations in the natural environment and observations in an experimental setting to determine the functional significance of a total of twelve challenging behaviours for five clients. Calculating agreement on function identification across the three methods for all behaviours produced a 35 per cent level of agreement for the presence of a function and a 37 per cent level of agreement for the absence of a function. Further analysis of the data revealed that analogue methodology was more likely to fail to identify a function for a behaviour when it is operative, while clinical interviews and natural observations increased the likelihood that a function will be ascribed to a behaviour when it is not functional.

In view of the lack of information on the predictive validities of each of these methods, coupled with the difficulties identified for each method, it is recommended that a combination of methods is utilised when conducting a functional analysis.

For high frequency behaviours, those which occur once an hour or more, using a semi-structured interview followed by naturalistic observations is recommended, while for behaviours of low frequency, those which occur less than once an hour, a combination of ABC charts followed by analogue observations is recommended. Semi-structured interviews and ABC charts act as useful screening devices which ensure that large time periods and a range of settings are sampled in the assessment. This information will assist the clinician in identifying activities, times of the day and other environmental factors which are associated with the occurrence of the behaviour. The functional significance of a behaviour may be identified at this stage but if not, then naturalistic or analogue observations will be useful in hypothesizing the likely components of the Antecedent–Behaviour–Consequences chain.

Given the plethora of information regarding how to carry out a functional analysis, it is interesting to learn from Lundervold and Bourland's (1988) review of intervention studies in this area that fewer than 13 per cent of their sample of published articles carried out a functional analysis prior to intervention. The vast majority, nearly 62 per cent, did not report using any method for determining the functional significance of a behaviour and also failed to provide a rationale for their chosen intervention plan. Nearly 13 per cent of studies relied on past treatment effects to determine their selection. Indeed, even those studies which state that functional analysis was used as an assessment tool to guide intervention choices gave insufficient detail of the methods used or neglected to carry out a complete analysis. This suggests that practitioners are still opting for techniques designed to decelerate intervention rather than basing their selection on the variables hypothesized to be controlling the target behaviour (Lennox and Miltenberger, 1989). Mace *et al.* (1988) have reported a single-case study which utilised functional analysis to develop a treatment strategy to reduce a young woman's bizarre speech. While they employed a combination of interviews with staff and analogue observations to carry out the functional analysis, this assessment focused on the relationship between the behaviour and its antecedents and failed to investigate events which followed the behaviour. Examination of the Antecedent-Behaviour relationship provides an incomplete picture of the ABC chain and does not demonstrate the functional significance of a behaviour.

In summary, this section has described the various methods of conducting a functional analysis focusing on the usefulness of the information obtained and the practical utility of each method when applied in a clinical setting. The paucity of research to investigate the reliability and validity of these methods has been highlighted, along with some proposals aimed at guiding practitioners in their choice of method.

DIFFICULTIES WITH FUNCTIONAL ANALYSIS

The previous two sections have identified the rationale and methodology for conducting a functional analysis. They have hopefully also served to alert readers to the fact that the reinstatement of functional analysis in the intervention decision-making process is neither straightforward nor the answer to all clinicians' problems with challenging behaviour. The methodology section above outlined a number of difficulties posed by each possible assessment method. Even if a combination of methods is used to overcome the drawbacks of individual methods this, in itself, raises its own problems. The more techniques that are used, the longer the assessment period will take and it can be difficult to convince carers of the value of assessment activities when the short-term implication is a delay in the start of treatment. If carers' co-operation is lost at this stage of treatment it bodes ill for the implementation of the intervention. Without a committed and consistent approach by carers, the treatment plan is likely to fail. Staff training may be able to highlight the integral part assessment plays in designing intervention packages, but this too results in a delay in the application of an intervention.

A further difficulty which arises from performing a functional analysis involves the assumption that each challenging behaviour meets one specific need or has one specific function for each individual. Given that individuals

Table 7.1   *Levels of challenging behaviour expected in different conditions given three different maintenance hypotheses* (Carr and Durand, 1985)

Hypothesis Condition	Attention maintained	Demand escape maintained	Attention and Demand escape maintained
1. Easy task and 100% attention	Low	Low	Low
2. Easy task and 33% attention	High	Low	High
3. Difficult task and 100% attention	Low	High	High

with learning difficulties have the same needs as everybody else but limited skills to meet these needs, it is likely that: the same behaviour may serve different 'purposes' at different times; the 'reason' for the behaviour may change over time; different topographies of challenging behaviour will have different functions for the same individual (Oliver, 1990). These possibilities need to be kept in mind when carrying out a functional analysis and addressed at the level of intervention. Carr and Durand (1985) investigated the functional qualities of a range of aggressive and self-injurious behaviours in four children by observing them in three different conditions: 1) an easy task plus 100 per cent adult attention; 2) an easy task plus 33 per cent adult attention; 3) a difficult task and 100 per cent adult attention. They hypothesized that children whose behaviour was maintained by adult attention would show high rates of challenging behaviour in condition (2) but low rates in conditions (1) and (3), while children whose behaviour was maintained by escaping from demands would show high rates of challenging behaviour in condition (3) and low rates in conditions (1) and (2) (see Table 7.1).

Two of the four children showed patterns of behaviour consistent with an escape maintained hypothesis, one child showed a pattern of behaviour consistent with an attention maintained hypotheses and one child showed a behaviour pattern which was consistent with both hypotheses. The interventions for these three groups of children consisted of teaching communicative phrases which were functionally equivalent to their challenging behaviours: 'I don't understand', for the escape responders and 'Am I doing good work?' for the attention maintained group. The child who showed both patterns of behaviour was taught both phrases.

The above example illustrates two points: firstly the importance of matching treatment strategy to the function of the behaviour and secondly, the role functional analysis has to play in the promotion of a constructional, non-aversive approach to intervention in contrast to a purely punitive approach. Adopting a constructional approach has obvious ethical advantages and it also maximises the chances that treatment gains will generalise and be maintained. Inappropriate behaviours become relegated to the bottom of an individual's behavioural repertoire and are substituted by new, socially appropriate skills which are maintained at the top of the repertoire by the new contingencies operating on them. It is worth pointing out, however, that these new skills will only continue to be utilised for as long as they meet the individual's needs. As soon as carers fail to respond appropriately to the new acceptable behaviours individuals will resort to more powerful behaviours which are guaranteed to have an impact, namely the previously employed challenging behaviours.

In theory, the substitution of undesirable behaviours for more desirable skills should not present clinicians with many problems. The children in the Carr and Durand study were able to learn verbal equivalents for their challenging behaviour. However, many individuals with learning difficulties and challenging behaviour have a very limited skills base on which to build new behaviours. It is precisely these people who have failed to learn appropriate skills for getting their needs met who are most at risk of developing challenging behaviour. The teaching of new skills to severely and profoundly disabled people is a major challenge for clinicians and may remain an ideal which cannot be achieved for all individuals, as the following case example illustrates.

Stuart was an 11 year-old-boy with profound learning disabilities. The functional analysis of his self-injurious eye-poking was complicated by the fact that he spent 95 per cent of his school day in straight arm splints due to the severity of his self-injury. This effectively prevented his SIB occurring and made its functional characteristics difficult to define. Several sources of data were used to generate hypotheses regarding its maintenance. Direct observation in the natural environment showed the eye-poking to occur immediately the splints were removed, regardless of environmental contingencies; the impression of care staff was that Stuart enjoyed eye-poking and the results of the Motivation Assessment Scale also supported a self-stimulation function. To test the hypothesis that Stuart's eye-poking was maintained by sensory feedback, five sensory extinction trials were conducted by blocking contact between Stuart's hands and eyes when his splints were removed. This both prevented the eye-poking generating feedback and prevented physical damage from occurring. Each session was continued until a minute free of all attempts at eye-poking had occurred. The results are presented in Table 7.2. The length of time taken to achieve the target across the five trials dropped from eighty minutes to five minutes with a concurrent 84 per cent drop in rate per minute of eye-poking from baseline to trial five. These results suggested that the response prevention trials had brought about partial extinction of the behaviour and therefore not only supported the self-stimulation hypothesis but also suggested a possible intervention strategy. A combined sensory extinction and differential reinforcement of other behaviour (DRO) programme was implemented, which involved blocking any attempt to eye-poke whilst at the same time terminating a reinforcing stimulus (a tape of bird song) for a ten-second period of time contingent on eye-poking. The bird song was reinstated and continued to play until the next attempt to eye-poke occurred. This intervention was conducted on a sessional basis twice a day. It was hoped that differential reinforcement of incompatible behaviour (DRI) would eventually come to replace the DRO programme. Instead of gaining reinforcement for simply not engaging in eye-poking, the reinforcement would be made contingent on displaying alternative self-occupation skill such as hitting a musical mobile or playing with sand and water. In this way it was hoped that the new skill would provide an equally pleasurable substitute to the eye-poking. Unfortunately, this development of the behavioural programme did not occur. The failure was partly due to the difficulty of finding self-occupations which were as intrinsically reinforcing for Stuart as the eye-poking, and partly due to the increased risk of eye-poking which occurred if Stuart's hands were placed on a table attached to his wheelchair. If his hands were left to hang by his side or placed in his lap he could go for up to fifteen minutes without eye-poking, but as soon as they were raised to the level of a table on which activities could be placed this time period dramatically decreased.

As well as illustrating the difficulty of replacing challenging behaviour with socially appropriate behaviour, the above example also demonstrates that even when the function of the challenging behaviour has been reliably identified, the goal of intervention may not be the complete eradication of that behaviour. For Stuart the aims were twofold: firstly, to provide him with two fifteen minute sessions per day when his splints could be removed without the risk of eye-poking occurring, and secondly, to provide him with the opportunity of engaging in intrinsically enjoyable non-self-injurious activities. In the light of the failure of the DRI component of the intervention, the goal simply became to provide him with two sessions a day when he didn't have to wear his splints and would not eye-poke. This, of course, was not ideal as the motivation to eye-poke was difficult to combat in the absence of providing alternative stimulating occupation.

One final problem needs to be addressed regarding functional analysis. Despite the advances in methodology, the assessment of challenging behaviour occasionally fails to identify the function of that behaviour. Figure 7.1 shows the results of five sets of analogue conditions conducted with a 12-year-old girl, Amanda. Amanda had severe learning disabilities, a diagnosis of autism and displayed severe self-injury, which consisted mainly of fist to head

Table 7.2   *Results of five sensory extinction trials showing the time taken to achieve one minute free of all attempts to eye-poke and the concurrent percentage reduction in rates of eye-poking per minute from baseline*

	Baseline	Trial 1	Trial 2	Trial 3	Trial 4	Trial 5
Mean Freq per min	37	19	8	12	6	6
% reduction	—	49%	78%	68%	84%	84%
Time to extinction (mins)	—	Terminated prematurely	80	50	70	5

punching. The analogue conditions used were those proposed by Oliver (unpublished PhD): continuous attention (non-demanding, positive social contact from an adult); contingent attention (brief verbal reprimand given every time SIB occurred); ignore (two adults present in room talking to each other and ignoring client); no stimulation (no adult or activities in room); stimulation (preferred activity present but no adults); demands (adults interacting with client in demanding way using gestural, verbal and physical prompts to complete a task). Figure 7.1 shows that few consistencies emerged in the pattern of results obtained from one set of analogues to the next. There was some evidence for a self-stimulation component to Amanda's SIB; in two of the five analogue conditions an escalation of the SIB occurred in the no stimulation condition which declined when stimulation was provided and in two of the five analogue conditions SIB was lowest in the demand condition. No coherent pattern emerged in the three social manipulation conditions, making it impossible to draw conclusions regarding the role of social attention in maintaining Amanda's SIB. For this individual, functional analysis did not allow the making of data-based decisions regarding treatment.

Two options presented themselves to clinicians at this point. One was the construction of an intervention which provided sufficiently powerful reinforcement for the absence of the challenging behaviour or for the production of an alternative behaviour to overcome whatever contingencies were maintaining the undesirable behaviour. The other option was to consider aversive interventions. Neither of these were ideal as both failed to recognise that challenging behaviour can serve an adaptive purpose for individuals. Simply rewarding its absence or punishing its presence does not encourage the development of functionally equivalent skills. However, as the alternative to adopting one or other of these strategies was to do nothing then the dilemma of which to opt for was solved by opting for the non-aversive strategy first. A DRI programme was devised based on an assessment of Amanda's skills and her reinforcer preferences.

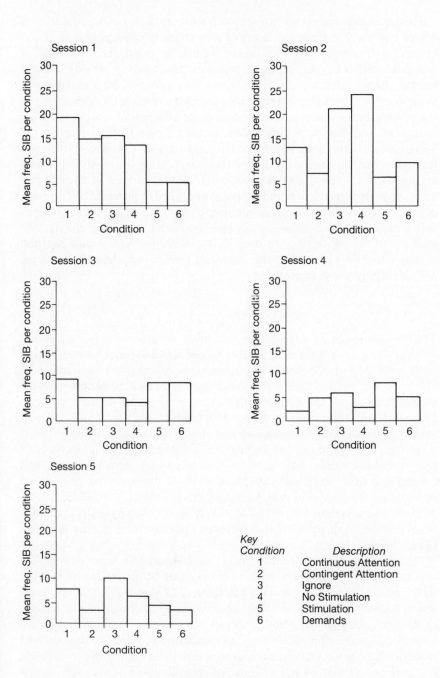

7.1 Mean frequency per minute of self-injurious behaviour in five analogue sessions

This intervention was run on a sessional basis and failed to produce either a decrease in her rate of the self-injury or an increase in incompatible skills. An aversive intervention was considered justifiable given the high rate of Amanda's SIB (5.5 per minute throughout the baseline period) and the intensity of her behaviour. Facial screening was chosen as the easiest aversive to apply and as the most potentially effective aversive in a pilot session where a range of other punishments were tested (brief physical restraint, verbal reprimand and forced arm exercises). In an attempt to both increase the aversiveness of the screening procedure and assuage the care team's own feelings of guilt at employing an aversive intervention the environment was arranged to be as reinforcing as possible outside of the screen by allowing free access to preferred activities and people as and when requested. Over a period of two months of the intervention running for 7 hours a day, Amanda's rate of SIB dropped from 5.5 per minute at baseline to less than 1 per minute. The intensity of the self-injury also decreased, her spontaneous communication increased and her social behaviour improved, even though these changes were not specifically 'programmed' for.

FORMULATING THE INTERVENTION PLAN

The formulation of an intervention plan must be carried out in conjunction with the client, his or her carers, parents, teachers and anyone else who is going to be involved with the plan. It is extremely important that practitioners are able to communicate their understanding of a client's behaviour and the proposed strategies for change with the group of people who are going to become the intervention team. Depending on the client's level of intellectual ability, proposals for intervention should also be discussed with him or her. If there are a number of options for intervention then these should be outlined and discussed within the team. All interventions demand effort and consistency from staff and parents and it is important to provide an opportunity for queries or criticisms to be raised at the outset. Indeed, some research indicates that care staff are less likely to perceive physically aggressive behaviour as 'challenging' if they have an understanding of why it occurs (Reed, 1990).

Discussion of outcome goals is also crucial. Affecting a 'cure' or complete suppression of the problem behaviour may not be an ethical or realistic treatment outcome. For example, Matthew, a 17-year-old young man with severe learning difficulties, showed high levels of masturbation across a range of different settings. The eradication of this behaviour would not be an appropriate goal for him but he does need to learn to confine the behaviour to settings where he has privacy, in order to maintain his dignity and to facilitate his continued participation in a number of community-based activities. As this behaviour occurs at a high rate the first consideration will need to be an assessment of Matthew's masturbation. During the assessment it will be important to establish whether Matthew has the necessary skills to be able to masturbate to ejaculation and whether pharmacological or physiological factors could be impairing his performance. It may be that he would benefit from a programme of skills training. Then, helping Matthew to discriminate between 'private' and 'non-private' settings might involve prompting him to go to his bedroom or to the toilet when at home or at school, and developing an intervention based on the differential reinforcement of other incompatible behaviour (DRI) when out in the community. This could involve a variety of possibilities including encouraging Matthew to take responsibility for carrying the shopping bags, prompting him to use Makaton signs to label features of the environment and asking him to collect items from the shelves in order to provide another, perhaps incompatible, behaviour and decrease his opportunity to masturbate. Thus it can be seen that the intervention plan will involve a number of components including a further, more detailed assessment of the presenting behaviour, helping Matthew to discriminate between settings and increasing his self-occupation skills. It is very important that all members of the team share a common view regarding what constitutes a positive outcome for the client.

Willis and LaVigna (1988) also suggest that intervention plans derived from functional analysis should adopt a multi-faceted approach comprising a number of different elements. At the time of referral carer concerns are likely to be focused on the situational management of the challenging behaviour and the promotion of carer and client safety within the setting. There are a number of articles and book chapters describing situational management techniques which seek to minimise the potential for carer and client injury while maintaining dignity and respect for the individual exhibiting challenging behaviour. However, in order to decrease the frequency and intensity of the problem behaviour over a longer time period this will be insufficient, and a treatment package involving three additional components needs to be drawn up. First, a direct treatment strategy based on the functional analysis of the topography needs to be formulated. Second, a constructional approach must be employed. Donnellan, LaVigna, Negri-Shoultz and Fassbender (1988) emphasise the need for positive programming, that is, teaching plans aimed at the acquisition of new skills and abilities. Positive programming may focus on the development of skills which are functionally equivalent or functionally related to the target behaviour, but may also involve more general skills training or the enhancement of coping skills, e.g. relaxation training. Third, it may be necessary to initiate ecological changes to the client's physical and social environment in order to ensure that the intervention plan is effective.

A further case example may help to illustrate these points. Patrick, a 45-year-old man with severe learning disabilities, no functional communication and right-sided hemiplegia was referred to the Psychology Department as a result of his self-injurious behaviour. At the time of referral, Patrick lived on a hospital ward with twenty-five other residents and a low staff:resident ratio.

Like Patrick, the majority of the residents needed a considerable amount of support in completing daily living skills. Assessment of the functional significance of Patrick's self-injury began with interviews and the completion of ABC charts and was followed by direct observations of Patrick's self-injury in the ward setting. From the information obtained by interviewing staff and maintenance of ABC records, it became clear that Patrick's self-injurious behaviour was composed of two separate topographies: hitting his forehead with his left hand (closed fist) which typically occurred when staff were engaged in assisting Patrick to get out of bed in the morning, and hitting his head against a pipe on the wall which occurred while he was sitting on the toilet.

Direct observation revealed that Patrick was the first to be helped to wash and dress as his bed was nearest to the dormitory door. However, as Patrick was slow to to wake up this may not have been the ideal routine for him. Carr and Durand (1985) advocate that many challenging topographies have a direct communicative intent. Encouraging the intervention team to generate ideas for Patrick's communicative aims in showing each self-injurious behaviour helped to promote the involvement of other staff in the intervention process and produced a number of possible functions for each topography. From the suggestions and subsequent discussion of observational data it was proposed that Patrick might be wanting to say 'Leave me alone and let me sleep a bit longer', or 'I'm not properly awake' when he hit his head with his fist. The logical test of this hypothesis was to implement an ecological change in Patrick's environment where he was given more time to adjust to waking up while staff attended to other residents. This ecological strategy alone was effective in decreasing Patrick's hand to head hitting. Functional analysis of Patrick's head to pipe banging suggested two possible functions. As a result of the low staffing levels and the low levels of continence among the residents on Patrick's ward, there were set toileting times during the day when residents were prompted and assisted to use the toilet. Several residents appeared to need to spend 15 minutes or more in the toilet before they were able to perform and this led to staff giving this same time period to all the residents who needed physical assistance to use the toilets. Again, staff were asked to generate ideas about what Patrick might be wanting to say, while also considering other assessment formations. 'I've finished and I want to get off', and 'This pipe makes a great noise!' were two suggestions which seemed to have face validity in this set of circumstances. Taking the first suggestion that Patrick wanted to leave the toilet area, he was given a buzzer and taught to press it in order to attract staff attention to help him to leave. This was a positive programming intervention which involved the development of a functionally equivalent skill. It was successful: the rate of Patrick's head to pipe banging decreased and he was effective in using the buzzer to communicate his needs. There was no change in his level of continence or use of the toilet. The success of this intervention supported the first suggested communicative aim, 'I'm finished and I want to leave'. However, if this intervention had not succeeded then further consideration would need to be given to Patrick's cognitive awareness of the goal of the teaching programme and to the possible utility of the second hypothesis, which is suggestive of a sensory function to his self-injurious behaviour.

There are a number of concerns which are frequently raised by staff and parents when intervention plans are discussed with them. Firstly, the team may object that the intervention plan has been tried in the past but with little positive effect. In these circumstances, it would be important for the practitioner to obtain access to any records and documentation describing previous intervention programmes which may prove helpful in reviewing the proposed plan. It is important to point out that achieving significant behaviour change is likely to be a lengthy process, especially if a client's problem behaviour has been shaped and refined over many months or years or sustained by very intermittent social reinforcement. Staff and parents may have had previous experience of implementing programmes involving extinction. Such procedures, which are likely to be perceived as aversive by the client when used in isolation, may result in a temporary increase in the frequency or duration of the client's challenging behaviour before any diminution occurs. These concerns need to be discussed within the team in order to maximise consistency of programme implementation.

Secondly, staff may raise concerns about the acceptability of the proposed intervention plan. Wolf (1978) asserts that behavioural interventions need to be considered in terms of their social validity, that is, the social significance of the goals, the social appropriateness of the procedures and the social importance of the effects. In a useful review of this developing area of research, Reimers, Wacker and Koeppl (1987) identified and described a number of factors which influence the acceptability of a treatment plan. Problem severity is a potential mediator, with most studies demonstrating that the amount of time needed to carry out the intervention shows a negative correlation with its acceptability. Positive treatment approaches are considered to be more acceptable than approaches aimed at behaviour suppression. Treatments which have potentially negative side-effects are more likely to be seen as unacceptable. Finally, the cost of interventions is likely to have an effect on ratings of acceptability. Further work in this area needs to define the set of parameters which determine treatment acceptability in order to inform the practice of those working in this area.

Thirdly, staff may be concerned that the methods of intervention are incompatible with a service philosophy of social role valorisation (Wolfensberger, 1983). Several authors have argued that social role valorisation and behaviour therapy-based interventions can operate together in a complementary way as described in a useful article by Emerson and McGill (1989). Again, this topic may demand considerable discussion within the intervention team in order to decide on a methodology which is acceptable to everyone who will be involved with its implementation.

We suggest that an exploration of these considerations will make a significant impact on the maintenance of the intervention plan by the team and the client's ability to generalise his or her newly acquired skills across time and settings.

SUMMARY

Functional analysis aims to elucidate the relationships between behaviours, their antecedents and their consequences. Increased understanding of these relationships facilitates the development of logical intervention plans which will hopefully provide long-term solutions to challenging behaviours. Interventions based on functional data should not only focus on decreasing the undesirable behaviour but also on promoting appropriate behaviour which is functionally equivalent to the declared target.

A number of methods exist to carry out a functional analysis: clinical interview, ABC charts, questionnaires, natural observations and observations made in analogue conditions. Each method has advantages and disadvantages and a combination of methods is likely to provide the most comprehensive data. Carrying out such an assessment, however, is neither easy nor guaranteed to enhance the intervention decision-making process. Difficulties include the time-consuming nature of such an assessment and the assumptions which have to be made when data is equivocal. On the positive side, functional data can lead to the implementation of multifaceted intervention plans which seek to change the motivation for, setting events and consequences of undesirable behaviour, in addition to promoting appropriate skills to substitute for the inappropriate behaviour.

References

Bird, F., Dores, P. A., Moniz, D. and Robinson J. X. (1989), 'Reducing severe aggressive and self-injurious behavior with functional communication training', *American Journal on Mental Retardation*, 94, 37–48.

Carr, E. G. and Durand, V. M. (1985), 'Reducing behavior problems through functional communication training', *Journal of Applied Behaviour Analysis*, 18, 111–26.

Christie, R., Bay, C., Kaufman, I. A., Bakay, B, Barden, M. and Nyhan, W. L. (1982), 'Lesch-Nyhan disease: clinical experience with nineteen patients', *Developmental Medicine and Child Neurology*, 24, 293–306.

Clare, I. C. H., Murphy, G., Cox, D. and Chaplin, E. H. (in press), 'Assessment and treatment of fire-setting: a single-case investigation using a cognitive-behavioural model', *Criminal Behaviour and Mental Health*.

DeLissovoy, V., (1963), 'Head banging in early childhood: a suggested cause', *Journal of Genetic Psychology*, 102, 109–14.

Donnellan, A. M., LaVigna, G. W., Negri-Shoultz, N. and Fassbender, L. L. (1988), *Progress without Punishment: Effective Approaches for Learners with Behavior Problems*, Teachers College Press, New York.

Durand, V. M. and Carr, E. G. (1987), 'Social influences on 'self-stimulatory' behavior: analysis and treatment application', *Journal of Applied Behavior Analysis*, 20, 119–32.

Durand, V. M. and Crimmins, D. B. (1988), 'Identifying the variables maintaining self-injurious behavior', *Journal of Autism and Developmental Disorders*, 18, 99–117.

Edelson, S. M., Taubman, M. T. and Lovaas O. I. (1983), 'Some social contexts of self-destructive behavior', *Journal of Autism and Developmental Disorders*, 18, 99–117.

Emerson, E. and McGill, P. (1989), 'Normalization and applied behaviour analysis: values and technology in services for people with learning difficulties', *Behavioural Psychotherapy*, 17, 101–17.

Felce, D., Saxby, H. and DeKock, U. (1987), 'To what behaviours do attending adults respond? A replication', *American Journal of Mental Deficiency*, 91, 496–504.

Iwata, B. A., Dorsey, M. F., Slifer, K. J., Bauman, K. E. and Richman, G. S. (1982), 'Toward a functional analysis of self-injury', *Analysis and Intervention in Developmental Disabilities*, 2, 3–20.

Kiernan, C. (1974), 'Behaviour modification' in A. M. Clarke and A. D. B. Clarke (ed.), *Mental Deficiency: The Changing Outlook*, Methuen, London.

Lennox, D. B. and Miltenberger, R. G. (1989), 'Conducting a functional assessment of problem behavior in applied settings', *Journal of the Association for Persons with Severe Handicaps*, 14, 304–11.

Lundervold, D. and Bourland, G. (1988), 'Quantitative analysis of treatment of aggression, self-injury and property damage', *Behavior Modification*, 12, 590–617.

Mace, F. C., Webb, M. E., Sharkey, R. W., Mattson, D. M. and Rosen, H. S. (1988), 'Functional analysis and treatment of bizarre speech', *Journal of Behavior Therapy and Experimental Psychiatry*, 19, 1–8.

McReynolds, P. (1968), *Advances in Psychological Assessment*, I, Science & Behaviour Books, Palo Alto, CA.

Murphy, G. and Wilson B. (1981), 'Long-term outcome of contingent shock treatment for self-injurious behaviour', in P. Mittler (ed.), *Frontiers of Knowledge in Mental Retardation*, II, University Park Press, Baltimore MD.

Oliver, C. (1988), 'Functional analysis of self-injurious behaviour: a comparison of methods', paper presented at the 3rd World Congress on Behavior Therapy, 5–10 September 1988, Edinburgh.

Oliver, C. (1990), 'Self-injurious behaviour: the lost cause', in V. Cowie and V. J. Harten Ash (eds.), *Current Approaches: Mental Retardation*, Dupher, Dorset.

Oliver, C. (1990), 'Self-injurious behaviour in people with mental handicap: prevalence, individual characterists and funtional analysis', Unpublished PhD, Institute of Psychiatry, University of London.

Oliver, C. and Head, D. (1990), 'Self-injurious behaviour in people with learning disabilities: determinants and interventions', *International Review of Psychiatry*, 892, 101–16.

Reed, J. (1990), 'Identification and description of adults with mental handicaps showing physically aggressive behaviours', *Mental Handicap Research*, 3(2), 126–36.

Reimers, T.M., Wacker, D.P. and Koeppl, G. (1987), 'Acceptability of behavioral interventions : a review of the literature', *School Psychology Review*, 16, 212–27.

188   *People with learning disability and severe challenging behaviour*

Richman, N., Stevenson, J. and Graham, P. J. (1982), *Pre-school to school: A Behavioural Study*, Academic Press, London.

Singh, N. N., Beale, I. L. and Dawson, M. J. (1981), 'Duration of facial screening and suppression of self-injurious behavior: analysis using an alternating treatments design', *Behavioral Assessment*, 3, 411.

Sturmey, P., Carlsen, A., Crisp, A. G. and Newton, J. T. (1988), 'A functional analysis of multiple aberrant responses: a refinement and extension of Iwata *et al*.'s (1982) methodology', *Journal of Mental Deficiency*, 32, 31–46.

Wing, L. (1987), 'The epidemiology and classification of behavioural disorders in people with mental retardation' in J. A. Corbett and C. Oliver (eds.), *Behavioural Disorders and Mental Retardation – Understanding and Management*, Collins, London.

Willis, T. J. and LaVigna, G. W. (1988), *Behavior Assessment and Intervention Plan*. Institute for Applied Behavior Analysis, Los Angeles.

Wolf, M. M. (1978), 'Social validity: the case for subjective measurement or how applied behavior analysis is finding its heart', *Journal of Applied Behavior Analysis*, 11, 203–14.

Wolfensberger, W. (1983), 'Social role valorisation: a proposed new term for the principle of normalisation', *Mental Retardation*, 21, 234–39.

Verbal self-regulation

'It is ironic but basic behaviour analysis may be building the kind of theoretical base that many of the 'non-behavioural' techniques have needed in order to tie clinical wisdom to scientifically validated principles' (Hayes, 1989).

As has been shown in previous chapters, until recently the most significant approaches and interventions used in relation to 'challenging behaviour' have been those which originate from a behavioural perspective. This chapter examines the influence of a new but complementary approach to challenging behaviour which has been variously called 'self-control', 'self-management' or 'self-regulation'. The origins of this approach are traced to a number of sources and the applications of self-regulation procedures to persons with challenging behaviour are examined using a number of case examples. Finally, some future directions are suggested.

Within the field of learning disabilities recent years have seen the growth of a wide and diverse literature which emphasises the dangers of regarding an individual as a passive recipient of environmental contingencies (Carr, 1991). Discussion has centred on the importance of dignity, status, choice, respect and self-determination for people with learning disabilities and yet in the field of challenging behaviour the majority of interventions have continued to rely on the use of external controls to regulate behaviour. This chapter argues that the direct application of operant principles, particularly those derived from studies of animal behaviour, may not be appropriate to all individuals who display challenging behaviours and indeed, that many such interventions do not take full account of the factors underlying the maintenance of the behaviour. This may be particularly the case with individuals who present with severe challenging behaviours but whose level of learning disability is in the mild to moderate range.

We begin by examining some of the criticisms of the behavioural approach which have led to the development of a more 'cognitive' type intervention being used with people with learning disabilities.

There can be little doubt that the application of techniques derived from the experimental analysis of behaviour, that is, applied behaviour analysis (ABA), revolutionised the care and treatment of individuals with learning disabilities. The theory underpinning it arose mainly from the work of B. F. Skinner, who, in developing the principles of operant conditioning, proposed that the behaviour of organisms could be explained as an 'orderly function of contingencies of reinforcement' (Skinner, 1938). By carefully controlling the relationship between these contingencies, it became possible to control or change a subject's behaviour. One of the most important influences on the emerging movement known as behaviour modification was the publication of *Schedules of Reinforcement*, by Ferster and Skinner (1957). This book described a wide variety of reinforcement schedules which could be programmed to control operant behaviour, and it identified operant principles as having a major role to play in achieving behaviour change.

Since this technology provided an apparently powerful means of controlling and shaping behaviour, it was adopted by those involved in clinical and educational psychology to modify a range of behaviours in a variety of situations (Kiernan, 1985). It is inappropriate here to chart in detail the enormous influence of the behavioural approach on the lives of people with learning disabilities but a number of reviews are readily available. The interested reader is referred to Remington and Evans (1988) and Remington (1991) for discussions of this influence.

CRITICISMS OF THE BEHAVIOURAL APPROACH

Despite the undoubted success of ABA in enhancing the lives of people with learning disabilities there have been numerous criticisms of it. These have ranged from empirical observations of the difficulty in maintaining and generalising treatment gains to theoretical criticisms that the field of behaviour modification ignores many of the recent trends in the experimental analysis of behaviour. We shall briefly examine these criticisms.

Difficulties with contingency analysis

In their early work, Skinner and others showed that animal behaviour was an orderly function of contingencies of reinforcement so that any particular performance, on a schedule of reinforcement, for instance, could be analysed within the framework of the 'three term contingency', that is, the relationship between responses, reinforcers, and discriminative stimuli. This model became the accepted theoretical base for workers in the field of behaviour modification. Focused as it was on observable behaviour and environmental stimuli, this model was taken by many to exclude all consideration of covert or 'cognitive' events. It was thought that basic conditioning principles had now been established, and all that remained was the development of an appropriate technology for their application to clinical and other social problems. In recent years, however, it has become apparent that in spite of this early confidence, the power to predict and control complex human behaviour has proved elusive (Lowe, 1983; Lowe, Horne and Higson, 1987). Indeed, although most behaviour modification procedures used in the area of learning disabilities are based on work originating in the animal laboratory, evidence has been accumulating in recent years that seriously questions the assumption that the principles of conditioning derived from the study of animal learning are sufficient to account for human behaviour. Much of this evidence is concerned with the effects of language.

The role of language in controlling behaviour

When one of the present authors (Lowe, 1979) first reviewed the literature on human operant behaviour, he found that the behaviour of adult human subjects bore very little resemblance to that of animals. On schedules of reinforcement, for example, it was not a case of there being minor departures from the patterns of performance found in animals, but rather that the classic patterns of behaviour associated with particular schedules such as fixed-interval and fixed-ratio simply did not exist. Humans behaved in very strange and often unpredictable ways on reinforcement schedules and they showed few of the phenomena with which researchers had become familiar in animal experimentation. For example, on the fixed-interval (FI) schedules, where the first response is reinforced after a stated interval has elapsed since the previous reinforcement, adult human behaviour bears little resemblance to that of animals and often takes one of two forms – either a continous and high rate of responding (the high-rate pattern) or a very low rate consisting of just one or two responses at the end of the inter-reinforcement interval (the low-rate pattern). The FI scallop, and the sensitivity of performance to variations in the schedule value, characteristic of animal behaviour, are virtually never seen (Leander, Lippman and Meyer, 1968; Lowe, 1979; Weiner, 1969; but see also Lowe, Harzem and Bagshaw, 1978, and Lowe, Harzem and Hughes, 1978). In addition to these marked differences in performance on the basic schedules, humans also differ from animals in the way they are affected by their previous history of reinforcement. Adult human subjects exposed to different schedules frequently show a rigidity of performance in the face of altered reinforcement contingencies that is often maladaptive in terms of reinforcement gain or response output, and this too is uncharacteristic of animal behaviour.

A series of studies by Lowe and colleagues (Bentall, Lowe and Beasty, 1985; Lowe, 1983; Lowe, Beasty and Bentall, 1983) has shown that these distinctive features of adult human operant behaviour are absent in pre-verbal infants, who perform on FI, fixed-ratio (FR) and differential-reinforcement-of-low-rate (DRL) schedules in a manner indistinguishable from that of animals. On the FI schedule, for example, it was found that human infants show scalloped patterns of responding and sensitivity to the schedule parameters just like that of animals. In contrast, children aged five years or older, who have the verbal skills to describe the schedule contingencies to themselves and to formulate rules for responding, show high-and low-rate patterns like adult humans, with similar insensitivity to alterations in schedule value. Children in an intermediate age range of two-and-a-half to four years, with less well-developed verbal skills, produce neither adult-like nor animal-like patterns of responding (Lowe *et al.*, 1983; Bentall *et al.*, 1985). Experiments showing that the developmental sequence can be accelerated by appropriate verbal instruction provide further evidence that the acquisition of linguistic skills is the variable responsible for these age-related changes in operant behaviour (Lowe, 1983; Bem, 1967; Luria, 1961).

The emergence of untrained behaviour

The results of these and other experiments suggest that verbally formulated rules for responding, whether overt or covert, are major determinants of human behaviour (Lowe and Horne, 1985; Davey and Cullen, 1988, Hayes, 1989). A related area of considerable importance concerns recent work on stimulus equivalence, a phenomenon that is of particular importance in the study of challenging behaviour. Matching-to-sample procedures are often employed in the study of equivalence. Typically, the subject sits in front of a response panel and the trial begins with the presentation of a sample stimulus on the centre key (e.g. the word GREEN). When the subject touches the sample a number of comparison stimuli are presented on the outer keys (e.g. colour patches red and green); a response on the 'correct' key (the green colour patch) is reinforced. These conditional discriminations can be easily established with both human and animal subjects. According to what we know of the three-term contingency, however, there is no reason to expect that when we now present the colour green as the sample that the word GREEN will be picked as the comparison. But Sidman and colleagues (Sidman, Rauzin, Lazar and Cunningham, 1982; Sidman and Tailby, 1982) have found that children of five years and upwards pass this test of what Sidman terms *symmetry*. The children spontaneously, as it were, reverse the relation between the stimulus pairs. Moreover, if we now teach another stimulus pair, where the colour green is the sample and the Welsh word for green, GWYRDD, is the comparison (we would also teach other pairs such as colour red – coch, coch being the Welsh for red), we find that children not only show symmetry with respect to GWYRDD and colour green, but that two new relations will be formed, again spontaneously (certainly the behaviour was not reinforced): when the word GREEN is presented as the sample, *GWYRDD* will be selected as the comparison and when *GWYRDD* is presented as sample, the word GREEN is selected. Thus for any three stimuli A, B and C, if we teach A-B and B-C, children will spontaneously acquire B-A, C-B, A-C, and C-A. As Sidman expresses it, all three stimuli form an equivalence class and are substitutable one for the other.

When an equivalence class is formed it is interesting because although we teach a limited number of relations we get many more for free, as it were; in this case we have got four extra, and Sidman and colleagues (Sidman and Cresson, 1973; Sidman, Cresson and Willson-Morris, 1974) have shown that it is comparatively easy to establish very large stimulus classes in children and people with learning difficulties. So teaching via equivalence relations may be very effective since it is not necessary to reinforce every relationship. Equivalence relations, and particularly, symmetry are also interesting because they appear to some people to come very close to defining what we mean by terms such as 'symbolising', or, indeed, 'meaning' itself, as opposed to mere conditional relations (see Catania, 1984; Lowe, in press). The additional theoretical interest for the present discussion, however, lies in the fact that, within the framework of the three-term contingency, equivalence relations are actually *illegitimate*; they should not exist. The three-term contingency specifies one-way relationships, which animal experiments have shown can indeed be very complex, but it cannot encompass reversals of the kind we see in symmetry tests. Indeed, several studies have now failed to find any evidence of stimulus equivalence with animal subjects, including pigeons, monkeys, baboons and chimpanzies (for example, Dugdale and Lowe, 1990; Sidman *et al.*, 1982). In a recent series of experiments Lowe and Beasty (1987, and see Dugdale and Lowe, 1990) showed that some children younger than 4 years of age initially fail equivalence tests but when they are taught to name the sample-comparison pairings on baseline trials they then go on to pass the tests of equivalence. These data, together with the rest of the literature on equivalence, indicate that this phenomenon is brought into being by language and in particular by the development of naming skills (see Dugdale and Lowe, 1990).

Implications of these findings

Taken together, the findings from the above experiments have had important implications for applied work with humans. They suggest that much of what could be termed traditional behavioural analysis might be of only indirect relevance when it comes to the modification of human behaviour. Furthermore, it seems that human subjects' ability to symbolically represent environmental stimuli and their own behaviour has major effects on the organisation and control of that behaviour. The field of behavioural analysis has been undergoing a profound if quiet revolution from within, the effects of which are only now beginning to influence applied work with clinical populations. Interestingly, at the same time as the revolution within behavioural analysis has been proceeding, other criticisms of the behavioural approach have also surfaced.

THE COGNITIVE REVOLUTION

As evidence has accumulated which questions the applicability of animal-based interventions, the supremacy of the behavioural model has also been challenged by the growing influence of the cognitive approach in applied psychology. Again, space precludes detailed description of this influence here but the interested reader is referred to Salkovskis (1986) for a detailed discussion of this 'cognitive revolution'.

In the field of learning disabilities and challenging behaviour a growing interest in 'cognitive' procedures probably began as elements of 'self-control' were incorporated into operant-based treatment approaches. In general, however, as regards people with learning disabilities, the research and clinical literature concerning self-control is significantly delayed in comparison with that for other client groups. Gardiner and Cole (1989) have suggested that this delay reflects a widespread attitude that those with learning disabilities are not capable of managing aspects of their own behaviour, and that the development of self-control is inconsistent with the external control integral to institutional management. Consequently, while much relevant research into the development of self-management strategies has occurred within the last two decades, only a minority of this research has directly addressed challenging behaviour.

Three areas are of prime interest in analysing the effects of self-management with people with learning disabilities. These are: self-monitoring; self-evaluation and self-reinforcement. These will be dealt with briefly in turn.

Self-monitoring

This refers to an individual's systematic recording of one or more of his or her own specific behaviours. For some individuals monitoring itself exerts such a powerful effect upon the rates of the monitored behaviour that there is no need for further intervention (Gardiner and Cole, 1989), although the specific mechanisms underlying the phenomenon are not fully understood (see Cooper, Heron and Heward for a discussion of theoretical issues in this area).

In one of the first studies of the use of self-monitoring in the reduction of challenging behaviour in a person with learning disabilities, Zegiob, Klukas and Junginger (1978) trained a young woman to self-monitor her rate of self-injurious behaviour (nose and mouth gouging). Data was also presented on the stereotyped behaviour (head shaking) of a 15-year-old girl. Both subjects significantly reduced their levels of challenging behaviour while monitoring their own behaviour. When external consequences were added to the monitoring procedure, further reductions were noted. Similar results were reported by Reese, Sherman and Sheldon (1984). The addition of external consequences is an important but complex matter. As mentioned above, sometimes self-monitoring alone can have powerful effects on behaviour. In other cases, however, a number of studies have shown that self-monitoring alone has no apparent effect on the target behaviour (e.g. Foxx and Rubinoff, 1979) and this suggests that the addition of external consequences may be necessary to generate reliable reductions in all cases. However, an issue of both clinical and research interest is whether the monitoring has to be accurate to effect significant reductions in challenging behaviour. A considerable body of research suggests that although even quite young children can be taught to self-monitor their own behaviour without being externally reinforced for accuracy (e.g. Glynn, Thomas and Shee, 1973), accuracy is enhanced when there are specific consequences scheduled for the accuracy of the self-recording. This may be particularly important where external consequences are contingent on the outcome of the recording. If, for example, an individual is reinforced for reported reductions in the amount of time spent in self-injurious behaviour, it is not, perhaps, suprising to find that the individual tends to exaggerate the rate of reduction in order to maximise access to the reinforcer. What is surprising, however, is that the accuracy of the recording may not be crucial for the eventual reduction in the challenging behaviour (Shapiro, 1986). Several studies have found a low correlation between the accuracy of self-monitoring and its effectiveness in changing the behaviour that is being recorded (Kneedler and Hallahan, 1981) and this suggests that it is the process, rather than the outcome, of the monitoring which perhaps exerts the crucial effect in reducing the behaviours. The data concerning self-monitoring in this client group is sparse, however, and it is rare to find a study where the effects of the monitoring can be experimentally separated from other components of an intervention (but see Zegiob *et al.*, 1978). Thus conclusions regarding the effectiveness of self-monitoring are tentative. What can be concluded from this short review is that sometimes self-monitoring is an effective behaviour change technique and sometimes it is not (Cooper, Heron and Heward, 1987). The effects of self-monitoring can be transient and may require some form of external reinforcement to effect maintenance and generalisation. Finally, the role of accuracy in self-monitoring is unclear but it does not seem to be a crucial variable in accounting for successful reduction of behaviour.

Case example: self-monitoring

The following case example is taken from Reese, Sherman and Sheldon (1984) and illustrates the successful use of a self-monitoring intervention which combined self-monitoring with external reinforcement. A 22-year-old woman with moderate learning disabilities showed periodic aggressive and disruptive behaviours (attacking staff, throwing objects, yelling, swearing, etc.) in a community group home. This woman was instructed to monitor her own behaviour during specific intervals, using a small pocket timer. When the timer sounded the woman was instructed to tick a recording sheet which specified either 'Handled my temper', or 'Lost my temper'. Despite the fact that the woman *never* correctly recorded the rate and duration of her challenging behaviour (although she usually recorded her appropriate behaviour correctly), this procedure appeared to result in significant reductions in aggressive and disruptive behaviour. This supports the findings of the other studies mentioned earlier which suggest that the accuracy of the self-monitoring may not be crucial. As with much of the clinical material in this area, however, it is difficult to ascertain exactly what component of the treatment package was responsible for the therapeutic effect. The self-monitoring was carried out in the client's group home where there was also in operation an ongoing token economy, and related response cost procedure for agitated behaviours. In addition, the woman was reinforced both for accurate recording and for reductions in agitated behaviour. All that can definitely be concluded is that the introduction of the self-monitoring procedure coincided with a significant reduction in the woman's aggressive and disruptive behaviours. The authors, however, felt that stronger evidence was provided by the fact that 'the relatively immediate increase in agitated disruptive behaviour on the two occasions when the self-recording procedure was eliminated makes it unlikely that unknown variables accounted for the change' (Reese *et al.*, 1984, p. 97).

Self-evaluation

Self-evaluation has been explored as a method of encouraging self-management. This procedure involves teaching the individual to evaluate his or her own behaviour as either positive or negative (Smith, 1990). An individual must be able to be aware of, and accurately label, his or her own behaviour before being able to evaluate that behaviour against a socially accepted norm. Thus, self-monitoring is often regarded as an essential prerequisite for self-evaluation (Gardiner and Cole, 1989). The research literature suggests that self-evaluation itself can be a powerful reduction strategy for challenging behaviour. For example, Harvey, Karan, Bhargava and Morehouse (1978) found that teaching adults with moderate learning disabilities to make positive self-evaluations while using relaxation procedures could reduce aggression. As was mentioned previously, however, many studies use a self-management package which combines self-monitoring, self-evaluation and self-reinforcement and it is rare to find a study which assesses the effects of self-evaluation alone. A recent study by Bryon (1988), however, evaluated the specific effects of self-evaluation in a multiple baseline across-subjects design which clearly showed the therapeutic effects of the evaluation procedure compared to the self-monitoring phase alone. Bryon used four subjects with mild learning disabilities who attended an adult training centre and displayed behaviours which disrupted the workshop sessions. These behaviours included shouting and disruptive interruptions but did not include severe or life-threatening challenging behaviours. Using a four-phase, reversal design (baseline, self-monitoring, self-evaluation, baseline), Bryon found that all subjects showed some reductions in disruptive behaviour when the self-monitoring phase was implemented, but that these decreases were greatly enhanced for all subjects when the subjects were taught to self-evaluate their own behaviour as being either 'good' or 'bad'. Significantly, no external consequences were provided for evaluation, which suggests that the process of evaluation itself was responsible for the behavioural reductions. Often self-evaluation can be aided by the use of a positive behaviour checklist, that is, a sheet of paper on which are listed a series of specific positive behaviours. These checklists not only provide a reminder for future behaviour but also serve as a basis for the client's own evalution of his or her behaviour.

Case example: self-evaluation

The following case example is taken from Smith (1990) and illustrates the successful use of a self-evaluation procedure in the reduction of bizarre stereotyped behaviours. Recent research has suggested that although not always regarded as challenging behaviour, the presence of abnormal stereotyped behaviours can be viewed very negatively by the general public (Jones, Wint and Ellis, 1990), thus reducing a client's chances of community integration. Smith (1990) described the case of Harold, a 24-year-old man with autism and good verbal skills, who lived in a group home under supervision and had short periods of unsupervised time which included periods when he used public transport. When out on his own he displayed a number of peculiar behaviours. For example, at the bus-stop he was observed to talk to himself, rock, race rapidly, and swing his arms. Staff constructed a checklist for Harold and reviewed this with him before each outing. This checklist included a number of items incompatible with his inappropriate behaviour, such as 'arms at side, silent unless spoken to or in need of assistance, and good posture'. A staff member explained and demonstrated 'good posture' and the checklist was reviewed with Harold before he left home in the morning, before he left work and before any other independent outing. Harold evaluated his own behaviour at the end of each outing. After the checklist evaluation system was put into effect, Harold was covertly observed on outings and these observations revealed '100% compliance with his checklist items' (p. 117).

Self-reinforcement

A number of studies have included a self-reinforcement component as part of an overall self-management package. Litrownik, Freitas and Franzini (1978), for example, taught children with moderate learning disabilities to indicate when they had finished a task by placing a happy face in front of them (not finishing was indicated by displaying a green square). These children increased their performance compared to a control group. Most frequently, self-reinforcement studies have been conducted using schoolchildren with normal intelligence, and they have typically involved the students' self-determining the number of tokens, points, or minutes of free time they should receive based on a self-assessment of their own performance (Cooper, Heron and Heward, 1987). Again, however, it is often difficult to separate experimentally the effects of self-reinforcement from those of self-monitoring and self-evaluation, which are inevitably associated with the decision to self-reinforce. More fundamental criticisms, however, have been directed at the theory of self-reinforcement.

CRITICISMS OF SELF-CONTROL STUDIES

The studies have little relevance to individuals with severe learning disabilities

The literature on self-control is dominated by studies of individuals with normal intelligence. Of the smaller numbers of studies which include people with learning disabilities, subjects are almost exclusively described as having mild or moderate levels of mental handicap and there have been no clear studies of self-control with people with severe learning disabilities. Although it may seem almost self-evident that the use of a verbal self-regulation intervention presupposes a basic level of language development, the present authors do not regard this as a foregone conclusion. We will argue later that individuals with few communicative skills can be taught to regulate their own behaviour. However, the existing literature on self-control is of limited assistance in this regard and can be criticised as having little relevance for individuals with severe learning disabilities.

Studies do not include serious challenging behaviours

Of the limited number of studies on self-control which have been published in the field of learning disabilities, the majority deal with the acquisition of new behaviours or the reduction of minor challenging behaviours. Gardiner and Cole (1989) have stated that in contrast to the many studies on these topics . . . 'relatively minimal attention has been devoted to investigating the effects of self-management approaches on clinically significant aberrant behaviors displayed by persons with mental retardation' (p. 21). Even where inappropriate behaviours have been targeted (e.g. swearing; shouting), these behaviours are often not as serious as some of the challenging behaviours mentioned elsewhere in this volume. Although not common, however, there are a small number of studies where self-control methods have been applied to more serious challenging behaviours. As mentioned previously, for example, the study by Zegiob *et al.* (1978), was one of the first studies to use self-control methods to reduce levels of self-injurious behaviour (gouging) and more recent examples of the procedures used to reduce self-injury and serious aggression can be found in Smith (1990) and in Gardiner and Cole (1989). Nevertheless, these examples are rare and the criticism that the literature fails to address complex or severe challenging behaviour seems justified, at least in the majority of studies reviewed.

Studies show little evidence of *self*-control

Skinner (1953), in one of the first theoretical analyses of self-control, made a distinction between operant reinforcement and self-control:

The place of operant reinforcement in self-control is not clear . . . Self-reinforcement of operant behaviour presupposes that the individual has it in his power to obtain reinforcement but does not do so until a particular response has been admitted. This might be the case if a man denied himself all social contacts until he had finished a particular job . . .
It must be remembered that the individual may at any moment drop the work in hand and obtain the reinforcement. (pp. 237–38)

Thus it seems necessary to invoke some concept of *choice* into any theoretical analysis of self-control. For example, an individual chooses to forsake immediate gratification (e.g. the reinforcement available for being negative to a fellow student who becomes irritating) in order to obtain a more distant reinforcer (e.g. access to a group outing at a weekend). An analysis of self-control in these terms, however, causes some problems when we examine the literature on self-reinforcement. Jones, Nelson and Kazdin (1977) have defined self-reinforcement as occurring when 'in the absence of external controlling influences, an individual has full control over certain contingencies for the self-administration of the reinforcing stimuli' (p. 151). Similarly, Bandura (1976) has defined self-reinforcement as involving three conditions, namely (a) free access to reinforcers, (b) a self-imposed standard of performance which the individual has decided to attain prior to self-reinforcement, and (c) the self-determination that the performance criterion has been satisfied prior to the administration of self-reinforcement. If we accept these definitions then it is arguable that there are *no* examples in the literature of individuals with learning disabilities using self-reinforcement to modify their own behaviour. There are, however, numerous papers and articles detailing studies where the performance standards are set by external agents and where the individuals do not have free access to reinforcers (see Gardiner and Cole, 1989 for a fuller discussion of these issues). Indeed much, if not all, of the literature on self-control refers to studies that include elements of significant external interventions. In many cases what is termed 'self-control' involves little more than the training of individuals with learning difficulties to cue external agents (experimenters, teachers etc.) to deliver stimuli which the external agents have previously labelled 'reinforcers'. At worst, this represents a form of tokenism which pays lip service to the true involvement of clients in their own educational progress. At best, these studies signify the beginnings of an attempt to shift behavioural control from the external environment and towards the individual. It is, however, premature to suggest that the literature contains any clear examples of true self-control being exhibited by people with learning disabilities.

Future directions

Taken together the above criticisms would suggest that the self-control literature so far does not address the needs of individuals with severe learning disabilities who display serious challenging behaviour. We are of the opinion that emerging evidence from a number of different fields suggests that individuals with severe learning disability *can* be helped to self-regulate their own behaviour, but that therapeutic endeavour needs to move away from the rather fossilised approaches to 'self-control' mentioned earlier and towards a more radical interpretation of learning disability. At this stage, however, concrete evidence is limited and much research needs to be completed before firm predictions can be made regarding treatment efficacy. The remainder of this chapter will, therefore, attempt to pull together a number of disparate strands into a comprehensive set of recommendations which may guide future research.

Rule-governed behaviour

Much of the work of Lowe and colleagues supports the notion that the development of language in humans with the consequent emergence of *rule-governed*, as opposed to *contingency-shaped*, behaviour has a profound effect on behavioural relationships generally. The distinction between contingency-shaped and rule-governed behaviour will be vital to the subsequent discussion. In essence, the distinction can be stated thus: behaviour which is under the direct control of schedules of operant reinforcement or punishment is contingency controlled; when individuals learn to describe their own behaviour and the particular contingencies in operation then their behaviour is said to be mediated by verbal behaviour and to be rule-governed. Of central importance here is the suggestion that the formulation of verbal rules may, under particular circumstances, render human behaviour insensitive to the immediate consequences that are central to the acquisition and maintenance of contingency-shaped behaviour. In a very real sense, if a person creates a rule to explain the influences of their environment upon their own behaviour, then that internal rule may, under certain conditions, exert more of a controlling influence over the person's behaviour than the actual environmental contingencies in operation. In a recent publication, Remington (1991), discussing the research findings related to the influence of rule-governed behaviour, summarised the implications of this research as follows:

It is unclear at present what the implications of this rapidly developing line of research will be for intervention with people with mental handicap, but several foci are likely to emerge. First, to the extent that clients have functional language skills, the impact of contingencies may be indirect, depending on the relations between instructions (or self-instructions), and the consequences that are provided for behaviour change. Secondly, the effect of an intervention that creates functional language skills must produce major changes in the functioning of people with mental handicap. Apart from simply enhancing efficient control over their environments, verbal behaviour opens a gateway to a completely different mode of relating to experience. Third, the behaviour of people who work as caregivers, teachers or clinical psychologists is often likely to be rule-governed. It may prove important to understand the ways in which interactions with clients may be mediated either through external instructions (e.g., the behaviour required of care staff) or self-instruction (e.g. the belief that 'all SIB is a way of getting attention'). (p. 16)

The last point here may be of considerable importance both in analysing the functions of staff training and in designing more effective interventions; space, however, does not permit a fuller discussion of this issue here. Of more relevance to the present discussion are Remington's other suggestions concerning the functional use of language and these will be dealt with in more detail.

Language and self-regulation

Whitman (1990) presented an analysis of learning disability as a 'self-regulatory disorder' (p. 348) and suggested that this re-formulation was consistent with previous descriptions of people with learning disability as being dependent and having an external locus of control (Zigler and Balla, 1982). This re-formulation suggests a number of directions which are related to the suggestions concerning the functional use of language mentioned earlier (Remington, 1991) and which augment these in important areas. Essentially, Whitman (1990) conceptualises the key deficit in learning disability as the inability to transfer learning from one situation to another, and sees language as an essential tool in facilitating this transfer. This emphasis on the importance of language in generalisation and maintenance (subsumed under the more general term 'transfer') is similar to that of Stokes and Baer (1977), who regarded language as meeting . . . 'perfectly the logic of a salient common stimulus, to be carried from any training setting to any generalisation setting that the child may ever enter. It also exemplifies the essence of the active generalisation approach . . .' (p. 362). Whitman (1990), like Remington (1991), emphasises the importance of teaching linguistic skills in the development of self-regulation. There can be little doubt that self-regulation can be developed more easily by individuals who show a linguistic competence, and that interventions which serve to increase functional language skills will produce major changes in the functioning of people with learning disability. This, however, is not the whole story. Firstly, we believe that individuals with severe learning disability can be helped to develop self-regulation even where there is little or no evidence of the presence of linguistic abilities and secondly, we also believe that the development of self-regulation can be considerably enhanced by focusing not only on language, but also (and perhaps most importantly) on aspects surrounding the motivation, self-esteem and sense of control of individuals with learning disabilities. This issue will be dealt with in detail in a later section. Firstly, however, some discussion of the relationship between self-regulation and learning disability is necessary.

Self-regulation and learning disability

Whitman (1990) stated that 'the procedures for teaching persons with retardation are fundamentally the same as teaching persons without retardation' (p. 360). Meichenbaum (1990) took issue with this statement and felt that 'mentally retarded individuals need specific supports and prompts' (p. 368). To talk, as both of these authors do, of the needs of groups of persons with a learning disability implies that there is some characteristic, attribute or deficit which all of these individuals have in common and which will differentiate them from other individuals who have not acquired this label. As Jones (1991), however, points out:

An underlying assumption behind this practice is that people with mental handicap represent a homogeneous group and therefore that they can be treated in a similar manner. Clearly, however, any large group of people will include individuals who have differing verbal abilities. It is likely, therefore that the responses of these individuals to particular interventions will differ on the basis of their ability to formulate and use verbal rules describing schedule contingencies. (p. 61)

Indeed, perhaps the single most outstanding characteristic of any group of individuals labelled learning disabled is their heterogeneity. This has significant implications for the development of self-regulation. From the discussion so far it seems clear that the ability of an individual to use language to describe and control his or her own behaviour represents one of the most important of all skills. Although many studies have been carried out in recent years which seek to use language as a medium whereby behaviour can be acquired and maintained these are, as we have seen, not without their difficulties. A more fundamental criticism, indeed, is that these studies do not fully exploit the extent to which language may be used to help in the development of persons with learning difficulties. Language has a much wider role than just self-regulation. Our understanding of the relevance of language to all aspects of development owes much to the work of the Soviet psychologists Luria (1961) and Vygotsky (1962). These researchers showed how children can be instructed by others and learn to instruct themselves to respond in certain prescribed ways and that this method of self-control becomes increasingly reliable as development proceeds. Employing data from a series of laboratory analogue studies, as well as material from naturalistic observations, Luria plotted the development of the regulatory function of speech in young children. From this work it would appear that there are several significant stages. Initially, children are unable to use speech to direct their own behaviour but speech has a general 'impellant' or initiating function. At later stages they use language to develop more complex control over their behaviour (i.e. they do what they say they will do) and gradually speech becomes covert and internalised. A factor of major relevance to the discussion of challenging behaviour is that the ability to inhibit ongoing action is a more developmentally advanced function of language. Luria (1961) has suggested that children need to be as old as five years before they can successfully inhibit their own behaviour *without extra assistance* (our italics). It is in determining the precise parameters of this extra assistance, however, that the most exciting areas of further research lie. This can be divided into three separate but related areas on the basis of the language abilities of the subjects receiving an intervention:

a) It seems clear that people with learning difficulties who have the ability to use language will continue to benefit from interventions which use their existing abilities to maximise the acquisition of new skills and the reduction of challenging behaviours, especially as the methodologies of these studies become more sophisticated (Woods and Lowe, 1986; Bryon, 1988).
b) The statistically smaller number of people with severe and profound learning difficulties will continue to benefit from the types of interventions which are at present referred to as behaviour modification. It should be stressed, however, that concurrent attempts to teach these subjects to use even the rudiments of language to control their own behaviour is essential.
c) A slightly larger population exists that may possess early language skills but these are such that the subjects are unable to use language to control behaviour. It is perhaps this population that represents the greatest challenge to available procedures. For example, Hobbs (1982) demonstrated that a group of people with learning disabilities were unable to learn a task which involved a simple conditional discrimination. This is in keeping with a number of studies which showed failure to learn conditional discrimination tasks in people with severe learning disabilities (e.g. Walsh, 1985). When Hobbs taught the subjects how to use verbal labels, however, they were able to learn the discriminations. In addition to labelling, a host of procedures hold potential to aid the development of rule-governed behaviour in this population. These include

the use of imagery, stimulus shaping, spatial location, and numerous non-verbal devices to aid the formation of verbal rules (Pressley, 1990). What seems vital in this endeavour is that individuals with severe learning disabilities should not be excluded on grounds related to their IQ, cognitive functioning or language ability levels (Kendall, 1990) from attempts to develop self-regulation. For example, Jones, Baker and Murphy (1988) found marked differences in the power of a differential reinforcement procedure to reduce stereotypy between individuals displaying high-rate challenging behaviour. They attributed these differences to the ability of one subject in their study to use verbal rules to modify his own behaviour. Similarly, Hughes and Rusch (1989) found that Self-Instructional Training (SIT) could be successfully used with individuals whose level of IQ was estimated to be 27 and 33. Despite the rather dubious validity of IQ scores in this range, this finding challenged the earlier work of Meichenbaum and Goodman (1971) and Agran, Fodor-Davis, and Moore (1986), which suggested that SIT is of maximum benefit to individuals with IQs above 60. Rather than use assessment to exclude people from interventions, it may be more important, if we are teaching a new skill, that we should do it through an appreciation of the language skills that already exist rather than by imposing a predetermined strategy. Again, however, this is rare in the literature. Existing research on developing self-regulation has not identified the precise subject characteristics which could predict the success of a self-regulation programme prior to its implementation. Potentially relevant characteristics might include expressive vocabulary, functional use of language, and ability to use language to control behaviour in a new situation. It is probable that successful interventions in the future will aim to establish the verbal abilities of subjects prior to an intervention in order to tailor the intervention to maximise the subjects' abilities to develop self-regulation. A further criterion of great importance, however, centres around the motivation of the individual.

Motivation and self-regulation

Although not often acknowledged, Vygotsky (1986) was one of the first theorists to recognise the vital importance which motivation plays in the development of learning disability. He regarded learning disability as a phenomenon which has both organic and social attributes, and suggested that society may respond to children who have organically traceable learning difficulties by depriving them of adequate communicative experiences, thus delaying their development still further. In this area (and indeed, in many others) Vygotsky was many years ahead of his time and the role which society plays in augmenting learning disability ('secondary handicap') is now widely acknowledged and has important implications for the development of self-regulation. One major reason, therefore, why individuals with learning disability may show a limited ability to self-regulate is that they are frequently isolated from 'normal' lifestyles in which independent decision-making skills are fostered. Evidence exists that people with learning difficulties are frequently encouraged from an early age to rely on others to guide their behaviour (Beveridge and Conti-Ramsden, 1987), to be less likely to trust their own cognitive resources (Zigler and Balla, 1982) and to have a concomitant dependence on external control (Whitman, 1990). Zigler and Balla (1982) also suggest that a history of frequent failure reinforces low self-esteem and a perception of external locus of control, which in turn leads to the expectation of further failure and limited belief in personal efficacy and self-control. Some authors have even suggested that some individuals *adopt* a secondary or 'opportunist' handicap as a defence or protective shield against societal demands (Sinason, 1986), while others (e.g. McGee, Menousek, and Hobbs, 1987) see challenging behaviour serving the same function. Clearly, these motivational dynamics do not set ideal conditions for the development of self-regulation. Vygotsky, however, regarded language development itself as being inexorably intertwined in the motivational dynamics of the individual. For Vygotsky language was not a side-effect or symptom of development, as was suggested by the Swiss psychologist Piaget, rather language itself was the driving force behind development and was itself influenced greatly by motivational factors. For Vygotsky, thinking was itself a social process centred on 'reflective awareness and deliberate control' (1962, p. 90) and this led him to advocate strongly for changes in the education of children with learning disability away from an emphasis on concrete thinking problems or look-and-do methods towards an emphasis on abstract thinking:

Precisely because retarded children when left to themselves, will never achieve well elaborated forms of abstract thought, the school should make every effort to push them in that direction and to develop in them what is intrinsically lacking in their own development. (Vygotsky, 1978, p.89)

This has major implications for the treatment of individuals with learning disability and suggests that the development of self-regulation is a long-term goal which cannot be expected to be achieved by simple, short-term, 'self-control' packages. It is rare for individuals with learning disability to have the opportunity to have self-regulatory skills gradually shaped in such a way that they experience a history of success. The importance of this process was outlined by Whitman (1990), who stated that:

From a developmental perspective attributional beliefs not only develop as a result of life experiences but also can be directly shaped by teaching individuals with retardation that success is a consequence of effort and proper strategy usage on their part and conversely that failure occurs through lack of effort and strategic inactivity. (p. 359)

As was mentioned previously, true self-regulation involves an individual having both control and choice over significant aspects of his or her own life. What Vygotsky alerts us to is that such familiar concepts as advocacy, self-determination, status, choice, and competence are not just slogans around which services for people with learning disabilities can develop but may represent the bedrock from which the development of cognitive competence can be facilitated and fostered.

CONCLUSIONS

Although the last twenty years has seen a steady increase in studies which claim to have researched the development of 'self-control' in people with learning disabilities, closer examination of the literature suggests that there is very little firm research evidence concerned with the development of true self-regulation in people with learning disabilities. Studies which address the needs of individuals with severe learning disabilities are fewer still, and research on the effects of verbal self-regulation in individuals with both severe learning disabilities and severe challenging behaviours is practically non-existent.

We have, however, outlined some areas where grounds for cautious optimism exist although evidence is scarce and much that has been discussed is still speculative. In summary, it appears that interventions which are based on the application of laboratory work with animals will be of only limited utility with individuals who display challenging behaviour. Techniques which encourage and augment functional language skills are likely to have considerable positive effects on the behaviour of individuals with a learning disability even when that disability is severe. Attempts to help subjects formulate rules to describe environmental contingencies are likely to enhance procedures designed to decrease challenging behaviour and increase appropriate responding. Although verbal mediation is the most obvious choice here, disabled individuals might also benefit from the use of mediators such as imagery or stimulus shaping. We have suggested that the use of 'self-control' packages will be of limited use in the development of effective self-regulation, and that a more long-term view is needed that envisages the acquisition of the skills necessary for self-regulation taking place over a number of years. Central to this process are the motivational dynamics of the individual. A personal sense of being in control may be crucial not just for the reduction of challenging behaviour, but also for the development of self-regulation, the acquisition of language and possibly even the development of thinking itself.

Because of the scarcity of published empirical data on the implementation of the ideas discussed in this paper, readers who wish to put these ideas into practice in working with individuals with learning disabilities and challenging behaviour will not find an easily available and accessible text outlining specific strategies. Hence the importance of conducting empirical investigations within the theoretical framework that we have outlined. As a starting point we suggest that the interested reader could find guidance in the work of Hayes (1989), Lowe (especially Lowe *et al.*, 1987 and Lowe, 1991) and Vygotsky (especially 1986 and 1978) and could find practical guidance in Bryon (1988), Hobbs (1982) and Smith (1990).

References

Agran, M., Fodor-Davis, J. and Moore, S. (1986), 'The effects of self-instructional training on job-task sequencing: suggesting a problem-solving strategy', *Education and Training of the Mentally Retarded*, 21, 273–81.

Bandura, A. (1976), 'Self-reinforcement: theoretical and methodological considerations', *Behaviorism*, 4, 135–55.

Bem, S. L. (1967), 'Verbal self-control: the establishment of effective self-instruction'. *Journal of Experimental Psychology*, 64, 485–91.

Bentall, R. P., Lowe, C. F. and Beasty, A. (1985), 'The role of verbal behavior in human learning II: developmental differences', *Journal of the Experimental Analysis of Behavior*, 43, 165–81.

Beveridge, M. and Conti-Ramsden, G. (1987), 'Social cognition and problem-solving in persons with mental retardation. *Australia and New Zealand Journal of Developmental Disabilities*, 13, 99–106.

Bryon, M. (1988), *The reduction of disruptive behaviour using self-management: A component analysis*, unpublished research dissertation, The British Psychological Society, Leicester.

Carr, J. (1991), 'Recent advances in working with people with learning difficulties', *Behavioural Psychotherapy*, 19, 109–20.

Catania, A. C. (1984), *Learning*, (2nd edn.) Prentice Hall, Englewood Cliffs, NJ.

Cooper, J. O., Heron, T. E. and Heward, W. L. (1987), *Applied Behavior Analysis*, Merrill, Colombus, Ohio.

Davey, G. and Cullen, C. (1988), *Human Operant Conditioning and Behavior Modification*, Wiley, New York.

Dugdale, N. and Lowe, C. F. (1990), 'Naming and stimulus equivalence' in D. E. Blackman and H. Lejeune (eds.), *Behaviour Analysis in Theory and Practice*, Lawrence Erlbaum Asociates Ltd, London.

Ferster, C. B. and Skinner, B. F. (1957), *Schedules of Reinforcement*, Appleton-Century-Crofts, New York.

Foxx, R. M. and Rubinoff, A. (1979), 'Behavioral treatment of caffeinism: reducing excessive coffee drinking', *Journal of Applied Behavior Analysis*, 12, 335–44.

Gardiner, W. I. and Cole, C. L. (1989), 'Self-management approaches' in E. Cipani (ed.), *The Treatment of Severe Behavior Disorders: Behavior Analysis Approaches*, American Association on Mental Retardation, Washington, DC.

Glynn, E. L., Thomas, J. D. and Shee, S. M. (1973), 'Behavioral self-control of on-task behavior in an elementary classroom', *Journal of Applied Behavior Analysis*, 6, 105–14.

Harvey, J. R., Karan, O. C., Bhargava, D. and Morehouse, N. (1978), 'Relaxation training and cognitive behavioral procedures to reduce violent temper outbursts in a moderately retarded woman', *Journal of Behavior Therapy and Experimental Psychiatry*, 9, 347–51.

Hayes, S. C. (1989), *Rule-Governed Behavior: Cognition, Contingencies and Instructional Control*, Plenum Press, New York.

Hobbs, S. D. W. (1982), *An investigation of the roles of verbal labelling in errorless discrimination learning with mentally handicapped adults*, unpublished research dissertation, The British Psychological Society, Leicester.

Hughes, C. and Rusch, F. R. (1989), 'Teaching supported employees with severe mental retardation to solve problems', *Journal of Applied Behavior Analysis*, 22, 365–72.

Jones, R. S. P. (1991), 'Reducing inappropriate behaviour using non-aversive procedures: evaluating differential reinforcement schedules', in B. Remington (ed.), *The Challenge of Severe Mental Handicap: A Behaviour Analytic Approach*, Wiley, Chichester.

Jones, R. S. P., Baker, L. J. V. and Murphy, M. (1988), 'Reducing stereotyped behaviour: the maintenance effects of a DRO reinforcement procedure', *Journal of Practical Approaches to Developmental Handicap*, 12, 24–30.

Jones, R. S. P., Wint, D. and Ellis, N. (1990), 'The social consequences of stereotyped behaviour', *Journal of Mental Handicap Research, 34*, 261–68.

Jones, R. T., Nelson, R. E. and Kazdin, A. E. (1977), 'The role of external variables in self-reinforcement', *Behavior Modification*, 1, 147–78.

Kendall, P. C. (1990), 'Challenges for cognitive strategy training: the case of mental retardation', *American Journal of Mental Deficiency*, 94, 156–63.

Kiernan, C. (1985), 'Behaviour Modification', in A. M. Clarke, A. D. B. Clarke and J. M. Berg (eds), *Mental Deficiency: The Changing Outlook*, Methuen, London.

Kneedler, R. D. and Hallahan, D. P. (1981), 'Self-monitoring of on-task behavior with learning disabled children: current studies and directions', *Exceptional Education Quarterly*, 2, 73–82.

Leander, J. D., Lippman, L. G. and Meyer, M. E. (1968), 'Fixed interval performance as related to subjects' verbalisations of the reinforcement contingency', *Psychological Record*, 18, 469–74.

Litrownik, A. J., Freitas, J. L. and Franzini, L. R. (1978), 'Self-regulation in mentally retarded children: assessment and training of self-monitoring skills', *American Journal of Mental Deficiency*, 82, 499–506.

Lowe, C. F. (1979), 'Determinants of human operant behaviour' in M. D. Zeiler and P. Harzem (eds.), *Advances in Analysis of Behaviour*, I Reinforcement and the Organisation of Behaviour, Wiley, Chichester.

Lowe, C. F. (1983), 'Radical behaviourism and human psychology', In G. L. C. Davey (ed.), *Animal Models and Human Behaviour: Conceptual, Evolutionary and Neurobiological Perspectives*, Wiley, Chichester.

Lowe, C. F. (1991), *From Conditioning to Consciousness: The Cultural Origins of Mind*, inaugural lecture, University of Wales (in press).

Lowe, C. F. and Beasty, A. (1987), 'Language and the emergence of equivalence relations: a developmental study', *Bulletin of the British Psychological Society*, 40, 42.

Lowe, C. F., Beasty, A. and Bentall, R. P. (1983), 'The role of verbal behaviour in human learning: infant performance on fixed-interval schedules', *Journal of the Experimental Analysis of Behaviour*, 39, 157–64.

Lowe, C. F., Harzem, P. and Bagshaw, M. (1978), 'Species difference in temporal control of behaviour: II. Human performance', *Journal of the Experimental Analysis of Behaviour*, 29, 351–61.

Lowe, C. F., Harzem, P. and Hughes, S. (1978), 'Determinants of operant behaviour in humans: some differences from animals', *Quarterly Journal of Experimental Psychology*, 30, 373–86.

Lowe, C. F. and Horne, P. J. (1985), 'On the generality of behavioural principles: human choice and the matching law' in C. F. Lowe, M. Richelle, D. E. Blackman and C. M. Bradshaw (eds.), *Behaviour Analysis and Contemporary Psychology*, Lawrence Erlbaum, London.

Lowe, C. F., Horne, P. J. and Higson, P. J. (1987), 'Operant conditioning: the hiatus between theory and practice in clinical psychology' in H. J. Eysenck and I. Martin (eds.), *Theoretical Foundaions of Behaviour Therapy*, Plenum, London.

Luria, A. R. (1961), *The Role of Speech in the Regulation of Normal and Abnormal Behaviour*, Pergamon Press, London.

Meichenbaum, D. (1990), 'Cognitive perspective on teaching self-regulation', *American Journal on Mental Retardation*, 94, 367–69.

Meichenbaum, D. and Goodman, J. (1971), 'Training impulsive children to talk to themselves: a means of developing self-control', *Journal of Abnormal Psychology*, 77, 116–26.

McGee, J. J., Menousek, P. E. and Hobbs, D. C. (1987), 'Gentle teaching: an alternative to punishment for people with challenging behaviours' in S. J. Taylor, D. Bicker, J. Knoll (eds.), *Community Integration for People with Severe Learning Disabilities*, Teachers College Press, New York.

Pressley, M. (1990), 'Four more considerations about self-regulation among mentally retarded persons', *American Journal on Mental Retardation*, 94, 369–71.

Reese, R. M., Sherman, J. A. and Sheldon, J. (1984). 'Reducing agitated-disruptive behavior of mentally retarded residents of community group homes: the role of self-recording and peer prompted self-recording', *Analysis and Intervention in Developmental Disabilities*, 4, 91–107.

Remington, B. (1991), 'Behavior analysis and severe mental handicap: the dialogue between research and application', in B. Remington (ed.), *The Challenge of Severe Mental Handicap: A Behaviour Analytic Approach*, Wiley, Chichester.

Remington, B. and Evans, J. (1988), 'Basic learning processes in people with profound mental retardations: review and relevance', *Mental Handicap Research*, 1, 4–23.

Salkovskis, P. M. (1986), 'The cognitive revolution: new way forward, backward somersault or full circle?', *Behavioural Psychotherapy*, 14, 278–82.

Shapiro, E. S. (1986), 'Behavior modification: self-control and cognitive procedures', In R. P. Barrett (ed.), *Severe Behavior Disorders in the Mentally Retarded*, Plenum, New York.

Sidman, M. and Cresson, O., Jr. (1973), 'Reading and crossmodal transfer of stimulus equivalences in severe retardation', *American Journal of Mental Deficiency*, 77, 515–23.

Sidman, M., Cresson, O., Jr. and Willson-Morris, M. (1974), 'Acquisition of matching to sample via mediated tranfer', *Journal of the Experimental Analysis of Behavior*, 22, 261–73.

Sidman, M., Rauzin, R., Lazar, R. and Cunningham, S. (1982), 'A search for symmetry in the conditional discrimination of Rhesus monkeys, baboons and children', *Journal of the Experimental Analysis of Behavior*, 37, 23–44.

Sidman, M. and Tailby, W. (1982), 'Conditional discrimination versus matching to sample: an expansion of the testing paradigm', *Journal of the Experimental Analysis of Behavior*, 37, 5–22.

Sinason, V. (1986), 'Secondary mental handicap and its relationship to trauma', *Psychoanalytic Psychotherapy*, 2, 131–54.

Skinner, B. F. (1938), *The Behavior of Organisms: An Analysis*, Appleton-Century-Crofts, New York.

Skinner, B. F. (1953), *Science and Human Behavior*, Macmillan, New York.

Smith, M. D. (1990), *Autism and Life in the Community: Successful Interventions for Behavioral Challenges*, Paul H. Brooks, Baltimore, MD.

Stokes, T. F. and Baer, D. M. (1977), 'An implicit technology of generalisation', *Journal of Applied Behavior Analysis*, 10, 349–67.

Vygotsky, L. S. (1962), *Thought and Language*, Wiley, New York.

Vygotsky, L. S. (1978), *The Development of Higher Psychological Processes*, Harvard University Press, New York.

Vygotsky, L. S. (1986), 'The problem of mental retardation (A tentative working hypothesis)', *Soviet Psychology*, 16, 78–85.

Walsh, P. G. (1985), 'Teaching colour discrimination to the mentally handicapped', *The Irish Journal of Psychology*, 7, 36–49.

Weiner, H. (1969), 'Human behavioural persistence', *The Psychological Record*, 20, 445–56.

Whitman, T. L. (1990), 'Self-regulation and mental retardation', *American Journal on Mental Retardation*, 94, 347–62.

Woods, P. A. and Lowe, C. F. (1986), 'Verbal self-regulation of inappropriate behaviour with mentally handicapped adults' in J. M. Berg, (ed.), *Science and Service in Mental Retardation*, Methuen, New York.

Zegiob, L., Klukas, N. and Junginger, J. (1978), 'Reactivity of self-monitoring procedures with retarded adolescents', *American Journal of Mental Deficiency*, 83, 156–63.

Zigler, E. and Balla, D. (1982), 'The developmental approach to mental retardation' in E. Zigler and D. Balla (eds.), *Mental Retardation: The Developmental-Difference Controversy*, Erlbaum, Hillsdale, NJ.

Psychopharmacological approaches to challenging behaviour

The prescription of psychoactive (psychotropic and anti-epileptic) drugs to people with learning disabilities is a subject which has provoked some controversy and resulted in much published research. Most studies agree that about 35 per cent of people with learning disabilities resident in hospitals receive psychotropic drugs (predominantly anti-psychotics) and about the same proportion receive anti-epileptic medications. Some studies have found lower rates of prescribing to people with learning disabilities resident in the community, but there are apparent inconsistencies which merit further investigation. For example, one study in the United States compared the use of anti-psychotic drugs in 'public residential facilities' (hospitals) and 'community residential facilities' (akin to large hostels) and concluded 'The decision as to whether or not a client is placed on an antipsychotic drug may be influenced as much by the characteristic of the client's environment as by the client's own behavior' (Intagliata and Rinck, 1985). However, another USA study found that demographic variables and those related to environment had very little influence (if any) on either the probability that a psychotropic drug would be prescribed, or the dose (Buck and Sprague, 1989). One UK study found that the people with learning disabilities resident in hospitals in the West Midlands were much more likely to receive drugs prescribed 'for behaviour' than people living in social services hostels or with their families, 40.2 per cent, compared to 19.3 per cent and 10.1 per cent respectively (Clarke, Kelley, Thinn and Corbett, 1990). However, another study by the same researchers found that when people with learning disabilities resident in hospital moved to live in the community, neither the number of people receiving anti-psychotic drugs, nor the doses prescribed, declined, despite follow-up after an average of 25 months of community living (Thinn, Clarke and Corbett, 1990).

It is natural that there should be concern about the use of medication, but research has unfortunately been unable to answer the key question concerning the prescription of psychotropic drugs to people with learning disabilities: how often is such use appropriate? The notion of appropriate (or rational) prescribing has received some attention (e.g. Bates, Smeltzer and Arnoczky, 1986), but to decide whether a prescription is appropriate or not requires detailed knowledge of the individual prescribed for, their current problems, past history and other strategies which have been employed to deal with the problem(s). This is an area which medical audit will probably illuminate more successfully than population-based research.

When considering the use of psychotropic drugs, it is important to separate the treatment of *challenging behaviour* from the treatment of *mental illness* such as manic-depressive (bipolar) or schizophrenic disorders. People with learning disabilities have an increased vulnerability to mental illness, the prevalence of mental illness among people with learning disabilities is about four times that found in the general population (Corbett, 1979; Lund, 1985), and the illnesses respond to the same interventions (including the use of psychotropic drugs) as those used for people without learning disabilities. Sometimes behaviour which might be considered 'challenging' arises as a result of mental illness (in which case the behaviour usually resolves as the mental illness remits) and sometimes a person has both a mental illness and challenging behaviour unrelated to the mental illness. The distinction might therefore seem arbitrary, but it is important because (for most behaviours) the evidence for the efficacy of medication in treating challenging behaviour is less well established than the evidence for efficacy in treating mental illness, which is very clearly established (e.g. Davis and Garver, 1978). Greater attention is therefore necessary to the risk/benefit ratio when using medication to manage challenging behaviour unrelated to mental illness.

This chapter reviews relevant assessment procedures, drugs commonly used to manage challenging behaviour unrelated to specific mental illness, their effects, and strategies which have been described for reviewing and optimising their use. The pharmacological management of three types of challenging behaviour (unacceptable or offending sexual behaviour, self-injurious behaviour, and abnormally aggressive behaviour) is then discussed. Aggression and unacceptable sexual behaviour are the commonest reasons for people with learning disabilities being detained under the Mental Health Act with a classification of 'mental impairment' or 'severe mental impairment'. Self-injury is a significant source of distress and morbidity for the individual concerned and distress for others, and is a not uncommon reason for people's opportunities being restricted.

The chapter concentrates on the use of pharmacological interventions alone, to avoid duplication of material: this should not be taken to implying that such interventions are always the treatment of choice. In practice, the combination of medication and other interventions is sometimes more efficacious than either intervention alone. For example, the combination of an anti-libidinal drug and psychotherapy is often superior to the use of medication (or psychotherapy) alone – the anti-libidinal lowers sexual drive, while concurrent psychotherapy addresses the reason for the behaviour and its consequences for the individual and others (Van de Merwe, 1979).

The issue of responsibility for behaviour needs to be considered when psychopharmacological treatment is offered; some people regard the prescription of medication as an indication that they no longer need to accept responsibility for the consequences of their behaviour. Whilst it is occasionally true that the person has little or no control over 'challenging' behaviour, the issue of responsibility can be usefully viewed as a continuum with people with no control over their actions (e.g. as a result of seizure activity interfering with consciousness) at one pole, and people with full awareness of (and responsibility for) their actions at the other pole. Many people with learning disabilities fall somewhere along the continuum with, for example, a lower threshold for loss of temper (resulting from changes in brain function), but with full awareness of their actions and the consequences, and the ability to curtail the behaviour in certain circumstances. These issues may need to be discussed with the person receiving the medication, and/or their carer, before treatment is started.

Full details of the possible adverse reactions to medications described are not given in the text: it is assumed that practitioners will refer to manufacturers' data sheets before prescribing.

ASSESSMENT

The assessment of a person who shows what appears to be challenging behaviour should include steps to exclude underlying illness (physical or mental), identify relevant initiating or maintaining factors, and decide how best the behaviour can be quantified and treatment effects evaluated. Because people with learning disabilities often have a concomitant speech or language problem, it is important to be alert to clues to the cause of changes in behaviour which the person cannot describe. Conditions which are associated with learning disability (such as epilepsy or autistic-like conditions) or are causes of developmental delay (such as Down's syndrome) may themselves predispose to unusual or unacceptable behaviours. Examples include:

1. Head banging by a young man with Down's syndrome in response to an ear infection (to which people with Down's syndrome are particularly vulnerable), which responded to treatment with antibiotics.
2. Sudden outbursts of temper and aggression by a young man with a pervasive developmental disorder (an autistic-like condition), which could be related to changes in the routine of his life, and mocking by other youths (because of his extremely eccentric appearance and habits). He accepted a move to different accommodation where his solitariness and eccentricity caused fewer problems, and he could re-establish a pattern to his week.

3. Incontinence and faecal smearing by a woman with Down's syndrome in her forties, whose cognitive abilities had declined over the year before the 'problem' behaviour started. After excluding a reversible cause of cognitive decline (such as hypothyroidism, to which people with Down's syndrome are vulnerable), a diagnosis of Alzheimer's disease was made. Although it was not possible to reverse the cognitive decline (or, for this particular lady, to change the behaviour), the knowledge of the cause (and that it was not just 'awkwardness') enabled her carers to accept and cope with the behaviour, with appropriate help from community services.

4. A middle-aged woman who started to steal from other people in the group home where she lived. She was also unusually talkative and somewhat disinhibited, and the other residents in the house regarded her as an unpleasant nuisance. She eventually became aggressive (partly as a result of the increasing friction in the house). She had a past history of episodes of depression, and had become hypomanic (hypomania is a mental disorder characterised by euphoria and overactivity). Her mental illness responded to treatment with anti-psychotic medication and subsequent prophylactic treatment with lithium.

5. A young man with short stature and lack of sexual development who had attended a special school mainly because of behaviour problems – he had an insatiable appetite and stole food or money to obtain food at any opportunity, and had sudden outbursts of extreme temper in response to quite trivial comments by his teachers, parents or other children. He was extremely overweight for his height. He was referred because his tempers were causing problems at home and at the day centre he attended. He had the characteristic small hands and feet and facial appearance seen in Prader-Willi syndrome. This accounted for his mild cognitive impairment, insatiable appetite, hypogonadism, and his low threshold for losing his temper. The explanation that people with Prader-Willi syndrome are more prone than most people to lose their temper, and have great difficulty controlling this was a help to him and to his parents and the day centre staff. His tempers continued, however, and he was offered treatment with carbamazepine, an anti-epileptic drug which also sometimes helps limit sudden outbursts of rage (see discussion below). The frequency and intensity of the outbursts declined, although the tempers did not stop completely.

Bridgen and Todd (1990) have described a 'pre-admission' checklist (with flow charts for appropriate action) which enable psychiatric and medical problems or disorders (together with a host of other possible causes, precipitants or factors perpetuating challenging behaviour) to be identified and acted on. An approach to assessment which is both thorough and methodical is essential if a person with challenging behaviour is to receive the best service, irrespective of whether a psychopharmacological approach is employed.

A further consideration where drugs are to be used is how to assess treatment effects. This obviously has to be tailored to the individual problems which are to be addressed, but a methodical approach is again necessary. The target behaviour should be defined as accurately as possible, and some measure (however crude) devised. One useful strategy is to use 10cm analogue scales to rate individual behaviours on a line with 'extreme problem' at one end, and 'no problem' at the other. By measuring the line, a 1 to 10 scale of behaviour can be transcribed. Alternatively, each behaviour can be rated as 'no problem', 'mild problem', 'marked problem' or 'extreme problem'. When devising scales, the usual considerations of subjectivity, tendency to central ratings, etc., should be borne in mind, but in general some measure is better than no measure at all! More than one rater may also be advantageous, especially if the initial impression is that the problem posed by a behaviour varies markedly according to the situation, or is estimated differently by different observers. Sturmey, Reed and Corbett (1991) have reviewed the standardised instruments available for rating psychiatric disorders, and instruments are also available for rating behaviour and behavioural change not due to specific mental illness, including adaptive behaviour (e.g. the Aberrant Behavior Checklist (Aman *et al.*, 1985); the Adaptive Behavior Scale (Nihira *et al.*, 1974) and the Challenging Behaviour Scales (Wilkinson, 1989). See Chapter 7 for a fuller discussion of assessment procedures.

DRUGS COMMONLY PRESCRIBED TO PEOPLE WITH CHALLENGING BEHAVIOUR

Anti-psychotics

The anti-psychotic drugs, also known as 'major tranquillisers' or 'neuroleptics' are relatively commonly prescribed (together with anti-epileptic drugs) for people with learning disabilities resident in hospital. They are of proven efficacy in the treatment of some forms of mental illness, including schizophrenia, paranoid psychoses (delusional disorders), manic illnesses, and depressive disorders where delusions or hallucinations are prominent. Their use to manage aggression or other forms of challenging behaviour is reviewed below. Anti-psychotics fall into four chemical classes, and (with the exception of the 'miscellaneous' group) their actions tend to be broadly similar. The four classes are the phenothiazines (e.g. chlorpromazine), the butyrophenones (e.g. haloperidol), the diphenylbutylpiperidines (e.g. pimozide) and the miscellaneous anti-psychotics (e.g. clozapine). Their unwanted effects vary in type and severity from compound to compound, but the most troublesome common adverse effects are those related to movement abnormalities. Most of the anti-psychotics can provoke acute dystonias (muscle spasms), pseudo-Parkinsonism (with rigidity and tremor), akathisia (restlessness) and tardive dyskinesias (a variety of abnormal movements, including tongue protrusion and other facial movements, and trunk movements, occurring after many months or years of treatment). The disorders resolve when treatment is stopped, with the exception of tardive dyskinesia, which may occasionally persist. Anti-Parkinsonian drugs can be used to overcome Parkinsonian side effects (stiffness and tremor), but at the expense of introducing another medication which may itself have adverse effects (e.g. constipation). Although the status of tardive dyskinesia is uncertain (in the sense that in some cases it may be a result of the illness for which treatment was given, rather than the drug used), the risk of producing an irreversible movement disorder is a strong incentive to limit the use of anti-psychotics to severe mental illnesses and other indications for which they are of proven benefit.

Carbamazepine

Carbamazepine is an anti-epileptic drug, but is also used in the treatment of bipolar affective disorders (it is structurally similar to tricyclic anti-depressant drugs) and a variety of behaviour disorders, especially those where there are sudden, explosive, outbursts of temper ('episodic dyscontrol syndrome'). The dose is usually decided by measuring the serum carbamazepine concentration and adjusting the dose to achieve a concentration within the recommended range. About 3 per cent of people treated with carbamazepine develop a rash, which disappears when treatment is stopped. Other adverse effects include drowsiness or dizziness (although sedation is much less marked than with older anti-epileptics such as phenobarbitone) and diplopia (double vision), which are usually dose-related. The person's blood count should be checked, especially during the early stages of treatment, as carbamazepine may (rarely) depress the production of certain blood cells.

Lithium

Lithium is a naturally occurring substance. Its salts (the form in which lithium is used in psychiatry) chemically resemble common salt. It is used (as lithium carbonate, citrate, etc.) to treat mania and prevent relapses of bipolar (manic-depressive) illness. It is highly effective and when the correct dose (ascertained by measuring the serum lithium concentration) is employed, is relatively free of adverse effects (the commonest are hand tremor, gastrointestinal disturbances and rashes). If the serum lithium level rises, however, (which may occur if an adequate fluid intake is not maintained, following severe diarrhoea or vomiting, and in some other circumstances), neurotoxicity will result. People with learning disabilities will often need help or supervision to ensure that they are not at risk of lithium toxicity, and their carer will usually be issued with a lithium information and record card when treatment is started.

Opiate antagonists

Naloxone and naltrexone are competitive antagonists of opiates such as morphine. They also reverse the effect of naturally occurring opiate-like compounds within the central nervous system, and this is thought to account for their proposed role in the management of self-injurious behaviour (reviewed below). Naloxone can only be administered parenterally (by intravenous, sub-cutaneous or intra-muscular injection) whereas naltrexone is given orally. Possible adverse reactions include vomiting, dizziness and drowsiness.

Beta-blockers

The beta-adrenoceptor blocking drugs ('beta-blockers') are widely used in the treatment of high blood pressure, angina, and a variety of other disorders. Some beta-blockers (notably propranolol) are also used to treat anxiety. They should not be used to treat people prone to asthma and some other forms of chest disease or heart disease, and may occasionally cause problems such as cold hands and feet, nausea or diarrhoea, and sleep disturbance. They do not cause dependence, which means they can be used for prolonged periods (unlike anxiolytics such as diazepam). Beta-blockers have been suggested as aids to the management of aggressive behaviour for some people with learning disabilities.

EFFECTS OF PSYCHOACTIVE MEDICATION ON LEARNING AND ADAPTIVE BEHAVIOUR

The effects of the psychoactive drugs most commonly prescribed to people with learning disabilities (the anti-psychotics) on cognition and adaptive behaviour are uncertain. Some drugs (such as chlorpromazine) have a sedating effect, but the degree of sedation varies markedly from person to person. One would expect, therefore, that at high doses such drugs would impair some people's cognitive functioning. This is obviously of concern where the person prescribed for has a pre-existing learning disability.

Reviews have been published which conclude (quite correctly on the basis of the information available) that anti-psychotic drugs adversely affect learning in people with learning disabilities, and may also exacerbate some maladaptive behaviours. The problem lies with the extent to which such conclusions are based on the work of Breuning, who purported to have carried out numerous investigations into the effect on learning and behaviour of thioridazine and other psychoactive drugs. Breuning's work has now been discredited (e.g. the editorial retraction by Matson and Schroeder (1988)), which means that a major proportion of the 'knowledge' about the effect of psychoactive drugs on learning must now be disregarded or treated with extreme caution (see Aman, 1987). There remains some work which implies that anti-psychotics may impair cognition (e.g. Sprague and Werry, 1971) and the other adverse effects of anti-psychotics are such that they should be used for the shortest time and in the lowest effective dose.

With regard to anti-epileptic drugs, the position is clearer; the older anti-epileptics such as phenytoin and phenobarbitone are associated with much greater impairments of cognition than newer compounds such as carbamazepine (Trimble, 1979; Aman, 1983).

Lithium does not usually impair cognition when used in therapeutic doses, neither do beta-blockers nor opiate antagonists.

AUDIT AND REVIEW OF PRESCRIBING

Several authors have now described methods of reviewing the use of psychoactive medication, in order to ensure that people who can derive benefit receive appropriate treatment, and that people who no longer require treatment (or who have failed to benefit) do not receive drugs unnecessarily. The latter is not only wasteful of resources and time; it also exposes the person treated to potential adverse effects without potential benefit. This is a particular concern where anti-psychotic drugs are used, and there is a risk of tardive dyskinesia. The strategies suggested include multidisciplinary review, and reports have suggested that the involvement of a pharmacist in regular reviews can promote rational treatment, and reduce overall use of psychoactive medication.

Inoue (1982) found that the involvement of a hospital pharmacist to review psychotropic drug use over a five-year period resulted in a significant decline in prescription. Inoue felt that a lack of feedback to prescribers about responses to drugs was something which could be overcome if the pharmacist co-ordinated the gathering of information about residents' behaviour, and the relationship of changes in behaviour to changes in prescriptions. Briggs (1989) found that the use of psychotropics in an institution in the United States was reduced, and maintained at about 20 per cent, over an eight-year period when a monitoring system (with interdisciplinary review, identification of target behaviours, and use of alternatives) was operating. Glaser and Morreau (1986) and Findholt and Emmett (1990) have also considered the effect of multidisciplinary team review on psychotropic drug prescribing to people with learning disabilities.

PSYCHOPHARMACOLOGICAL MANAGEMENT OF SPECIFIC BEHAVIOURS

1. The reduction of sexual drive

In many instances, unacceptable or illegal sexual activity by someone with a learning difficulty is a consequence of lack of knowledge, either about the law, or about which behaviours are usually regarded as acceptable in particular social settings. This obviously calls for the relevant knowledge to be imparted, in a manner appropriate to the individual's level of comprehension. In most other cases, unacceptable sexual activity can be managed through the use of counselling, psychotherapy, or behavioural interventions. Sometimes the concept of what is 'unacceptable' needs to be clarified, and the attitudes of parents or carers (rather than the person with a learning disability) may need to be addressed. There are, however, a number of people (particularly men), who benefit from the prescription of medication to reduce their sexual drive;

such medication can also be of value for some men with learning disabilities, who might otherwise find themselves in conflict with the law (with a threat to their liberty), or whose behaviour is such that it poses a significant danger to other members of society.

Sex offences and men with learning disabilities

Early studies of criminal behaviour found an excess of people with learning disabilities among offenders, especially those convicted of arson or sexual offences. These studies are now thought to be methodologically unsound, and more recent studies with better methodology have found the prevalence of learning disabilities among male offenders to be little different to that in the general population (MacEachron, 1979). However, among people with learning disabilities who do offend, sex offences and arson are disproportionately common (Lund, 1990). Sexual offending is also a relatively common reason for a man with a learning disability to be admitted to a semi-secure or specialist unit; of the men described by Day (1988) in his description of a hospital-based service, 40 per cent had committed sexual offences. Sex offences are also the commonest category of offence committed by men with learning disabilities who are detained under Section 37 of the Mental Health Act, i.e. with a Home Office 'Restriction Order', (Gibbens and Robertson, 1983). Prescription of an anti-libidinal may therefore be of great help to some men with learning disabilities, whose sexual drive would otherwise lead them into conflict with the law or have other serious adverse consequences.

Assessment

The assessment of a man with a learning disability and unacceptable or offending sexual behaviour should include an assessment of knowledge and attitudes regarding sexual behaviour, which may be best carried out by using a standardised instrument such as the Socio-Sexual Knowledge and Attitude Test (Wish, McCombs and Edmonson, 1980), together with a developmental, psychiatric and forensic history. This will enable people with other requirements (such as counselling or behavioural interventions) to be identified, and allow a decision about how helpful anti-libidinal treatment is likely to be. An assessment of sexual responsiveness can be carried out using penile plethysmography, if this is judged useful, and before starting treatment with one anti-libidinal (cyproterone acetate) the manufacturers recommend that a baseline sperm count is carried out (this is recommended as a medico-legal safeguard for the prescriber, and seldom seems to be acted on).

Preparations available and mode of action

Two drugs account for most anti-libidinal drug prescriptions in the UK at present: cyproterone acetate (CPA), and benperidol. CPA is a steroid analogue with two actions which contribute to its anti-libidinal effect: it is a competitive antagonist of testosterone (at receptors located within cell nuclei), and it has progestagenic activity. The latter (through negative feedback) decreases hypothalamic gonadotrophin release and so reduces production of testosterone by the gonads. Its administration results in a reduction in serum concentrations of testosterone, luteinizing hormone and follicle-stimulating hormone, and a rise in prolactin. Benperidol is an anti-psychotic (or 'neuroleptic') chemically related to haloperidol. It is said to exert a relatively specific anti-libidinal effect, but the mechanism for this is uncertain. One author has suggested that it may reduce sexual fantasies, rather than exert any effect on potency (Haslam, 1976).

Testosterone, and other factors influencing aggressive sexual behaviour
The relationship between plasma testosterone concentration and 'sexual aggression' in men is not a simple one: testosterone is one factor which influences aggressive sexual behaviour, along with social and psychological factors (including personality factors) and other organic factors (such as disinhibition following frontal lobe damage). Evidence for this multifactorial model for aggressive sexual behaviour comes from a variety of sources, including case studies and follow-up studies of men who have undergone castration. The former include Raboch, Černá and Zemek's (1987) account of two men with demonstrably low plasma testosterone who committed sexually motivated murders. Follow-up studies have demonstrated that although the reduction in plasma testosterone which follows castration is associated with a marked reduction in recidivism among men who have committed sexual offences (Bremer, 1959), castration does not *invariably* eliminate sexual drive and sexual responsiveness (Heim and Hursch, 1979). Drugs such as CPA, which reduce testosterone, can therefore not be guaranteed to abolish sexual drive (this should be explained to the patient at the same time that an explanation of wanted and unwanted effects is given), but even a small reduction in sexual drive may allow some men to achieve more control over their sexual behaviour.

Efficacy
There are numerous uncontrolled studies which indicate that CPA effectively reduces sexual drive and sexual responsiveness, and two placebo-controlled studies have reached a similar conclusion. The evidence for the efficacy of benperidol is less convincing, and one set of authors concluded that the libido-reducing effects of benperidol were weak, and unlikely to be sufficient to control serious anti-social sexual behaviour (Tennant, Bancroft and Cass, 1974).

There have been relatively few studies of the use of anti-libidinal drugs among men with learning disabilities; the studies which have been performed have been reviewed by Clarke (1989). There is no reason to think that the outcome of treatment is any different to that for men without learning disabilities; motivation for change and compliance with treatment are probably much more important factors than intellectual ability.

CPA could in theory be used to reduce female sexual drive, but it is not licensed for this indication, and one would have to be sure that the woman to be treated was not likely to become pregnant (because of the potential risks to the foetus of anti-androgen treatment).

Precautions and adverse effects

CPA should not be prescribed to young men whose bone or testicular development may not be complete. It is also contra-indicated for men with malignant or wasting diseases, or liver disease, and should be used with caution if there is a history of thrombo-embolic disease. It inhibits spermatogenesis and usually produces reversible infertility (spermatogenesis returns to normal within months of treatment being discontinued). The commonest unwanted effect is transient fatigue (for the first few weeks of treatment). Gynaecomastia (breast enlargement) affects up to 20 per cent of men treated, but is usually reversed when treatment is stopped. Other adverse effects occur rarely.

Benperidol has the adverse effects which would be expected of an antipsychotic drug related to haloperidol. Sedation and movement disorders – acute dystonias, akathisia (restlessness), Parkinsonism and tardive dyskinesia (abnormal involuntary movements, which may be irreversible) occur, and other adverse effects also occur more rarely.

Legal and ethical issues

(a) The Mental Health Act

It is often thought that the Mental Health Act has special provisions concerning the use of anti-libidinal drugs; in fact the Act recognizes one subcategory of treatment (which is very rarely used) as a 'treatment of special concern', namely the surgical implantation of hormones to reduce sexual drive, which is specified in section 57 of the Mental Health Act. This section of the Act applies to treatments for mental disorder, and lists treatments which require not only the patient's consent, but also a second medical opinion in favour of treatment, and certification by the independent second-opinion doctor and two non-medical persons (appointed by the Secretary of State) that the patient's consent is valid.

The Mental Health Act also specifies procedures which must be adhered to when prescribing for a patient who is unable to consent, or who refuses to consent, to treatment intended to alleviate a mental disorder which has resulted in the patient being compulsorily detained. These same provisions would apply to the use of an anti-ibidinal (as to the use of an anti-psychotic or anti-depressant) if it was used to treat a mental disorder. Many psychiatrists would, however, be reluctant to impose treatment with an anti-libidinal if a patient did not or could not consent.

(b) Consent

For patients not detained under the Mental Health Act (and with the exception of 'Section 57' treatments), the same legal principles apply to the use of anti-libidinal drugs as to other medication.

The Department of Health has issued guidelines about procedures to be adopted when dealing with patients who are incapable of consenting to treatment because of mental disorder (including severe learning disability). These centre on multidisciplinary consultation, and a decision about what is in the patient's best interest. However, the use of an anti-libidinal obviously impinges more fundamentally on someone's life than most other interventions, such as the surgical correction of a sight defect, or the treatment of a depressive illness. The individual clinician has to decide how best to proceed in the interests of his/her patient in such circumstances, but my own practice is not to use an anti-libidinal unless the patient understands the reason for its use and the likely effects (wanted and unwanted) and agrees to treatment, *unless* the patient is in danger of suffering serious adverse consequences as a result of sexual behaviour which is unequivocally unacceptable or illegal *and* other methods have either been tried and have failed or are not possible *and* all concerned with the patient's care agree that treatment is in his interest. In the latter case I would consider treatment if the patient was unable to consent (for example, because of a communication problem) but not if he actively refused treatment.

In practice, the issue of consent does not give rise to as many problems as might be thought. By far the majority of men with learning disabilities who would be considered for treatment with an anti-libidinal have mild learning disabilities, and can give valid consent to treatment if sufficient time is taken to explain its nature and purpose.

(c) Alternatives

It is most important that the pre-treatment assessment considers other methods of managing the behaviour which has given rise to concern. An anti-libidinal should usually only be prescribed if other courses of action (education, counselling, behavioural techniques, etc.) have either been tried without success, or are obviously inappropriate. In some instances the assessment will uncover an underlying psychiatric disorder (an example being a young man who indecently exposed himself when he became disinhibited as a result of a hypomanic illness). Treatment of the underlying illness, rather than anti-libidinal treatment, is then indicated.

(d) Conclusions

A careful assessment is needed to ensure that a man with a learning disability has behaviour which is of a nature and degree that justifies offering treatment with an anti-libidinal. Some men are greatly helped by such treatment. Issues of consent require careful attention. The consequences for the individual of continuing with the unacceptable behaviour have to be balanced against the consequences of treatment, and the individual informed as far as possible about potential consequences of the behaviour, the reason treatment is recommended, and the likely effects of treatment.

The evidence for the efficacy of anti-libidinal drugs is based largely on clinical observation, rather than controlled study, and many studies have included men with a heterogeneous group of behaviours (e.g. varying from excessive masturbation to serious sex offences) and have used poorly defined outcome criteria. Cyproterone acetate is the drug which appears most effective; its efficacy has been demonstrated in double-blind studies, and it has a more favourable adverse reaction profile than benperidol.

Few studies have specifically investigated the use of antilibidinals for men with learning disabilities, but the likelihood of treatment being beneficial seems to be the same as for men without learning disabilities. A small reduction in sexual drive may allow a man to avoid offending or otherwise unacceptable behaviour, and such treatment is often usefully combined with psychotherapy (to address issues related to the direction of sexual drive, and the consequences for the individual receiving treatment and others).

2. The management of abnormal aggression

The majority of studies concerning the management of people with learning disabilities and abnormally aggressive behaviour with drugs describe the use of anti-psychotics, lithium, or carbamazepine. Other medications have been used, but more rarely (e.g. the use of beta-adrenergic blockers, referred to in the section on self-injury).

(i) Antipsychotics

Studies concerning the effectiveness of chlorpromazine in reducing maladaptive behaviours started almost as soon as the drug became widely available. One of the earliest studies evaluated the effect of chlorpromazine, reserpine, and the two drugs in combination on the behaviours of forty children with learning disabilities and severe behaviour disorders. This double-blind, crossover trial found chlorpromazine alone to be the most effective, and placebo the least effective (Adamson, Nellis, Runge, Cleland and Killian, 1958). Unfortunately (as with many pharmacological studies in the 1950s and 1960s), the data are not presented in a way which would enable definite conclusions about specific effects on aggressive behaviour to be drawn. Chlorpromazine has a multitude of effects (hence the first trade name, Largactil), and the same applies to many other anti-psychotics which have been used to manage aggressive behaviour. It is therefore difficult, even when studies are of sound design, to draw conclusions about specific effects of the drug (such as dopaminergic blockade), as opposed to non-specific effects such as sedation, effects on other neurotransmitter systems, or increased staff or carer attention. There are fewer problems when evaluating pharmacologically more specific agents, which usually have fewer effects and cause less sedation. Of these, clopenthixol has received particular attention, and several studies have evaluated its effect on aggressive behaviour. Carney and Rutherford (1981) reported an improvement in aggressive behaviour among twenty patients with chronic schizophrenia who were treated with clopenthixol decanoate (a depot-injectable form), and Yar-Khan (1981) subsequently reported a beneficial effect on the aggressive behaviour of fifteen people with learning disabilities. A further study of the effect of clopenthixol (Mlele and Wiley, 1986) documented marked reductions in aggressive behaviour among 10 patients with learning disabilities, but acknowledged that non-specific factors (such as wards being renovated and upgraded during the treatment period) may have contributed to the observed effect. They called for further studies, with operational definitions of aggressive behaviour and standardised methods of selection and evaluation.

(ii) Lithium
Several reports in the 1970s suggested that lithium might reduce aggressive and/or self-injurious behaviour among people with learning disabilities. Cooper and Fowlie (1973) described a woman with severe self-injury who responded well to treatment with lithium (although her self-injury may have been related to an underlying affective disorder, for which lithium is an established treatment). Micev and Lynch (1974) gave a subjective account of an improvement in the behaviour of ten patients with severe learning disabilities and maladaptive behaviours. Worrall, Moody and Naylor (1975) treated eight women with learning disabilities and aggressive behaviour with lithium in a double-blind, placebo-controlled study and reported 'The group as a whole showed a reduction in aggression scores while on lithium (p < 0.01): three patients became less aggressive, one became worse and two were unchanged'. Dale (1980) described an improvement in the aggressive behaviour of eleven out of fifteen people with learning disabilities treated with lithium, although the study was not controlled, and ratings of aggression were subjective (a retrospective analysis of ward reports confirmed the clinical impression in five cases). A double-blind trial of the effect of lithium on forty-two people with learning disabilities and aggression showed that 73 per cent of patients showed a reduction in aggression during the period of lithium treatment (Craft *et al.*, 1987). This trial was conducted at five centres, and care was taken over methodological issues such as the standardisation of ratings and the maintenance of blindness; even so the study is open to some criticism (e.g. the five-point scale used included the ambiguous phrase 'mood uncertain'; ratings were made by nursing staff at each centre; the patients entering the study had a mixture of aggressive and self-injurious behaviours). Langee (1990) reported a ten-year retrospective study of seventy-four institutionalised residents with severe or profound learning disabilities and 'various behaviour disorders' which had not responded to other treatments. Thirty-one demonstrated 'a sustained major reduction or elimination of behavioral symptoms'. Of the thirty-one, four had aggressive behaviour, compared to eleven of the thirty-five non-responders. Langee concluded that older age and psychotic symptoms predicted a better response, but that 'all characteristics studied were seen in both the responder and nonresponder group'.

Pary (1991) reviewed the literature concerning the use of lithium to treat mental illness and behaviour disorders in people with learning disabilities, and concluded that 'of the various indicators for lithium, the most solid are for aggression, although the type of aggression is not specified', and cited Tupin (1975) who suggested that the main characteristic of patients whose aggression shows a good response to treatment with lithium is a 'short fuse' – implying similarities with those responding to treatment with carbamazepine.

(iii) Carbamazepine

Carbamazepine is an anti-epileptic which is effective in the treatment of both generalised and focal epilepsy. The latter use includes the treatment of epilepsy originating in the temporal lobes ('psychomotor epilepsy'), which occasionally gives rise to bizarre or aggressive behaviour, although the association is probably not as strong as was once believed (Rodin, 1973). Several reports suggested that some people with violent behaviour of sudden onset ('episodic dyscontrol') had electro-encephalogram (EEG) abnormalities, and that the aggressive behaviour may be lessened by treatment with an anti-convulsant, especially carbamazepine, (e.g. Stone, McDaniel, Hughes and Hermann, 1986). Carbamazepine has been used successfully to treat sudden outbursts of behaviour both in people with EEG abnormalities (Tunks and Dermer, 1977) and people with sudden rages and normal EEGs (Mattes, Rosenberg and Mayes, 1984). Mattes (1986) reviewed the psychopharmacology of temper outbursts, and concluded that there was good case-study evidence (and some evidence from controlled studies) that carbamazepine reduced aggressiveness regardless of the condition with which it was associated (e.g. abnormal EEG, the presence of schizophrenia, etc.), but that additional placebo-controlled trials were necessary.

Reports have also suggested that carbamazepine may be of benefit to people with learning disabilities and aggressive behaviour which is 'explosive' in nature; Langee (1989) in a retrospective study of seventy-six people with learning disabilities and 'behaviour disorders' found that thirty people had complete or almost complete loss of the abnormal behaviour, ten improved slightly, and thirty-one derived no benefit from treatment. Of the thirty people who responded, twenty-seven had an EEG abnormality or epilepsy. Langee described the 'target symptoms' of his study population; these included aggression and 'a key factor in this assessment was that the behavioural disturbance did not appear to be under the patients' conscious control. That is, it was neither escape behavior, manipulative, attention seeking, a product of physical distress, nor a response to environmental stimuli'. Laminack (1990) re-tabulated some of Langee's data, and suggested that carbamazepine probably improved the efficacy of other drugs given concomitantly (e.g. lithium), that it was unlikely to be of benefit to people without epilepsy and with a normal EEG, and that an EEG would be a useful screening procedure prior to treatment. Other case reports have described successful treatment of people with developmental disorders and rages with carbamazepine (e.g. Gupta, Fish and Yerevanian, 1987), or a combination of carbamazepine and lithium (e.g. Buck and Havey, 1986).

(iv) Conclusions

There is some evidence for the efficacy of anti-psychotics (notably clopenthixol), carbamazepine and lithium when used to treat some forms of aggression. A response to psychopharmacological interventions seems to be most likely where the behaviour is of sudden onset, and the individual appears to lack control over the behaviour once it starts. Carbamazepine may be more effective for people with seizure disorders or abnormal EEGs. Further research is necessary to define the factors predicting response to psycho-pharmacological intervention and to compare the effects of different drugs.

3. The management of self-injurious behaviour

The pharmacological treatment of self-injurious behaviour (SIB) was initially limited to the use of sedative agents (to depress overall activity and limit tissue damage). Over the past two decades, more specific treatments have been proposed. At present, the evidence suggests that some pharmacological agents (in particular, the opiate antagonists) may have a very useful role in stopping (or reducing the frequency or severity of) SIB among some people with learning disabilities.

In 1979, Primrose published a study detailing the treatment of SIB with baclofen (a gamma-aminobutyric acid analogue marketed for the reduction of spasticity) among twenty-two patients, of whom eighteen were felt to have benefited. The finding that baclofen beneficially affects SIB has not been confirmed, but the following decade saw a marked increase in reports suggesting drugs which might have a use in limiting SIB. Many of these reports concerned the use of opiate blocking drugs.

Endogenous opiates and SIB

Self-injury can serve many functions (such as communication or self-stimulation; see Chapter 7 for a full discussion), but there is some evidence that biological factors play a part in predisposing some people to self-injury (e.g. in Lesch-Nyhan syndrome) or in maintaining SIB that may have started for some other reason. One theory concerns the role played by endogenous opiates, which are released following injury, and produce both analgesia and euphoria (thus promoting further SIB).

The endogenous opiates are neuropeptides, short chains of amino acids which are derived from larger peptide precursors. An example is beta (B-) endorphin, an opioid with analgesic and euphoriant effects which is a 31-amino acid fragment of pro-opiomelanocortin. Studies in the mid-1970s demonstrated that B-endorphin and other opioids induce dependence; a characteristic opiate withdrawal syndrome occurs if they are administered for some time and then withheld (Wei and Loh, 1976).

In 1978 Kalat pointed out some similarities between behaviours seen in autism and those occurring during chronic opiate administration (Kalat, 1978). Several authors have explored this theme (e.g. Deutsch, 1986; Sahley and Panksepp; 1987). The features which Deutsch (1986) considered included insensitivity to pain, diminished crying, poor clinging, reduced socialization, episodes of increased motor activity alternating with quiescence, affective lability and repetitive, stereotyped behaviour. Deutsch noted:

In view of the beneficial effects of haloperidol in autism and its synergism with naloxone, the ability of neuroleptics to increase levels of B-endorphin in plasma, the presence of "autistic" features in opiate addicts and opiate-treated animals, and the dysregulation of opioid activity in autism, a rationale exists for a clinical trial of opiate antagonist administration to autistic patients . . . Thus, in addition to their possible role in enhancing attention in autistic patients, opiate antagonists may also have a specific indication for autistic patients exhibiting self-injurious behavior.

Evidence does appear to be strongest for a connection between the *self-injury* which some people with autism display and opioid neuroregulatory abnormalities; the same abnormalities probably occur in non-autistic people with learning disabilities and SIB. For example, Gillberg, Terenius and Lonnerholm (1985) found that children with autism did not have abnormal cerebrospinal fluid B-endorphin concentrations, but children with autism who self-injured had higher CSF B-endorphin concentrations than those who did not; Sandman, Barron, Chicz-Demet and Demet (1990) found that (compared to matched controls) patients with learning disabilities, stereotyped behaviour and SIB had elevated plasma B-endorphin levels.

Further evidence linking SIB to opioid neuroregulatory systems comes from studies where people with learning disabilities and SIB have been treated with opiate antagonists. Three such studies, describing the use of the opiate antagonist naloxone, were published in 1983. One report described a great reduction in the SIB and stereotyped behaviour of two people with learning disabilities (Sandman *et al.*, 1983), another that the intensity of SIB in one patient with a learning difficulty was reduced following treatment with naloxone (Davidson, Kleene, Carroll and Rockowitz, 1983) and the third that infusions of naloxone over six hours for two days produced a two-day elimination of a patient's SIB (Richardson and Zaleski, 1983). Further reports of the use of naloxone followed (e.g. Sandyk, 1985; Bernstein, Hughes, Mitchell and Thompson, 1987). However, the clinical relevance of these studies was limited by the need to administer naloxone parenterally (in most studies it was given by intravenous injection or infusion). More recent studies have investigated the use of naltrexone, a long acting, orally administered opiate antagonist. Campbell *et al.* (1988) treated seven children with autism (aged between 3 and 7) with naltrexone. They judged five children to have benefited, with reduced self-injury and aggressive behaviour. Herman *et al.* (1987) treated three children with naltrexone, and observed a dose-dependent reduction in SIB. Two studies of four patients failed to find a response of SIB to treatment with an opiate antagonist; one study used naloxone (Beckwith, Couk and Schumacher, 1986) and one naltrexone (Szymanski, Kedesdy, Sulkes, Cutler and Stevens-Our, 1987).

Thus, of the published studies, most suggest that opiate antagonists reduce SIB, although some reports describe treatment which was unsuccessful. The reports include double-blind studies (e.g. Szymanski *et al.*, 1987; Barrett, Feinstein and Hole, 1989; Sandman, Barron and Colman, 1990) and it can be concluded that there is good evidence for the efficacy of opiate antagonists in the treatment of *some* people with learning disabilities' SIB. Because of the small number of people in most studies, however, little can be deduced about the factors which predict successful treatment.

Other drugs

The study of baclofen by Primrose (1979) has been referred to above. The study was of double-blind crossover design, and twenty-two people with learning disabilities and SIB were treated, of whom eighteen were thought to have benefited; however, the assessment of improvement was made by the author and ward staff in an unsystematic way. A review by Singh and Millichamp (1985) considered the evidence for the use of a variety of drugs to treat SIB by people with learning disabilities. The studies reviewed included those using anti-psychotics, stimulants, anxiolytics, and anti-manic drugs. Singh and Millichamp commented that 'the bulk of the research is clinical in nature, with few of the necessary methodological controls being employed. The results reported in clinical papers are usually very encouraging of the efficacy of pharmacotherapy. However, subsequent but better controlled evaluative studies have usually reported less than enthusiastic outcomes'. They concluded that there was some evidence that anti-psychotic and anti-manic drugs 'may prove to be useful in the management of self-injury and warrant further investigation'. They also emphasized the need for method-ologically sound studies, consideration of dose-related effects, comparative studies, and the 'question of maintenance of treatment gains and the long-term effects of psychotropic medication', in view of studies indicating that most people with learning disabilities in institutions who received anti-psychotic medication to control maladaptive behaviour were likely to receive prolonged treatment. Aman (1987) also reviewed the evidence for the efficacy of anti-psychotics in treating SIB, and felt that the evidence was strongest for the efficacy of thioridazine. He added that it was difficult to be sure whether the anti-psychotics had a specific effect, or whether SIB was reduced as part of a general reduction in all behaviours.

Ruedrich, Grush and Wilson (1990) described a 25-year-old man with severe learning disabilities, aggressive and other maladaptive behaviours and SIB who responded to treatment with propranolol, and reviewed the literature concerning the use of beta-adrenergic blocking drugs for such problems. In a conclusion resembling that of Singh and Millichamp (1985), they argued that 'despite the methodological limitations of the papers reviewed, it appears that the beta-adrenergic blocking medications do benefit some percentage of aggressive or self-injurious retarded persons who have failed to respond to a multitude of other treatment approaches. What is now necessary is to examine the efficacy of these medications in double-blind placebo-controlled studies, using subjects who are otherwise unmedicated or behaviorally modified and using standardized rating instruments to assess behavior' (Ruedrich *et al.*, 1990). One recent review considered that 'support is emerging, however, for the use of lithium and carbamazepine with self-injuring mentally retarded patients . . .' (Winchel and Stanley, 1991), but the authors acknowledge the problem of disentangling the effects of lithium and carbamazepine on SIB from effects on mood and aggressive behaviour.

Conclusions

There is evidence from methodologically sound studies that opiate antagonists such as naltrexone benefit some people with learning disabilities and SIB. Other drugs, including anti-psychotics and beta-blockers may also be effective, but the evidence for their efficacy is less well documented, and their use may be associated with more long-term adverse effects, especially tardive dyskinesia in the case of anti-psychotics. Where a patient causes severe tissue damage due to repeated self-injury, however, the balance may be tilted towards treatment of any kind which may minimise further damage.

General conclusions

The use of psychotropic medication can be of great benefit to people with learning disabilities and challenging behaviour, and advances in understanding of the mechanisms underlying behaviours such as self-injury and some inappropriate sexual behaviour have allowed more specific drug treatments. As with all potent interventions, however, the potential benefits have to be weighed against potential adverse reactions ('side-effects'), and other unwanted effects of treatment (such as an unwillingness to accept responsibility for behaviour).

The prescription of medication to someone with a learning disability and challenging behaviour should therefore be accompanied by an assessment of the behaviour (preferably in a quantitative way), an explanation of the intended effect (including its likely magnitude and a consideration of issues such as responsibility and consent), an assessment of efficacy, and review to ensure ineffective treatments are not continued. Treatment reviews involving pharmacists appear to be particularly effective.

In view of their unwanted effects (especially tardive dyskinesia) the use of anti-psychotics should be confined to treating psychotic illnesses and to use as adjuncts in the management of challenging behaviours (where they should be used for the shortest possible time, in the lowest effective dose). Other drugs with relatively few adverse effects do not give rise to the same degree of concern. Most medications fall somewhere between the two, and require a careful assessment of the risk/benefit ratio for the person for whom treatment is proposed.

People with learning disabilities have a right to psychopharmacological treatments which are judged to be of potential benefit; they also have a right to be protected from the adverse effects of treatments which are ineffective or used inappropriately. Psychiatrists and others have a duty to ensure that their practice reflects the need to offer up-to-date psychopharmacological expertise and the need to balance benefits against risks in the interests of those receiving treatment.

Glossary

Psychotropic medication – medication prescribed with the intention of altering emotional state or behaviour (eg antidepressant medication)

Antiepileptic – A class of drugs used to treat epileptic seizures of all kinds.

Antipsychotic – A class of drugs (also called 'neuroleptics') which reduce or abolish some symptoms of psychotic mental illness such as delusions or hallucinations.

Pervasive developmental disorders – A group of conditions including autism, characterised by language abnormalities, impairments in social interaction and a restricted, stereotyped repertoire of interests and activities.

Psychoses – A class of mental illnesses characterised by loss of contact with reality ('impaired reality testing'), often with hallucinations, false beliefs, abnormal states of depression, elation, etc.

References

Adamson, W. C., Nellis, B. P., Runge, C. and Killian, E. (1958), 'Use of tranquillizers for mentally deficient patients', *Journal for Diseases of Children*, 96, 156–64.

Aman, M. G. (1983), 'Psychoactive drugs in mental retardation', in: J. L. Matson and F. Andrasik (eds.), *Treatment Issues and Innovations in Mental Retardation*, Plenum Press, New York.

Aman, M. G. (1987), 'Overview of pharmacotherapy: current status and future directions', *Journal of Mental Deficiency Research*, 31, 121–30.

Aman, M. G., Singh, N. N., Stewart, A. W. and Field, C. J. (1985), 'The Aberrant Behavior Checklist: a behavior rating scale for the assessment of treatment effects', *American Journal of Mental Deficiency*, 89, 485–91.

Barrett, R. P., Feinstein, C. and Hole, W. T. (1989), 'Effects of naloxone and naltrexone on self-injury: a double-blind, placebo-controlled analysis', *American Journal on Mental Retardation*, 93, 644–51.

Barron, J. and Sandman, C. A. (1983), 'Relationship of sedative-hypnotic response to self-injurious behavior and stereotypy by mentally retarded clients', *American Journal of Mental Deficiency*, 88, 177–86.

Bates, W. J., Smeltzer, D. J. and Arnoczky, S. M. (1986), 'Appropriate and inappropriate use of psychotherapeutic medications for institutionalized mentally retarded persons', *American Journal of Mental Deficiency*, 90, 363–70.

Beckwith, B. E., Couk, D. I. and Schumacher, K. (1986), 'Failure of naloxone to reduce self-injurious behavior in two developmentally disabled females', *Applied Research in Mental Retardation*, 7, 183–88.

Bernstein, G. A., Hughes, J. R., Mitchell, J. E. and Thompson, T. (1987), 'Effects of narcotic antagonists on self-injurious behavior: A single case study', *Journal of the American Academy of Child and Adolescent Psychiatry*, 26, 886–89.

Bremer, J. (1959), *Asexualization*, Macmillan, New York.

Bridgen, P. and Todd, M. (1990), 'Challenging behaviour: introducing a preadmission checklist, problem analysis flow chart, and intervention flow chart to guide decision-making in a multidisciplinary team', *Mental Handicap*, 18, 99–104.

Briggs, R. (1989), 'Monitoring and evaluating psychotropic drug use for persons with mental retardation: a follow-up report', *American Journal on Mental Retardation*, 93, 633–39.

Buck, J. A. and Sprague, R. L. (1989), 'Psychotropic medication of mentally retarded residents in community long-term care facilities', *American Journal on Mental Retardation*, 93, 618–23.

Buck, O. D. and Havey, P. (1986), 'Combined carbamazepine and lithium therapy for violent behavior'. *American Journal of Psychiatry*, 143, 1487.

Campbell, M., Adams, P., Small, A. M., Tesch, L. M. and Curren, E. L. (1988), 'Naltrexone in infantile autism', *Psychopharmacology Bulletin*, 24, 135–39.

Carney, M. W. P. and Rutherford, P. (1981), 'Clopenthixol decanoate in schizophrenia', *Current Medical Research and Opinion*, 7, 205–11.

Clarke, D. J. (1989), 'Anti-libidinal drugs and mental retardation: a review', *Medicine, Science and the Law*, 29, 136–46.

Clarke, D. J., Kelley, S., Thinn, K. and Corbett, J. A. (1990), 'Psychotropic drugs and mental retardation: 1. Disabilities and the prescription of drugs for behaviour and for epilepsy in three residential settings', *Journal of Mental Deficiency Research*, 34, 385–95.

Cooper, A. F. and Fowlie, H. C. (1973), 'Control of gross self-mutilation with lithium carbonate', *British Journal of Psychiatry*, 122, 370–71.

Corbett, J. (1979), 'Psychiatric morbidity and mental retardation', in P. Snaith and F. E. James (eds.), *Psychiatric Illness and Mental Handicap*, Headly Brothers, Ashford.

Craft, M., Ismail, I. A., Krishnamurti, D., Mathews, J., Regan, A., Seth, R. V. and North, P. M. (1987), 'Lithium in the treatment of aggression in mentally handicapped patients: a double-blind trial', *British Journal of Psychiatry*, 150, 685–89.

Dale, P. G. (1980), 'Lithium therapy in aggressive mentally subnormal patients', *British Journal of Psychiatry*, 137, 469–74.

Davidson, P. W., Kleene, B. M., Carroll, M. and Rockowitz, R. J. (1983), 'Effects of naloxone on self-injurious behavior: a case study', *Applied Research in Mental Retardation*, 4, 1–4.

Davis, J. M. and Garver, D. L. (1978), 'Neuroleptics: clinical use in psychiatry', in L. L. Iversen and S. D. Iversen (eds.), *Handbook of Psychopharmacology, Neuroleptics and Schizophrenia*, Plenum Press, New York.

Day, K. (1988), 'A hospital-based treatment programme for male mentally handicapped offenders', *British Journal of Psychiatry*, 153, 635–44.

Deutsch, S. I. (1986), 'Rationale for the administration of opiate antagonists in treating infantile autism', *American Journal of Mental Deficiency*, 90, 631–35.

Findholt, N. E. and Emmett, C. G. (1990), 'Impact of interdisciplinary team review on psychotropic drug use with persons who have mental retardation', *Mental Retardation*, 28, 41–6.

Gibbens, T. C. N. and Robertson, G. (1983), 'A survey of the criminal careers of restriction order patients', *British Journal of Psychiatry*, 143, 370–75.

Gillberg, C., Terenius, L. and Lonnerholm, G. (1985), 'Endorphin activity in childhood psychosis', *Archives of General Psychiatry*, 42, 780–83.

Glaser, B. A. and Morreau, L. E. (1986), 'Effects of interdisciplinary team review on the use of antipsychotic agents with severely and profoundly mentally retarded persons', *American Journal of Mental Deficiency*, 90, 371–79.

Gupta, B. K., Fish, D. N. and Yerevanian, B. I. (1987), 'Carbamazepine for intermittent explosive disorder in a Prader-Willi syndrome patient', *Journal of Clinical Psychiatry*, 48, 423.

Haslam, M. T. (1976), 'Psycho-sexual disorders and their treatment', Part III, 'Sexual Deviation', *Current Medical Research and Opinion*, 3, 726–35.

Heim, N. and Hursch, C. J. (1979), 'Castration for sex offenders: treatment or punishment? A review and critique of recent European literature', *Archives of Sexual Behavior*, 8, 281–304.

Herman, B. H., Hammock, M. K., Arthur-Smith, A., Egan, J., Chatoor, I., Werner, A. and Zelnick, N. (1987), 'Naltrexone decreases self-injurious behavior', *Annals of Neurology*, 22, 550–52.

Inoue, F. (1982), 'A clinical pharmacy service to reduce psychotropic medication use in an institution for mentally retarded persons'. *Mental Retardation*, 20, 70–4.

Intagliata, J. and Rinck, C. (1985), 'Psychoactive drug use in public and community residential facilities for mentally retarded persons', *Psychopharmacology Bulletin*, 21, 268–78.

Kalat, J. W. (1978), 'Speculations on similarities between autism and opiate addiction', *Journal of Autism and Childhood Schizophrenia*, 8, 477–79.

Laminack, L. (1990), 'Carbamazepine for behavioral disorders', *American Journal on Mental Retardation*, 94, 563–64.

Langee, H. R. (1989), 'A retrospective study of mentally retarded patients with behavioral disorders who were treated with carbamazepine', *American Journal on Mental Retardation*, 93, 640–43.

Langee, H. R. (1990), 'Retrospective study of lithium use for institutionalized mentally retarded individuals with behavior disorders', *American Journal on Mental Retardation*, 94, 448–52.

Lund, J. (1985), 'The prevalence of psychiatric morbidity in mentally retarded adults', *Acta Psychiatrica Scandinavica*, 72, 563–70.

Lund, J. (1990), 'Mentally retarded criminal offenders in Denmark', *British Journal of Psychiatry*, 156, 726–31.

MacEachron, A. E. (1979), 'Mentally retarded offenders: prevalence and characteristics', *American Journal of Mental Deficiency*, 84, 165–76.

Matson, J. L. and Schroeder, S. R. (1988), 'Editorial: A retraction', *Research in Developmental Disabilities*, 9, 1–2.

Mattes, J. A., Rosenberg, J. and Mayes, D. (1984), 'Carbamazepine vs. propranolol in patients with uncontrolled rage outbursts: a random assignment study', *Psychopharmacology Bulletin*, 20, 98–100.

Mattes, J. A. (1986), 'Psychopharmacology of temper outbursts: a review', *Journal of Nervous and Mental Disease*, 174, 464–70.

Micev, V. and Lynch, D. M. (1974), 'Effect of lithium on disturbed severely mentally retarded patients', *British Journal of Psychiatry*, 125, 110.

Mlele, T. J. J. and Wiley, Y. V. (1986), 'Clopenthixol decanoate in the management of aggressive mentally handicapped patients', *British Journal of Psychiatry*, 149, 373–76.

Nihira, K., Foster, R., Shellhaas, M. and Leland, H. (1974), *AAMD Adaptive Behavior Scale*, (rev. edn.), DC: American Association on Mental Deficiency, Washington, DC.

Pary, R. J. (1991), 'Towards defining adequate lithium trials for individuals with mental retardation and mental illness', *American Journal on Mental Retardation*, 95, 681–91.

Primrose, D. A. (1979), 'Treatment of self-injurious behaviour with a GABA (gamma-aminobutyric acid) analogue', *Journal of Mental Deficiency Research*, 23, 163–73.

Raboch, J., Cern, H. and Zemek, P. (1987), 'Sexual aggressivity and androgens', *British Journal of Psychiatry*, 151, 398–400.

Richardson, J. F. and Zaleski, W. A. (1983), 'Naxolone and self-mutilation', *Biological Psychiatry*, 18, 99–101.

Rodin, E. A. (1973), 'Psychomotor epilepsy and aggressive behavior', *Archives of General Psychiatry*, 28, 210–13.

Ruedrich, S. L., Grush, L. and Wilson, J. (1990), 'Beta adrenergic blocking medications for aggressive or self-injurious mentally retarded persons', *American Journal on Mental Retardation*, 95, 110–19.

Sahley, T. L. and Panksepp, J. (1987), 'Brain opioids and autism: an updated analysis of possible linkages', *Journal of Autism and Developmental Disorders*, 17, 201–16.

Sandman, C. A., Barron, J. L., Chicz-Demet, A. and Demet, E. M. (1990), 'Plasma B-endorphin levels in patients with self-injurious behaviour and stereotypy', *American Journal on Mental Retardation*, 95, 84–92.

Sandman, C. A., Barron, J. L. and Colman, H. (1990), 'An orally administered opiate blocker, naltrexone, attenuates self-injurious behavior', *American Journal on Mental Retardation*, 95, 93–102.

Sandman, C. A., Datta, P., Barron, J. L., Hoehler, F., Williams, C. and Swanson, J. (1983), 'Naloxone attenuates self-abusive behavior in developmentally disabled clients', *Applied Research in Mental Retardation*, 4, 5–11.

Sandyk, R. (1985), 'Naloxone abolished self-injuring in a mentally retarded child', *Annals of Neurology*, 17, 520.

Singh, N. N. and Millichamp, C. J. (1985), 'Pharmacological treatment of self-injurious behavior in mentally retarded persons', *Journal of Autism and Developmental Disorders*, 15, 257–67.

Sprague, R. L. and Werry, J. S. (1971), 'Methodology of psychopharmacological studies with the retarded', in N. R. Ellis (ed.), *International Review of Research in Mental Retardation*, Academic Press, New York.

Stone, J. L., McDaniel, K. D., Hughes, J. R. and Hermann, B. P. (1986), 'Episodic dyscontrol disorder and paroxysmal EEG abnormalities: successful treatment with carbamazepine', *Biological Psychiatry*, 21, 208–12.

Sturmey, P., Reed, J. and Corbett, J. (1991), 'Psychometric assessment of psychiatric disorders in people with learning disabilities (mental handicap): a review of measures', *Psychological Medicine*, 21, 143–55.

Szymanski, L., Kedesdy, J., Sulkes, S. and Cutler, A. (1987), 'Naltrexone in treatment of self injurious behavior: a clinical study', *Research in Developmental Disabilities*, 8, 179–90.

Tennant, G., Bancroft, J. and Cass, J. (1974), 'The control of deviant sexual behavior by drugs: a double-blind controlled study of benperidol, chlorpromazine and placebo', *Archives of Sexual Behavior*, 3, 261–71.

Thinn, K., Clarke, D. J. and Corbett, J. A. (1990), 'Psychotropic drugs and mental retardation: 2. A comparison of psychoactive drug use before and after discharge from hospital to community', *Journal of Mental Deficiency Research*, 34, 397–407.

Trimble, M. (1979), 'The effect of anti-convulsant drugs on cognitive abilities. *Pharmacology and Therapeutics*, 4, 677–32.

Tunks, E. R. and Dermer, S. W. (1977), 'Carbamazepine in the dyscontrol syndrome associated with limbic system dysfunction', *Journal of Nervous and Mental Disease*, 164, 56–63.

Tupin, J. P. (1975), 'Management of the violent patient', in R. I. Shader (ed.), *Manual of Psychiatric Therapies*, Little & Brown, Boston.

Van de Merwe, T. J. (1979), 'Cyproterone acetate and hypersexuality', *South African Medical Journal*, 55, 113.

Wei, E. and Loh, H. (1976), 'Physical dependence on opiate-like peptides', *Science*, 193, 1262–63.

Wilkinson, J. (1989), 'Assessing the challenge: development of the Challenging Behaviour Scales', *Mental Handicap Research*, 2, 86–104.

Winchel, R. M. and Stanley, M. (1991), 'Self-injurious behavior: a review of the behavior and biology of self-mutilation', *American Journal of Psychiatry*, 148, 306–17.

Wish, J. R., McCombs, K. F. and Edmonson, B. (1980), 'The Socio-Sexual Knowledge and Attitude Test', Stoelting, Wood Dale, IL.

Worrall, E. P., Moody, J. P. and Naylor, G. J. (1975), 'Lithium in non-manic-depressives: anti-aggressive effect and red cell lithium values', *British Journal of Psychiatry*, 126, 464–68.

Yar-Khan, S. (1981), 'The psychiatrically violent patient', *British Medical Journal*, 282, 1400–01.

Do the ends justify the means? Aversive procedures in the treatment of severe challenging behaviours

INTRODUCTION

In 1965 Lovaas *et al.* claimed to have succeeded in eliminating severe self-injurious behaviour by means of contingent electric shock. Their treatment programme included a client whose fingers had been so badly bitten that amputation was required. This study was reviewed some twenty years later by Owens (1987) in the context of ethical issues raised by radical behaviourism. He concluded: 'Few people are particularly critical of the use of punishment when such extreme benefit can be shown and where the cost of failing to punish is so high. When, however, punishment is used with less severe problems, there is inevitably some disquiet' (p.97).

The appearance of consensus across nearly a quarter of a century is deceptive however. For this period has seen not only a proliferation of studies of severe challenging behaviour, but also an increasingly heated debate about the use of aversive procedures, which continues today unabated. Owens' comments about punishment certainly typify one school of thought – namely, that it is justified for the treatment of severe problem behaviour, where demonstrably effective. But they also raise two major questions:

Are the benefits of aversive treatment for challenging behaviour clear-cut?
Does failure to punish lead to 'high costs' – or are there alternatives?

In order to attempt to answer these questions some working definitions must first be offered. The term 'aversive' is rarely defined explicitly in the literature, but there are at least two separate points of view:

1. That aversive stimuli can only be defined in terms of operant conditioning – there are no universal punishers;
2. That certain stimuli are intrinsically aversive, generally on the grounds that they are painful or noxious (for example, electric shock, slapping, vinegar spray in the mouth).

The first view is generally associated with a behaviourist approach, within which the outcome of punishment[1] is typically defined as: '. . . behavior showing an orderly decrease in probability when followed by stimuli with certain properties . . .' (Mulick, 1990a, p. 145).

In other words, punishment is analogous to reinforcement, a consequence of behaviour that affects the probability of its occurrence in future. In each case, the consequences themselves are regarded as intrinsically neutral: there are no universal reinforcers, so no stimuli should be treated as inherently aversive.

The second view is perhaps more easily acceptable to the lay-person – that certain stimuli used in treatment are aversive by their nature. This thinking clearly underlies the resolutions issued by a number of voluntary organisations, calling for the elimination of specified aversive treatments judged to be painful or noxious (for example, the Canadian Association for Community Living, quoted by Rioux, 1988, pp. 11–12). But a similar outlook appears to be shared tacitly by many of those involved in the behavioural treatment of challenging behaviours. Certainly it seems common in the literature for a treatment (say electric shock) to be selected with no particular justification, but evidently on the assumption that it will prove aversive.

We are left with a rather confusing picture, in which there are two distinct conceptions of what is meant by aversive. Horner (1990) adopts the first (operant) definition of aversive stimulation and agrees with Mulick (1990a) that all stimuli may be aversive. But he sides with the non-aversive camp in asking for three criteria to be adhered to in applying behavioural techniques: no delivery of physical pain; no treatment effects which may require medical attention; the use of norms that are subjectively in line with the relevant society's code of conduct. Evans and Meyer (1990), taking a very extreme non-aversive position, criticise Horner for arguing '. . . from what would be called the narrow operant perspective . . .' (p. 134). They prefer the term aversive to be '. . . defined in terms of subjective judgement, individual responses and the health and well-being of the individual (cf. Archer & Nilsson, 1989)' (p. 134). Unfortunately, neither Evans and Meyer nor Horner provide any guidance as to how such subjective variables are to be measured. Not surprisingly, these various definitions of what constitutes an aversive therapeutic intervention lead to uncertainty about the categorisation of some behavioural treatments. Two particular cases in point are the procedures of extinction and over-

---

[1] Punishment is but one form of *aversive conditioning*. Negative reinforcement, '. . . behaviour showing an orderly increase in probability where pre-existing stimuli [are] stopped or lessened in some of their properties . . .' and avoidance conditioning, '. . . when behavior probability increases as long as contingent stimuli with certain properties are postponed or never happen at all . . .' (Mulick, 1990a, p. 145) are two other functional relations classified as aversive. However, the current debate largely concerns punishment procedures as they are most widely used in planned clinical interventions for people with learning difficulties and severe challenging behaviours.

correction. Both are regarded as aversive treatments by Gorman-Smith and Matson (1985), but according to Harradence and Hartlebury (1983) these are non-aversive techniques.

It is not within the scope of this chapter to resolve these difficulties. Rather an inclusive view of the term aversive will be adopted, in an attempt to draw out the major features of the debate about the treatment of challenging behaviour. In particular, we will deal in turn with:

- a historical perspective of the use of aversives in relation to challenging behaviour
- the effectiveness of aversive procedures;
- the ethical issues involved in such treatment techniques;
- alternatives to punishment – the current debate about non-aversives and finally
- possible ways for the future.

The greater part of the literature discussed to this end concerns severe self-injurious behaviour (SIB). This is because the physical consequences and therefore the ethical issues are often most pertinent in cases where people are seriously harming themselves.

A HISTORICAL PERSPECTIVE

According to Yule and Carr (1987), the use of behavioural techniques in therapeutic interventions with people with learning difficulties dates from the mid-1960s, originating in the United States. From this time to the present, a number of developments can be traced in the application of aversive procedures to challenging behaviour. Changes in attitude and practice are inevitably gradual. But for convenience, three separate periods can be distinguished: i) the mid-1960s to the mid-1970s; ii) the mid-1970s to the early 1980s; and iii) the early 1980s to the present day. In many respects, the trends in Britain have reflected those in North America, with a certain time lag.

The mid-60s to mid-70s

The dominant belief during this period was that aversive techniques were effective in treating challenging behaviour. A helpful review of the period is provided by Corbett (1975), who summarises published reports of aversive treatments for serious SIB (8 in all) dating from 1966 to 1975. Corbett acknowledges the inadequacies of much of the clinical data, particularly in reporting previous treatment, and the length of follow-up period. But he concludes that: 'In most cases, the intensity of self-injury has been considerable and the aversive treatment has, invariably, been effective in eliminating or reducing it considerably, in a way which cannot easily be accounted for by spontaneous remission or the action of other variables'. He does not include details of the treatment procedures used, but comments that 'almost all' cases involved contingent electric shock. He notes further that most of the studies report few, if any, side effects and are '. . . almost universally enthusiastic in their accounts of the general improvement and relief from other symptoms'. It is also worth mentioning that he devotes considerable space to discussion of the technical requirements for an 'ideal' punishing stimulus – for example, the importance of specifying levels of voltage and amperage, and the relative merits of a hand-held probe as against remotely controlled devices. Corbett draws a distinction between milder forms of SIB and severe life-threatening behaviour; but for the latter, aversive techniques are regarded as the treatment of choice.

Further confirmation of the attitudes prevalent during this period is given by Ewen (1988):

During the early 70s, there was a major trend towards the use of cold showers, wooden spoons, cattle prods and remote shock apparatus . . . Throughout Canada and the United States, people were advised that punishment was the best way to help their offspring and many were trained in the use of the tools of aversive therapy (p. 91).

The mid-70s to the early 80s

This second period saw a change of emphasis. Aversive procedures were still held to be effective but typically were regarded as a last resort. Gorman-Smith and Matson (1985) offer a useful overview of the period in a summary of treatment research (aversive and non-aversive) for self-injurious and stereo-typed behaviour from 1976 to 1983. The initial trawl for their study included all articles referenced for this period in *Psychological Abstracts*. And it is interesting to note that they too remark on a change of climate in the mid–1970s: 'Studies prior to 1976 were not reviewed given marked changes in the approach to the treatment of these problems (for example, contingent electric shock which was popular is now only rarely used)' (p. 297).

Like Corbett before, Gorman-Smith and Matson comment on the poverty of follow-up data in the studies. But nevertheless they attempt a comparison of the treatments used, in terms of their effectiveness. From this they observe that the most frequently used treatments (over-correction, facial screening and physical restraint) were not the most effective – these were said to be DRO, lemon juice therapy, and time-out. The prominence of DRO prompts them to conclude that:

Reinforcement may be better than punishment for some . . . self-injurious behaviour. This finding is of note since effective reinforcement would be a more desirable approach than punishment. These findings also run . . . contrary to the common belief that punishment is the most preferred treatment method (p. 303).

They also comment, however, that: 'The recalcitrant nature of the problems argues for punishment procedures when they are the only recourse for effective treatment' (p. 302).

It is worth noting that other research from this period was starting to explore the utility of different reinforcement procedures. For example, Tarpley and Schroeder (1979) report a study in which reinforcement of incompatible behaviour (DRI) was more effective than DRO in suppressing the rate of head-banging. But the broad-based review by Gorman-Smith and Matson seems to reflect the dominant attitude – that aversives should still be retained as a last resort.

The early 80s to the present day

The third and final period is marked by a definite split in opinion. On the one hand, there are those sticking to the 'last resort' argument, for example Carr and Lovaas (1983) and Matson and Keyes (1988). But there are others who regard aversive procedures as completely unacceptable, either on the grounds of ethics or pragmatics, or a mixture of both. Just why this change occurred is not entirely clear; it seems to have been a conflux of factors. In the United States the 1970s saw a number of privately brought court cases against the use of punishment. There were increasing restrictions on aversive procedures in both individual facilities and some entire states, for example, Michigan (Yule and Carr, 1987, p.133). Repp and Deitz (1974) report growing concern at many facilities about the use of contingent shock. And by 1979, Tarpley and Schroeder suggest that the ethical doubts about shock: '... make its utility as a workable clinical procedure questionable'.

Then in the 1980s this trend drew strength from the growing interest and confidence in the power of non-aversive techniques even with severe behaviour problems. This culminated in a range of exclusively constructional approaches whose origin can be traced back to Goldiamond (1974). There followed a number of positional statements issued by organisations concerned with disability, rejecting the use of aversives completely. These included the American Association on Mental Retardation in 1986 (AAMR 1988) and the Association for Persons with Severe Handicaps (TASH 1988). All the evidence so far is from North America. But the attitudes described are clearly reflected in Britain as well. Harradence and Hartlebury (1983) in a literature review of *Difficult and Disruptive Behaviour*, record their own belief that aversive stimulation can never be justified.

All this seems to represent a strong current of opinion against aversive procedures. Yet the 'last resort' argument is still well established. Lennox *et al.* (1988) report in a literature review from 1981 to 1985 that over 60 per cent of treatments for challenging behaviour involved some aversive component. It is also interesting to note that in 1988 the AAMR were obliged to withdraw their resolution rejecting aversives, on finding a marked lack of agreement among their members (both about the principle involved, and also the definition of aversive).

The controversy in the United States has been fuelled yet further by the development of SIBIS, the 'Self-Injurious Behavior Inhibiting System'. This is a mechanical device which is worn by the client and which: '. . . automatically provides a mild aversive electrical stimulation to the leg in response to self-injurious blows to the head' (manufacturer's advertisement, *Journal of Applied Behavioral Analysis*, Winter 1988).

Evans and Meyer (1990) strongly condemn the use of SIBIS and criticise studies such as Linscheid *et al.* (1990) for not consistently performing functional analyses of the target behaviour in order to decide on a 'positive' treatment plan, and for continuing the shock treatment without achieving immediate results. Mulick (1990a) argues that painful stimuli can only be justifiably used if they contribute to an 'immediately effective procedure'. The Linscheid *et al.* study reports on an individual who, during a fourteen-month treatment phase, had received 3,640 SIBIS controlled shocks and was still hitting himself, although at a statistically lower rate. This raises the question whether obtaining statistically significant pre-/post-treatment differences is sufficient to meet Mulick's criteria of efficacy. Most clinicians would argue that a decrease in severe SIB needs to be more than statistically significant to be clinically relevant.

Butterfield (1990), as editor of the *American Journal of Mental Retardation*, attempts to summarise and draw his own conclusions from a heated debate presented in the same journal issue:

Harmful [Butterfield refers here to psychological as well as physical harmfulness] treatments should be tried only if usually efficacious harmless ones fail to eliminate serious self-injury and then only if it is judged that the harmful procedure, if effective in a typical long course of treatment, and its side-effects will result in less damage and harm than the untreated self-injurious behavior and if appropriate informed consent and committee approvals are received. (p.140)

The vigorous controversy which characterises this third period in the history of the debate looks set to run for some time.

THE EFFECTIVENESS OF AVERSIVE PROCEDURES

The very existence of the debate about aversive approaches indicates that they must be effective to some extent. If they simply were ineffectual they would not be used and there would hardly be such concern about ethical issues. But what is the nature of their effectiveness? Should efficacy be judged purely in terms of deceleration of challenging behaviours? Horner (1990) argues for new 'outcome standards', not just a reduction in target behaviours for a limited period of time in a limited setting but also an increase in 'adaptive options' and 'valued life style patterns'.

A number of studies record the apparently successful use of aversive stimuli, mainly electric shock – in the treatment of challenging behaviour. For example, Lovaas and Simmons (1969) report that severe hand-to-head hitting in three children was 'immediately suppressed' by contingent shock. When the procedure was discontinued, however, the behaviour recurred. In a comparative study involving two of the children, an extinction procedure was also found to reduce self-injury to near-zero levels, but only after a period of several days, during which there was risk of serious damage. Corté *et al.* (1971) report a comparison of procedures used with four adolescents displaying face-slapping, face-banging, hair pulling and finger biting. In this case, extinction was ineffective; reinforcement (DRO) was partially successful with one subject, while contingent shock effectively eliminated self-injury in all four subjects. Or again, Young and Wincze (1975) describe a single case study of a woman exhibiting two forms of head-banging, head-to-object and hand-to-head. Two types of reinforcement procedures were attempted: DRO which was ineffective; and DRI, which led to an increase in one kind of head-banging, while the other decreased. An unplanned final phase of contingent shock was introduced, which rapidly suppressed the form of head-banging to which it was applied.

These three studies all focus on the benefits of electric shock. But other aversive procedures have been used as well. For example, Goldiamond (1974) gives a moving account of an institutionalised girl exhibiting head-banging, who was successfully treated with facial slaps combined with verbal reprimand. Non-aversive reinforcement techniques had previously had no effect, but shortly after the aversive regime began, physical restraints and a protective helmet could be removed, and the girl started to develop a range of appropriate social behaviours. Murphy and Wilson (1985) provide a summary of other aversive techniques applied successfully to self-injury, including lemon juice therapy, ammonia, and (based on the operant definition of aversive) over-correction and facial screening. There seems to be widespread agreement that of all aversive procedures, contingent shock is the single most effective treatment. Harradence and Hartlebury (1983) cite three independent sources supporting this view. And Murphy and Wilson (1985) conclude: 'It is certainly more rapid than extinction and there can be little doubt that, as a first time treatment, shock can be very effective in reducing or eliminating self-injurious behaviour for a six to twelve month period' (p. 243).

So the main stated benefit of an aversive approach, particularly contingent shock, relates to the speed and degree of effect. It can apparently offer dramatic improvements quite rapidly. There are, however, recorded cases where the technique simply fails. Jones *et al.* (1974) describe the case of a young girl, where the use of shock led to an *increase* in self-destructive responding, to complete suppression of spontaneous feeding, and to the necessity for constant physical restraint. This intervention is reported as part of the earlier treatment history, however. The programme actually implemented by Jones, an extinction procedure, was in part successful. This article raises an important point, namely, the inevitable bias in reported results towards positive outcomes. It is impossible to know how many unsuccessful cases involving aversive methods have gone unreported. What the relevant published studies clearly demonstrate, however, are several major drawbacks, in particular, problems relating to generalisation, side-effects of treatment, and durability.

Generalisation

In two of the studies mentioned above, the generalisation of treatment was clearly limited. Lovaas and Simmons (1969) and Corté *et al.* (1971) both report that the effects of shock were largely specific to the setting in which it was given and to the person who administered it. This leads Corte to conclude: 'Treatment of self-injurious behavior with punishment must include the active generalization of the effects through a planned program of treating the behaviour under as many different conditions as necessary' (p. 202).

How far this approach is practical is not addressed. There is also a possibility that the person administering the treatment becomes, by association, an object of fear, a risk acknowledged by Lovaas and Simmons and by Corbett (1975).

Other studies suggest that contingent shock may make it possible to gain experimental control over challenging behaviour but not clinical control. In other words, effects seen in a laboratory setting may not generalise to a natural environment (Romanczyk and Goren, 1975; Williams and Surtees, 1975). According to Romanczyk and Goren, shock as the treatment of choice for self-injury is based largely on extrapolation from its effects in experimental settings.

Side effects of treatment

The possible side-effects of aversive procedures are contentious in the extreme. A monograph published by TASH in 1987 suggests that they include: '. . . emotional reactions – crying, grimacing, screaming and wincing. Aggression – struggling, arm flapping and leg extensions. Escape or avoidance behaviours'. (quoted by Ewen, 1988, p. 93). Mulick (1990a) acknowledges that undesirable side-effects of reduction methods are a problem and more difficult to prevent or remedy than those produced by accelerative methods.

However, a number of positive side-effects have also been reported, notably an increase in social behaviours, including eye contact, smiling and physical contact (Lovaas and Simmons, 1969). Indeed, Matson and Taras (1989), who reviewed twenty-three relevant journals over a twenty-year period, counted 212 reported positive side-effects versus sixteen negative side effects associated with aversive (punishment) procedures. But (as the authors acknowledge) reporting bias may account for these results.

Durability

Early learning experiments (using animals) showed that punishment suppresses but does not eliminate behaviour and that once the punishing procedure is stopped, the behaviour may return. Although Matson and Gardner (1991) argue that there is a substantial body of evidence of maintenance over at least several months, there are also many studies which suggest that aversive procedures are not long-lasting in their effects.

Corté *et al.* (1971) found that with at least one subject, the effects of shock had disappeared at two-month follow-up. Tanner and Zeiler (1975) report a case in which self-injury had been suppressed by shock, but returned when the programme finished. Their own treatment with ammonia apparently succeeded, but the follow-up period was only twenty days. Studies recording any long-term follow-up are sparse. Lennox *et al.* (1988) attempted to evaluate the effectiveness of different procedures, and were obliged to accept short-term results as their main criterion, because of a lack of maintenance data in many of the studies reviewed.

One of the few studies of longer term effectiveness was carried out by Murphy and Wilson (1981) in a two-year follow-up of thirteen people treated with contingent shock. They found that relapse after the first treatment was common and that only two subjects showed no relapse, two years after treatment ceased.

The limitations of aversive treatment, in terms of generalisation, side-effects and durability, are therefore considerable. The best case that can be made is that intervention may buy a breathing space – a brief remission to self-injury, in which constructional techniques can be attempted. A number of studies suggest that an effective approach is to combine different treatments, aversive and non-aversive, in a single package. For instance, Tate and Baroff (1966) paired shock with DRO in the treatment of face-slapping. Matson and Keyes (1988) used physical restraint with DRO to treat head-banging and self-biting. Solnick *et al.* (1977) found that time-out punishment for SIB was only effective if 'time-in' conditions were used for accelerative procedures. Harradence and Hartlebury (1983) also cite a number of studies combining positive reinforcement with time-out procedures.

THE ETHICS OF AVERSIVE PROCEDURES

The ethical arguments surrounding the use of aversives in treating people with learning difficulties are many and tangled. The nub of the difficulty is the absence of informed consent to treatment, other than at best by the relative or advocate of the person concerned. We will review some of the efforts to sort out the rights and wrongs of aversive treatment, in the context of clinical practice. The range of views expressed on the issue could hardly be wider. At one extreme, aversive procedures are regarded as inhumane and hence completely unacceptable. McGee (1986) states that:

Punishment practices are similar to the torture of political prisoners . . . The rationales are different, but the means are similar – a calculated, deliberate assault on human dignity through isolation, control over the person, degradation, and finally, submission (p. 7).

Similarly, Konarski (1990) strongly criticises anyone (and in particular Mulick, 1990a) who uses treatment efficacy as a critical factor in the justification of aversive practices. He maintains that ideological issues can never be ignored.

Others regard the use of aversives as justified on balance, in the case of severe self-injury. Thus B. F. Skinner, quoted by Griffin *et al.* (1988): 'If brief and harmless aversive stimuli, made precisely contingent on self-destructive or other excessive behavior, suppress the behavior . . . I believe it can be justified' (p. 104). The real mistake, he later comments, is: 'to remain satisfied with punishment without exploring non-punitive alternatives' (p. 104).

This position is broadly in line with the principle of the least intrusive intervention, which proposes that aversive or restrictive techniques should only be used when other methods have been tried and failed. The principle is based on a hierarchy of interventions from least to most intrusive, first developed by Roos in 1972 (see Bird *et al.*, 1989). It is worth noting, incidentally, that this kind of hierarchy could be used to justify an aversive procedure like shock, on the grounds of being *less* intrusive than medication. For example, Lennox *et al.* (1988) categorised medication regimes as most restrictive as they result in continuous control and intrusion (Aman and Singh, 1986, but see also Chapter 9).

The National Institutes of Health Consensus Development Conference statement summarised by Bijou (1990) also recommends that reduction procedures are only used if enhancement methods have failed and only for short periods of time and in the context of a behaviour enhancement treatment package. Also, treatment should be reviewed and informed consent obtained. Psychopharmacological agents are only justified if a specific psychiatric syndrome has been diagnosed.

A third view regards it as unethical *not* to use aversives, the overriding concern being effective treatment. Thus Foxx (1986) suggests that the failure to consider punishment as a viable alternative might be considered a violation of a client's right to treatment (quoted by Spreat *et al.* 1989).

It is difficult to see how a conflict caused by such wide-ranging views can be resolved. An appeal to the legal situation hardly makes matters any clearer. The court cases in North America, contesting the use of aversives, have already been mentioned. They have resulted in some states (including Massachusetts) banning certain behavioural procedures (Matson and Taras, 1989) and many states requiring therapists to demonstrate that non-aversive treatments have not worked before implementing aversive conditioning (O'Brien and Repp, 1990). But in 1986 a court in Massachusetts issued an injunction *against* a state official who had halted the use of aversive therapy with disturbed adults (Behaviour Research Institute v. Leonard). In this confusing situation, a number of attempts have been made to establish a framework for clinical practice. These include:

1. definition of safeguards against abuse 2. research into social acceptability 3. appeals to the principle of normalisation 4. the concept of social validity.

1. Safeguards against abuse

Perhaps the most common way of attempting to devise safeguards is to establish a local ethics committee, responsible for overseeing behavioural programmes (Yule and Carr, 1987, p.196). This approach is fairly well established in Britain and is evidently preferred to legislation. Another approach is to develop a set of ethical guidelines, again a practice in use in Britain as well as the United States. For example, in the US Lovaas and Favell (1987) produced a set of guidelines which preclude aversive procedures except in extremely unusual cases, and then only if carried out by well-trained and well-monitored staff. However, Evans and Meyer (1990) observe that the Lovaas and Favell guidelines have failed as safeguards against abuse as the use of aversives is still widespread and not bound by their strict criteria. Although Horner (1990) welcomes the Lovaas and Favell guidelines, he also raises the problem of 'drift' in the application of aversive behavioural intervention. That is, when time-out, slaps or shock are introduced into an environment, the potential for misuse or even abuse is clearly present.

La Vigna and Donnellan (1986) also argue that even the most careful guidelines are unable to solve the problem of abuse. Owens (1987) takes a similar view and suggests that ethical guidelines merely serve to indicate the potential for exploitation, against which clients need protection. He regards the nub of the problem to be imbalance of power between the client and therapist, exacerbated when there is no direct consent to treatment. As a possible safeguard, he invokes Skinner's notion of countercontrol – an attempt to restore some control to the client, or at least ensure that client and therapist are subject to similar contingencies. He develops this idea in relation to aversive procedures, and suggests that any therapist administering shock might by 'yoked' to the client and experience the treatment as well. How far this idea would find favour is doubtful. But the concept of countercontrol seems worth exploring further.

2. Social acceptability

Several attempts have been made to sample opinion about the acceptability of different treatments for challenging behaviour. While having no explicit links with ethical considerations, these studies represent attempts to establish a clinical *modus operandi*. Spreat *et al.* (1989) report that a group of professionals in learning difficulties tended to regard shock as appropriate treatment if the behaviour problem was severe, and had been unresponsive to less aversive methods. Tarnowski *et al.* (1989, 1990) found that accelerative methods of treatment were more acceptable to direct care staff than reductive methods, and that generally shock was the least acceptable procedure. However, Harris *et al.* (1991) found that professionals working with young people with autistic characteristics and using 'strong aversives' (e.g. slap, shock, noxious odour) had lower job stress ratings and higher personal accomplishment ratings than their colleagues who used 'mild aversives' (e.g. time-out, facial screening, response cost)! The latter staff group reported greater and more frequent 'emotional exhaustion'. And finally Pickering and Morgan (1985) report a study of parental attitudes to treatments for self-injury. Differential reinforcement was consistently regarded as the most acceptable technique, while shock was the least acceptable. But interestingly, shock was also rated as the most potent and active treatment. These findings encapsulate neatly the dilemma between ethics and effectiveness. Overall, however, these studies take us little further forward. They simply reflect the uncertainties of the current debate.

3. Appeals to normalisation

It has been suggested by Tennant *et al.* (1978) that the use of punishment in behavioural interventions is in accordance with principles of normalisation or social role valorisation (Wolfensberger and Thomas, 1983). Their central point is that much of 'normal' social behaviour is under the control of avoidance contingencies. A clinical intervention may succeed in establishing new behaviours by means of accelerative reinforcement, but if these behaviours are typically controlled by punishment in the natural environment, there will be difficulties with maintenance. In the case of teaching good table manners, they argue, it is artificial to use reward. Instead, the behaviour should be made subject to the social (punishing) contingencies in ordinary life.

This argument raises two major questions. First, it is unclear whether the authors are making an ethical appeal to the *principles* of normalisation. Or are they simply concerned with the pragmatics of behaviour maintenance? Secondly, an appeal to normalisation can be used to support a radically different position. For example, Emerson and McGill (1989) have suggested that the principles of normalisation should lead to an increasing use of non-aversive, constructional interventions. But Emerson (1990) warns against rejecting the use of structured, individualised ('powerful' but not aversive) treatments in the name of normalisation. He criticises Wolfensberger (1989) for suggesting that people with severe SIB can only be helped '. . . when somebody takes them in and patiently loves and 'gentles' them for long periods of time, perhaps without any technology whatever' (p.183).

4. Social validity

The point at issue here is summarised clearly by Schroeder and Schroeder (1989) 'Should only those procedures used for people without handicaps be permitted for people with handicaps?' (p. v).

The significance of this question is illustrated by a study by Powell and Azrin (1968), in which contingent shock was used in an attempt to reduce smoking in a group of non-disabled adults. At an early stage in treatment, seventeen out of twenty subjects dropped out. This raises the issue – are people with learning difficulties always in a position to drop out from such interventions? The answer is probably 'no'. Evans and Meyer (1990) argue that aversive methods used in the past for the psychological symptoms of other populations, such as substance abuse or deviant sexual behaviour, have all but disappeared. They query whether the persistent use of aversives for people with severe learning difficulties is due to their weak (and in many cases non-existent) consumer voice.

None of the studies described above amount, of course, to a formal evaluation of the ethical issues involved. But some interesting ideas have emerged from them. Within the field of safeguards, it seems worth looking further at a concept of countercontrol. And the question raised about the social validity of aversive treatment needs to be addressed further.

ALTERNATIVES TO PUNISHMENT – THE CURRENT DEBATE

During the 1980s a number of behavioural interventions have been gathering momentum, all firmly committed to non-aversive strategies. Although they constitute separate developments, they share the belief that even severely challenging behaviour can be treated successfully without recourse to punishment. In a sense, they represent a way of side-stepping the debate about ethics and effectiveness, by claiming that aversive procedures are not only undesirable, but unnecessary. Three major examples of these new approaches will be briefly reviewed, namely gentle teaching, positive programming and functional communication training. All have been subject to criticism to some degree, and an outline of these will be given in each case.

Gentle teaching

As the name implies, gentle teaching is primarily an instructional technique. But it goes beyond skill teaching to embody a style of personal interaction between therapist and client. It is described most fully by its originators, McGee *et al.* (1986, 1987). A concept central to this approach is 'bonding' with the individual client or learner. Indeed, according to McGee (1986) 'The goal of all teaching is bonding . . . literally teaching reciprocal and mutually humanising ties of affection between ourselves and the person' (p. 7).

For bonding to occur, the reinforcing value of social interaction must be established for the client. Once achieved, this enables the teacher to gain interactional control over the client's behaviour. Specific teaching techniques include the use of gestures and physical prompts, rather than verbal instruction, and enthusiastic praise for any compliance. The suggested response to SIB is to so arrange the environment as to prevent or reduce the behaviour, and to work for interactional control by the strategy Ignore – Redirect – Reward. McGee reports that gentle teaching has been successfully used with over 650 clients. In particular, he presents a study of 73 persons with severe SIB, of whom 69 are claimed to have shown marked improvement on discharge and at five-year follow-up.

A major published criticism of gentle teaching is in an article by Jordan *et al.* (1989). The two main charges are:

a)   Faulty methodology, for example, treatment results are often reported as informal observations, without baseline data;
b)   Lack of originality – the basis of the approach being differential reinforcement combined with 'simple management techniques' (see also Turnbull, 1990).

The study carried out by Jordan *et al.* is a comparison of gentle teaching with visual screening (which they regard as an aversive procedure) in the treatment of three adults with stereotypy. The results suggest that visual screening is more effective and, more importantly, that 'bonding' between therapist and client occurred equally in both treatment conditions.

This design was replicated for two people with SIB by Jones *et al.* (1990), who reported that visual screening and gentle teaching were equally effective for one subject and equally ineffective for the other. 'Bonding' occurred at low levels under both types of treatment. Again, Jones *et al.* (1991) compared visual screening gentle teaching and no-treatment control conditions after training a 44-year-old man with severe SIB in age-appropriate tasks. The training sessions alone resulted in only a minimal reduction in SIB. Both visual screening and gentle teaching reduced the target behaviour but visual screening more so than gentle teaching. 'Bonding' again occurred at low levels in both conditions.

These replicated results are a serious indictment of gentle teaching. McGee (1990) attributes these negative findings to deviations in methodology and too strong a focus on reducing target behaviours rather than on the interpersonal behaviours. But clearly further research from both 'sides' is required to disentangle the various components in the gentle teaching technique, which may or may not be effective.

McGee's (1990) defence against Jordan *et al.* (1989) and Turnbull's (1990) criticisms (that his methods are nothing more than a collection of well-tested behaviour modification procedures) is that gentle teaching provides *unconditional* reward as opposed to contingent reinforcement. McGee emphasises 'human valuing' because he is convinced that everyone, however aggressive or withdrawn, has an inherent longing for affection. Other authors (e.g. Paisey *et al.*, 1989) maintain that affectionate responses (e.g. hugs and smiles) may well be perceived as aversive by some. Thus, they argue, it is possible that in certain instances gentle teaching may be experienced as highly aversive and intrusive!

Positive programming

The term 'positive programming' is applied for convenience to a range of non-aversive intervention strategies developed by La Vigna and Donnellan (1986). None of the techniques they suggest is in itself original. Their contribution is to combine these techniques within a single framework and to propose an intensive method of implementation. The framework they suggest consists of detailed functional analyses of the target behaviours, followed by a four stage programme. This comprises:

a)   Ecological manipulation – changes to the stimulus conditions or setting of the behaviour.
b)   Teaching alternative skills or behaviours – possibly functionally equivalent to the target behaviours.
c)   Direct treatment – including a variety of differential reinforcement techniques, instructional control, and covert conditioning.
d)   Situational management – a reactive strategy in case the target behaviour occurs, despite the proactive methods already described.

The particular elements of an individual programme are determined by the functional analysis. And the programme is usually implemented in the client's natural environment by a specialist team, handing over where possible to carers or family (see Chapters 3 and 4).

La Vigna and Donnellan's book *Alternatives to Punishment* attracted a volley of critical reviews, notably by Axelrod (1987), Bailey (1987) and Mulick and Linscheid (1987). The major charges against their work include a lack of convincing empirical data, reliance on unpublished papers and personal communications, lengthy and complex treatment procedures and failure to address severe behaviour problems, particularly SIB.

The only point with which the critics agree is the central importance of functional analysis. It is certainly true that many of the examples used in the book concern milder forms of behaviour problem. But studies reported elsewhere redress the balance. Donnellan *et al.* (1985) describe an intensive intervention programme to maintain sixteen clients with severe behaviour problems in community placements. Their single reported failure involved SIB, but the results are still impressive.

Functional communication training

This approach, developed by Carr and Durand (1985), has a number of similarities with the work of La Vigna and Donnellan. Both adopt a constructional approach to intervention, aiming to replace rather than eliminate behaviour. And both stress the importance of functional analysis. Carr and Durand also regard problem behaviour as a non-verbal means of communication. They illustrate this hypothesis in an elegantly designed study involving a group of four children with challenging behaviour. In the first of two experiments, they identify the situations in which the target behaviours are most likely to occur (these being low levels of adult attention, or high levels of task difficulty). Then in the second, they train the children to use relevant verbal responses in each of these situations (i.e. to make a request for either adult attention or for assistance with the task), with which the therapist complies. The results indicate a rapid and marked decline in the occurrence of behaviour problems. In a further refinement, the children were trained to use irrelevant communicative responses which results in the challenging behaviours occurring at their previous level. This demonstrates, according to Carr and Durand, that in some cases at least, problem behaviour is functionally equivalent to verbal communication.

Carr *et al.* (1990) firm up this position by stating that any treatment must:

1. be based on functional analysis
2. be pro-active (i.e. taking place when the person is not engaged in challenging behaviour)
3. make desirable responses more probable (deceleration of challenging behaviour is a critical side-effect)
4. be carried out indefinitely as the focus is on maintaining increases in desirable behaviour.

With this last point Carr *et al.* condemn any *non-functional* methodology, be it aversive or non-aversive. They argue that too much of the debate has been centred on reactive crisis management at the expense of long-term pro-active support and education. The latter must be firmly based on a clear understanding of the function of any challenging behaviour displayed. Non-functional non-aversive treatments are equally criticised as non-functional aversive ones because neither can be effective in substituting functional acceptable responses for functional unacceptable (and challenging) responses.

Taken together, these 'positive' approaches emphasise accelerative methods, social validation, and a strong rejection of certain classes of decelerative behavioural techniques. But far from resulting in a resolution, the debate is becoming increasingly bitter and personal. Sidman (1989) asserts baldly that 'people who use shocks become shocks'. While Schroeder and Schroeder (1989) quote a speaker addressing the aversive versus non-aversive treatment debate at a national convention as fearing for his life. Mulick (1990a and b) accuses the non-aversive camp of having 'a poor understanding of behavioural science', whereas Guess *et al.* (1990) (equally insulting) compare Mulick's arguments with those of an arrogant nineteenth-century phrenologist.

What underlies the evident strength of hostile feelings in what should be an academic, objective debate? There seem to be two possible factors. First, an obvious point, challenging behaviour is a highly charged, emotional issue for carers and families, and indeed for professionals. Secondly, for professionals the focus of the present debate is on competence and expertise, just as much as ethics. The non-aversive camp claims to have found all the answers, even for serious challenging behaviour: their opponents are evidently ignorant of the latest techniques (La Vigna and Donnellan, 1986). Those in the aversive camp accuse their critics not only of ignorance but of simply failing to tackle treatment of severe behaviour problems and thus depriving people of 'their right to effective treatment' (e.g. van Houten *et al.*, 1988). This is indeed the stuff of controversy.

WAYS FOR THE FUTURE

It is difficult to know when and how this debate will end. And it is equally difficult to recommend with conviction which principles should guide clinical practice in the meantime. In some ways, it is tempting to sit on the fence: to make a commitment to non-aversive approaches a general rule, while retaining an option on aversive measures in the case of resistant life-threatening behaviour. But is this entirely coherent as an argument? We tend to agree with Haring and White (1990), who suggest that efficacy research is irrelevant if one has taken an ideological stance against certain treatment methods. One cannot use empirical research either to defend or attack such a position. But they argue further that the onus then falls on the ideological campaigners (such as TASH) to use *scientific* methods to identify and test techniques that are (for them) acceptable. Haring and White fear that, after having provided us with a number of admirable ideologies, the advocates for the rights of people with learning difficulties will now neglect or lose their analytic powers and drive good researchers away from their ranks.

Some ideas emerging from several recent studies of challenging behaviour, at times almost by accident, are in our opinion attractive from a treatment as well as an ethical point of view. They share a single theme: returning control or the power of choice to the person with challenging behaviour.

It might seem naive to suggest that restoring control to someone displaying severe challenging behaviour will successfully 'cure' them. But a number of case reports appear to indicate some such process at work. Berkman and Meyer (1988) present a detailed study of a series of interventions with a forty-five-year old man who had lived in institutions for over thirty-two years. His challenging behaviour included head-banging, eye-poking and operant vomiting. The article is remarkable for describing the uncertainties which arose during treatment and for acknowledging that eventual success was due to a chance discovery. The first intervention involved DRO, the reinforcers being tokens, which could be exchanged for a walk away from the ward. This was combined with aversive treatment for any incident of self-injury, physical restraint in a chair facing towards a wall, with arm splints in position. This programme succeeded in reducing head-banging, but led to a serious increase in vomiting, to the point where major weight loss and dehydration occurred. Staff noticed, however, that neither vomiting nor head-banging occurred during the walks away from the unit. This chance observation led to a total revision of strategy. Direct treatment was discontinued and the client was offered increasing opportunities to leave the ward and visit the community. A programme was started to involve him in decision-making, initially about snacks and food, and later about daily activities. Several months later he moved to a house in the community and took up a work experience placement. Progress was maintained at twelve-month follow-up. Berkman and Meyer comment 'It was as if his intellectual abilities were concentrated upon a variety of increasingly negative and life-threatening strategies to effect control in an environment over which he had no control' (p. 84). The successful outcome, they argue, was due not to the mere fact of community living, but to the 'Positive program that . . . encouraged appropriate and long overdue choices and control in his daily life' (p. 84).

All this is based on a single case study, of course. But there is other evidence elsewhere. Smith (1985) stresses the importance of giving maximum control to the client in a programme of reinforcement. She describes the case of an underweight man who engaged in severe head-banging in the presence of food. The treatment consisted of immediate access to food on demand, provided it was requested verbally and without self-injury. The requests for food occurred at first very frequently. And Smith acknowledges that the programme involved a dense reinforcement schedule, which might be seen by some as over-indulgent. But at the outset, the client was forty pounds under-weight. During the programme, he approached his normal body weight, and his intake of food fell back by choice to the usual meals plus occasional snacks. At the same time the rate of head-banging decreased considerably. Smith presents this intervention as a process of substituting language for self-injury, and restoring control to the client over an important aspect of his life.

A very similar point is made by Bird *et al.* (1989) in a study of functional communication training applied to self-injury. They conclude from the results that control over access to reinforcers is a critical factor in success. Both the type of reinforcer used and the schedule of reinforcement should be 'determined by the subject's communicative requests', and not by anyone else. This underlines the point made by Carr and Durand (1985) that functional communication training offers the client the role of active participant rather than passive recipient.

Any attempt at restoring choice and control to the client is obviously appealing on the grounds of social validity. Choice is specified by O'Brien (1987) as one of the five accomplishments which services should aim to provide for their users. But the studies described here suggest that this approach may also be directly relevant to the treatment of challenging behaviour. If this is true, it puts the use of aversives – even as a last resort – in a different light. For of all techniques, those involving aversives appear to presume external control. They are conceptually apart from returning choice to the client.

CONCLUSIONS

Over the last few decades in which behavioural interventions have known general currency, the attitudes towards aversive techniques have changed significantly. At first they were viewed as an effective treatment for severe challenging behaviour. One of the concerns was how to achieve technical refinement, and produce the 'ideal' punishing stimulus. An element of doubt then entered the picture, and aversives were regarded as a last resort. In the early 1980s a split in opinion emerged, between the 'last resort' and 'right to treatment' camp and those regarding aversive treatment as unacceptable and unnecessary. The debate continues today, with supporters of each viewpoint now entrenched in their positions.

The treatments adopted include a variety of approaches which have been termed aversive, some based on an operant theory of punishment, and others on the assumption that certain punishers are universal. Of these, the single, most widely supported technique in the North American literature has probably been contingent shock. This is still favoured by some today, as evidenced by the wide use of 'SIBIS'. The strongest argument for contingent shock is that in certain cases of life-threatening behaviour it can lead to a rapid and marked improvement. This may on occasions offer a chance to implement a constructional programme (teaching other more appropriate behaviours to replace the challenging behaviour), and makes a case for a combined method of treatment, linking aversive with non-aversive methods in the same programme. There are serious drawbacks to contingent shock, however. At times it is ineffective or even makes matters worse. The effects are often specific to a single situation. And the benefits, if any, are of short duration. Various efforts have been made to unravel the ethical issues surrounding the use of shock, and other aversive procedures. But overall these have simply reflected the divided opinions which prevail. It is evidently hard to find a common framework for ethics on the one hand and treatment effectiveness on the other. Two useful ideas have emerged, however. The notion of countercontrol, as a safeguard against abuse, seems worth exploring. And questions about the social validity of treatment clearly need to be addressed.

The alternatives to punishment which started to emerge in the early 1980s have attracted interest and enthusiasm, but also considerable opposition. Some of their supporters seem to have done the cause more harm than good, by making extravagant claims for the success of the new methods, and adding an emotional charge to the debate. For example, *The Language of Pain* (Rioux, 1988) is in parts more like a polemical diatribe than a reasoned argument. As a philosopher and therefore a relative outsider, Oldenquist (1990) states that 'I confess to being surprised and shocked to find . . . apparently unsubstantiated speculation about bad motives as well as inflammatory analogies between aversive therapy and atrocities' (p. 171).

Nevertheless, there are several exciting developments, which give grounds for optimism. In particular, the two approaches emphasising functional analysis appear to have potential, the work of La Vigna and Donnellan (as reflected in journal articles as much as their handbook) and Carr and Durand's (1985) functional communication training. These apart, there are a number of hints in the literature that approaches aiming to restore choice and control to the client may offer a new way forward. If supported by further studies, these will certainly add weight to the arguments against aversives.

There are three further conclusions of a more general nature about this field of research:

1. The debate about aversive treatments for challenging behaviour is not simply, or even mainly, academic. Theoretical positions which look good on paper are unlikely to impress carers or families under pressure.
2. Neither side of the present debate has produced absolute 'proof' by case study. There are too many variables involved (not least the attitudes of therapists and carers), and in any case a tendency for mainly positive results to be published produces a biased picture of applied research findings.
3. There is no single key to challenging behaviour, no one right treatment for every individual. It is therefore crucial to avoid sweeping claims or over-generalisations and to focus instead on the particular. This point underlines the central importance of functional analysis to any intervention. Interestingly, this is an issue on which both sides of the debate appear to agree. But Lennox *et al.*'s (1988) study suggests that in practice functional analysis may be a minority activity. Carr *et al.* (1990) make a passionate plea for hypothesis-driven treatment by means of functional analysis 'Treatment failure is a bad thing, but being directionless is worse' (p.374).

As for the future, the most pressing needs are to defuse the current emotional exchanges, to encourage longer term evaluation of treatment outcomes and to establish a climate in which treatment effectiveness can be discussed in relation to social validity. As things stand at present, some of the non-aversive approaches to challenging behaviour seem to offer promise and reason for optimism. The greatest risk is that extravagant claims on their behalf will overshadow the genuine advances made and slow down the further research that is so vitally necessary in this field.

We agree with Emerson (1990) that openness of services to monitoring and evaluation will not only increase our body of knowledge but also provide a safeguard against abusive practices.

References

American Association on Mental Retardation (AAMR) (1988), 'The AAMR position statement on aversive therapy: the controversy', *Mental Retardation*, 26, 314–17.

Aman, M. G. and Singh, N. N. (1986), 'A critical appraisal of recent drug research in mental retardation: the coldwater studies', *Journal of Mental Deficiency Research*, 30, 302–16.

Archer, T. and Nilsson, L. G. (eds.) (1989), *Aversion, Avoidance and Anxiety*, Lawrence Erlbaum Associates, Hillsdale, NY.

Axelrod, S. (1987), 'Doing it without arrows: a review of La Vigna and Donnellan's *Alternatives to Punishment*', *Behavior Analyst*, 10, 343–51.

Bailey, J. S. (1987), 'Misguided Alternatives: a review of La Vigna and Donnellans's *Alternatives to Punishment*', *Contemporary Psychology*, 32, 571–72.

Behavior Research Institute *v.* Leonard (1986), 'Aversive therapy justified for severely ill', *Mental and Physical Disability Law Reporter*, 10, 358–59.

Berkman, K. A. and Meyer, L. H. (1988), 'Alternative strategies and multiple outcomes in the remediation of severe self-injury: going 'all out' non-aversively', *Journal of the Association for Persons with Severe Handicaps*, 13, 76–86.

Bijou, S. W. (1990), 'Review treatment of destructive behaviors in persons with developmental disabilities', National Institutes of Health Consensus Development Conference Statement, *Journal of Autism and Developmental Disorders*, 20, 43.

Bird, F., Dores, P. A., Moniz, D. and Robinson, J. (1989), 'Reducing severe aggressive and self-injurious behaviors with functional communication training', *American Journal on Mental Retardation*, 94, 37–48.

Butterfield, E. C. (1990), 'The compassion of distinguishing punishing behavioral treatment from aversive treatment', *American Journal of Mental Retardation*, 95 (2), 137–41.

Carr, E. G. and Durand, V. M. (1985), 'Reducing behavior problems through functional communication training', *Journal of Applied Behavior Analysis*, 18, 111–26.

Carr, E. G. and Lovaas, O. I. (1983), 'Contingent electric shock as a treatment for severe behavior problems' in F. Axrelrod and J. Apsche (eds.), *Punishment: Its Effects on Human Behavior*, Academic Press, New York.

Carr, E. G., Robinson, S. and Palumbo, L. W. (1990), 'The wrong issue: aversive versus nonaversive treatment. The right issue: functional versus nonfunctional treatment' in A. Repp and N. Singh (eds.), *Current Perspectives in the Use of Nonaversive and Aversive Interventions with Developmentally Disabled Persons*, Sycamore Press, Sycamore, IL.

Corbett, J. (1975), 'Aversion for the treatment of self-injurious behavior', *Journal of Mental Deficiency Research*, 19, 79–95.

Corté, H. E., Wolf, M. M. and Locke, B. J. (1971), 'A comparison of procedures for eliminating self-injurious behavior of retarded adolescents', *Journal of Applied Behavior Analysis*, 4, 201–13.

Donnellan, A. M., La Vigna, G. W., Zambito, J. and Thvedt, J. (1985), 'A time-limited intersive intervention program model to support community placement for persons with severe behavior problems', *Journal of the Association for Persons with Severe Handicaps*, 10, 123–31.

Emerson, E. (1990), 'Severe self-injurious behaviour: some of the challenges it presents', *Mental Handicap*, 18, 92–8.

Emerson, E. and McGill, P. (1989), 'Normalization and applied behaviour analysis: values and technology in services for people with learning difficulties', *Behavioural Psychotherapy*, 17, 101–17.

Evans, I. M. and Meyer, L. H. (1990), 'Reader response. Towards a science in support of meaningful outcomes: a response to Horner *et al.*', *Journal of the Association for Persons with Severe Handicaps*, 15 (3), 133–35.

Ewen, D. (1988), 'Aversive therapy' in M. H. Rioux, (ed.), *The Language of Pain*, q.v. (pp. 91–5).

Goldiamond, I. (1974), 'Toward a constructional approach to social problems', *Behaviorism*, 2, 1–84.

Gorman-Smith, D. and Matson, J. L. (1985), 'A review of treatment research for self-injurious and stereotyped responding', *Journal of Mental Deficiency Research*, 29, 295–308.

Griffin, J. C., Paisey, T. J., Stark, M. T. and Emerson, J. H. (1988), 'B. F. Skinner's position on aversive treatment', *American Journal on Mental Retardation*, 93, 104–5.

Guess, D., Turnbull, H. R., III., and Helmstetter, E. (1990), 'Science, paradigms, and values: a response to Mulick', *American Journal on Mental Retardation*, 95, 157–63.

Harradence, A. M. and Hartlebury, M. A. (1983), *Difficult and Disruptive Behavior: A Literature Review*, Sheffield Health Authority Mental Handicap Services.

Haring, N. G. and White, O. R. (1990), 'Comments on the TASH monograph and the Mulick review', *American Journal on Mental Retardation*, 95, 163–65.

Harris, S. L., Handleman, J. S., Gill, M. J. and Fong, P. L. (1991), 'Does punishment hurt? The impact of aversives on the clinician', *Research in Developmental Disabilities*, 12, 17–24.

Horner, R. M., Dunlop, G., Koegal, R. L., Carr, E. G., Sailor, W., Anderson, G., Albin, R. W. and O'Neill, R. E. (1990), 'Toward a technology of "nonaversive" behavioural support', *Journal of the Association for Persons with Severe Handicaps*, 15 (3), 125–32.

Horner, R. (1990), 'Ideology, technology, and typical community settings: use of severe aversive stimuli', *American Journal on Mental Retardation*, 95, 166–68.

Jones, F. H., Simmons, J. Q. and Frankel, F. (1974), 'An extinction procedure for eliminating self-destructive behaviour in a 9-year-old autistic girl', reprinted in Murphy and Wilson (1985), *Self-Injurious Behaviour*, q.v. (pp. 367–73).

Jones, J. L., Singh, N. N., and Kendall, K. A. (1990), 'Effects of gentle teaching and alternative treatments on self-injury' in A. Repp and N. Singh (eds.), *Current Perspectives on the Use of Aversive and Nonaversive Interventions with Developmentally Disabled Persons*, Sycamore Press, Sycamore, IL.

Jones, L. J., Singh, N. N. and Kendall, K. A. (1991), 'Comparative effects of gentle teaching and visual screening on self-injurious behaviour', *Journal of Mental Deficiency Research*, 35, 37–47.

Jordan, J., Singh, N. N. and Repp, A. C. (1989), 'An evaluation of gentle teaching and visual screening in the reduction of stereotypy', *Journal of Applied Behavior Analysis*, 22, 9–22.

Konarski, E. A. (1990), 'Science as an ineffective white knight', *American Journal on Mental Retardation*, 95, 169–71.

La Vigna, G. W. and Donnellan, A. M. (1986), *Alternatives to Punishment: Solving Behavior Problems with Non-Aversive Strategies*, Irvington Publishers, New York.

Lennox, D. B., Miltenberger, R. G., Spengler, P. and Erfanian, N. (1988), 'Declaration treatment practices with persons who have mental retardation: a review of five years of the literature', *American Journal on Mental Retardation*, 92, 492–501.

Linscheid, T. R., Iwata, B. A., Ricketts, R. W., Williams, D. E., and Griffin, J. C. (1990), 'Clinical evaluation of the self-injurious Behavior Inhibiting System (SIBIS)', *Journal of Applied Behavior Analysis*, 53–78.

Lovaas, O. I., and Favell, J. E. (1987), 'Protection for clients undergoing aversive/ restrictive interventions', *Education and Treatment of Children*, 10, 311–25.

Lovaas, O. I., Shaeffer, B. and Simmons, J. Q. (1965), 'Building social behavior in autistic children by the use of electric shock', *Journal of Experimental Research in Personality*, 1, 99–109.

Lovaas, O. I. and Simmons, J. Q. (1969), 'Manipulation of self-destruction in three retarded children', reprinted in Murphy and Wilson (1985), *Self-Injurious Behavior*, pp. 195–209.

Matson, J. L. and Gardner, W. I. (1991), 'Behavioral learning theory and current applications to severe behavior problems in persons with mental retardation', *Clinical Psychology Review*, 11, 175–83.

Matson, J. L. and Keyes, J. (1988), 'Contingent reinforcement and contingent restraint to treat severe aggression and self-injury in mentally retarded and autistic adults', *Journal of the Multi-handicapped Person*, 1, 141–53.

Matson, J. L. and Taras, M. E. (1989), 'A 20-year review of punishment and alternative methods to treat problem behaviors in developmentally delayed persons', *Research in Developmentally Disabilities*, 10, 35–104.

McGee, J. J. (1986), 'Gentle teaching' *Newsletter of the Association for Persons with Severe Handicaps*, September 1986, (p. 7).

McGee, J. J. (1990), 'Gentle teaching: the basic tenet', *Nursing Times*, 86 (32), 68–72.

McGee, J. J., Menolascino, F. J., Hobbs, D. C. and Menousek, P. E. (1987), *Gentle Teaching: A Non-aversive Approach for Helping Persons with Mental Retardation*, Human Sciences Press, New York.

Meinhold, P. M. and Mulick, J. A. (1990a), 'Risks, choices and behavioral treatments', *Behavioral Residential Treatment*, 5 (1), A.29–44.

Mulick, J. A. (1990a), 'The ideology and science of punishment in mental retardation', *American Journal on Mental Retardation*, 95 (2), 142–56.

Mulick, J. A. (1990b), 'Ideology and punishment reconsidered', *American Journal on Mental Retardation*, 95 (2), 173–81.

Mulick, J. A. and Linscheid, T. R. (1988), 'A review of La Vigna and Donnellan's Alternatives to Punishment: Solving Behavior Problems with Nonaversive Strategies', *Research in Developmental Disabilities*, 9, 317–27.

Murphy, G. H. and Wilson, B. (1981), 'Long-term outcome of contingent shock treatment for self-injurious behaviour', reprinted in Murphy and Wilson (1985), *Self-Injurious Behaviour*, q.v., pp. 403–08.

Murphy, G. H. and Wilson, B. (eds.) (1985), *Self-Injurious Behaviour*, BIMH Publications, Kidderminster.

O'Brien, J. (1987), 'A guide to personal futures planning' in G. T. Bellamy and B.

Wilcox, (eds.), *A Comprehensive Guide to the Activities Catalog*, Paul H. Brookes, Baltimore, MD.

O'Brien, S. and Repp, A. C. (1990), 'Reinforcement-based reductive procedures: a review of 20 years of their use with persons with severe and profound retardation', *Journal of the Association for Persons with Severe Handicaps*, 15 (3), 148–59.

Oldenquist, A. (1990), 'How not to make moral arguments', *American Journal on Mental Retardation*, 95, 171–72.

Owens, G. (1987), 'Radical behaviourism and the Ethics of clinical psychology' in S. Fairbairn and G. Fairbairn (eds.), *Psychology, Ethics and Change*, Routledge and Kegan Paul, London.

Paisley, T. J. H., Whitney, R. B., and Moore, J. (1989), 'Person-treatment interactions across nonaversive response-deceleration procedures for self-injury: a case study of effects and side-effects', *Behavioral Residential Treatment*, 4, 69–88.

Pickering, D. and Morgan, S. B. (1985), 'Parental ratings of treatments of self-injurious behavior', *Journal of Autism and Developmental Disorders*, 15, 303–14.

Powell, J. and Azrin, N. (1968), 'The effects of shock as a punisher for cigarette smoking', *Journal of Applied Behavior Analysis*, 1, 63–71.

Repp, A. C. and Deitz, S. M. (1974), 'Reducing aggressive and self-injurious behavior of institutionalised retarded children through reinforcement of other behavior', *Journal of Applied Behavior Analysis*, 7, 313–25.

Rioux, M. H. (ed.) (1988), *The Language of Pain: Perspectives on Behavior Management*, G. Allan Roeher Institute, Ontario.

Romanczyk, R. G. and Goren, E. R. (1975), 'Severe self-injurious behaviour: the problem of clinical control', reprinted in Murphy and Wilson (1985), *Self-injurious Behaviour*, q.v. pp. 374–85.

Schroeder, S. R. and Schroeder, C. S. (1989), 'The role of the AAMR in the aversives controversy', *Mental Retardation* (Guest Editorial: June 1989), iii–iv.

Sidman, M. (1989), *Coercion and its Fallout*, Authors' Cooperative Inc., Boston, MA.

Smith, M. D. (1985), 'Managing the aggressive and self-injurious behavior of adults disabled by autism', *Journal of the Association for Persons with Severe Handicaps*, 10, 228–32.

Solnick, J. V., Rincover, A., and Peterson, C. R. (1977), 'Some determinants of the reinforcing and punishing effects of timeout', *Journal of Applied Behavior Analysis*, 10, 415–24.

Spreat, S., Lipinski, D., Dickerson, R., Nass, R. and Dorsey, M. (1989), 'The acceptability of electric shock programs', *Behaviour Modification*, 13, 245–56.

Tanner, B. A. and Zeiler, M. (1975), 'Punishment of self-injurious behaviour using aromatic ammonia as the aversive stimulus', reprinted in Murphy and Wilson (1985), *Self-injurious Behaviour*, q.v., pp. 347–51.

Tarnowski, K. J., Rasnake, L. K., Mulick, J. A. and Kelly, P. A. (1989), 'Acceptability of behavioral interventions for self-injurious behavior', *American Journal on Mental Retardation*, 93, 575–80.

Tarnowski, K. G., Mulick, J. A. and Rasnake, L. K. (1990), 'Acceptability of behavioral interventions for self-injurious behavior: replication and interinstitutional comparison', *American Journal of Mental Retardation*, 95 (2), 182–87.

Tarpley, H. D. and Schroeder, S. R. (1979), 'Comparison of D.R.O. and D.R.I. on rate of suppression of self-injurious behavior', *American Journal of Mental Deficiency*,

84, 188–94.

TASH (1988), 'TASH joins with other organisations to protest electric shock device', *Newsletter of the Association for Persons with Severe Handicaps*, August 1988, pp. 1–2.

Tate, B. G. and Baroff, G. S. (1966), 'Aversive control of self-injurious behaviour in a psychotic boy', reprinted in Murphy and Wilson (1985), *Self-injurious Behaviour*, q.v., pp. 352–57.

Tennant, L., Hattersley, J. and Cullen, C. (1978), 'Some brief comments on the punishment relationship and its relevance to normalization for developmentally retarded people', *Mental Retardation*, 16, 42–44.

Turnbull, J. (1990), 'Gentle teaching: the emperor's new clothes?', *Nursing Times*, 86 (32), 64–68.

van Houten, R., Axelrod, S., Bailey, J. S., Favell, G. E., Foxx, R. M., Iwata, B. A. and Lovaas, O. I. (1988), 'The right to effective behavioral treatment', *Journal of Applied Behavior Analysis*, 21, 381–84.

Williams, C. and Surtees, P. (1975), 'Behaviour modification with children: mannerisms, mutilation and management', reprinted in Murphy and Wilson (1985), *Self-injurious Behaviour*, q.v., pp. 386–95.

Wolfensberger, W. (1989), 'Self-injurious behavior, behavioristic responses, and social role valorization: a reply to Mulick and Kedesley', *Mental Retardation*, 27, 181–84.

Wolfensberger, W., and Thomas, S. (1983), *PASSING: Program Analysis of Service Systems Implementation of Normalization Goals*, National Institute on Mental Retardation, Toronto.

Young, J. A. and Wincze, J. P. (1975), 'The effects of the reinforcement of compatible and incompatible alternative behaviors on the self-injurious and related behaviors of a profoundly retarded female adult', *Behavior Therapy*, 5, 614–23.

Yule, W. and Carr, J. (1987), *Behaviour Modification for the Mentally Handicapped*, (2nd ed.), Croom Helm, London.

Author Index

Subject Index